# FREE GRASS TO FENCES

## The Montana Cattle Range Story

## Robert H. Fletcher

### ILLUSTRATIONS BY CHARLES M. RUSSELL

*Published for the Historical Society of Montana*

UNIVERSITY PUBLISHERS INCORPORATED

NEW YORK

*Library of Congress Catalog Card Number: 60–12710*
Designed by MARSHALL LEE
Manufactured in the United States of America by
H. Wolff Book Manufacturing Company, New York.

*Free Grass to Fences*

*For Montana's finest—the old-time cowmen*

## THE TRAIL OF AN OLD-TIMER'S MEMORY

*There's a trail that leads out to the mountains*
*Through the prairie dust, velvety gray,*
*Through the canyons, the gulches, and coulees,*
*A trail that grows dimmer each day.*
*You can't make it without an old-timer*
*To guide you and make you his guest*
*For that trail is the long trail of memory*
*And it leads to the heart of the West.*

*Now it winds through the shadows of sorrow,*
*Now it's warmed by the sunlight of smiles,*
*Now it lingers along pleasant waters,*
*Now it stretches o'er long, weary miles.*
*But it never is lonesome, deserted,*
*As you journey its distances vast*
*For it always is crowded and peopled*
*With dim, phantom shapes of the past.*

*Freight wagons creaking and lurching,*
*Leaving the old trading posts,*

*And Indian war parties scouting*
*As silent and furtive as ghosts;*
*Cowpunchers driving the trail herds,*
*The stagecoach that swayed as she rolled*
*With her passengers, sourdough and pilgrim,*
*In quest of adventure and gold.*

*Cavalry trots through the dust clouds,*
*Hunter and trapper and scout,*
*Miner and trader and outlaw*
*All meet on this marvelous route*
*Where laughter and tears are found mingled,*
*Where a prince may be found in a shack*
*On this trail to the days 'most forgotten,*
*The days that will never come back.*

*Deer and elk drink at its waters,*
*And the dark, shaggy buffalo hordes*
*Graze on the range near its borders*
*While the antelope muddy its fords.*
*It's a wonderful trail to travel,*
*Of all trails it's the oldest and best—*
*The trail of an old-timer's memory,*
*And it leads to the heart of the West.*

ROBERT H. FLETCHER

# OF MY HELPFUL FRIENDS...

The debt of gratitude that I owe to many people for information and other help in connection with the compounding of this tome is like the national debt. It is astronomical, keeps increasing, and can probably never be discharged. It is impossible to cite each of them individually, but I hereby tender special thanks to the following for their sage advice and generous assistance:

President Gene Etchart and all the other Executive Committee members of the Montana Stockgrowers Association who initiated and authorized this book; Eddy Phillips, veteran former secretary, and Ralph Miracle, present secretary of that organization; Mike Kennedy, director of the Historical Society of Montana and editor of *Montana, The Magazine of Western History;* the past and present librarians of the Society's Historical Library, Anne McDonnell, Rita McDonald, Virginia Walton, and Mary Dempsey; the heirs of the Kohrs estate, who so graciously permitted use of material from Con Kohrs' unpublished works; Lee Ford, of Great Falls, who has thoughtfully preserved invaluable records of his father, Robert S. Ford, pioneer cattleman;

old-timers Austin Middleton, Julian Terrett, and Ed Holt, who rode the Power River Range long, long ago; Miles City residents Casey Barthelmess, photographer, writer, rancher and humorist extraordinary; Henry Sawtell, banker and stockman; Nick Monte of grazing district fame, and Jim Masterson, master artist and depicter of the Old West with brush, pen, and pencil; Frank McDowell, Fred Hirschy, and the Clemow brothers of the Big Hole Basin; Jack Brenner, past-president of MSGA and active stockgrower of the Horse Prairie country; G. R. ("Jack") Milburn, of the N Bar, Angus breeder immediate past-president of the American National Cattlemen's Association; Bill Armington, who grew up in the cow business along the High Line; Rial Havens, Deer Lodge Valley rancher, partner and manager of the Montana Livestock Auction Company; Lyman Brewster, top rider and scion of a prominent cowland family; Fred S. Willson, head of the Department of Animal Industry and Range Management, Montana State College; R. D. Nielson, State Supervisor, Bureau of Land Management; Favre Eaton, Supervisor, Deer Lodge National Forest; and Mrs. Helen Flowerree, of Great Falls, whose data concerning D. A. G. Flowerree and her father-in-law, W. K. Flowerree, were most helpful; and not forgetting Bud (A. B.) Guthrie, writer and Pulitzer Prize winner, who gave me so much encouragement.

Tribute is paid to members of cowland's top echelon: the owners, ramrods, and plain pounders of leather with whom I once had the privilege of friendship or contact, but who are now camped in the Elysian Fields where the grass grows stirrup-high. Most of them were my seniors. I learned much from them—sometimes while bending an elbow. You will meet some of them in the following pages. I name them here at random:

John Survant, State Senator and theater owner, who ramrodded the Circle Diamond in its prime; Tom Mix, cowboy, movie actor, circus owner; Wallace Coburn, "cowboy poet-lariat," and foreman Jake Myers, both of the Circle C; Territorial Governor Sam T. Hauser, Henry Sieben, U.S. Senator T. C. Power, banker T. A. Marlow and his ranching partner, C. J. McNamara; rugged Bill Flowerree, Sr.; A. B. Cook, breeder of blue ribbon Herefords; Governor Elmer Holt; Harold Hoover and Bill Sullivan of the Highwoods; dynamic Jack Burke; Bud Story, whose father brought the first herd of Texas cattle to Montana; Teddy Blue, Ott Cassidy, and Long Henry Plott, colorful characters who came up the Texas Trail; Charley Stuart, son of Granville; Dan Raymond, Madison Valley rancher and long-time secretary of the Montana Livestock Commission; Johnny Ritch, newsman, historian, story teller, and recorder of "early times" in salty prose and verse.

To these seasoned hands, whose laughter, tales, and times I can't forget, I doff my Stetson in respectful memory.

ROBERT H. FLETCHER

# SPEAKING OF COW PEOPLE...

Charlie Russell was about as visionary as anyone who ever ranged these parts. He surely had someone like the author of this book in mind when his mouthpiece, Rawhide Rawlins, stated: "Speakin' of cowpunchers I'm glad to see in the last few years that them that know the business have been writin' about 'em. It begin to look like they'd be wiped out without a history. Up to a few years ago there's mighty little known about cows and cow people. . . ."

It was, indeed, a happy set of circumstances—like cattle in deep grass, warm rain, and money in the bank—that brought Bob Fletcher and the Montana Stockgrowers Association into the same corral, determined to rope, tie, and brand the facts that would make up this significant book. Although this fine organization of cattlemen is in no danger of being "wiped out"—as a matter of fact, they have flourished, and matured to the point where the preservation of heritage and history becomes a part of their complex structure of public service—yet it is commendable that they would undertake an extra chore as herculean as this. In Bob Fletcher the Montana Stockgrowers certainly found the ideal roundup captain.

Here is a writer who knows the rangeland and its landmarks without a map (his Montana historical highway markers are the best in the business). Many of the old-timers have been his friends or acquaintances and some of them were his relatives. In addition, he possesses a keen sense of history; understanding the empathy and interrelationship of Territorial explorers, fur-traders, gold miners, and the multitude of other frontier and western types and events so intertwined with Montana cowboys and cowmen. Above all, Bob Fletcher has the poet's instinct. (Is there a better western verse than "Don't Fence Me In"?) This accounts for his rare feeling for local idiom and beauty, and his sensitivity to the tragedy, laughter, strength, bravery, rugged individualism, and other splendid nuances which set the cowmen apart as a rare breed even in their own bailiwick of uncommon northern Great Plains rawhide characters.

When Ralph Miracle, representing the Stockgrowers Association, and Bob Fletcher invited us to ride along, "after the roundup was over and the cattle bedded down," it came as an honor and a gracious gesture. But the Montana Stockgrowers spawned this book and Robert Fletcher nurtured it. They alone should get full credit for the splendid quality of meat, bone, and heart that it possesses. We of the Historical Society of Montana simply provided an open range of raw source material and rare records, and a picture pasture by means of our files of documentary photographs and illustrations.

It is a happy circumstance that Montana can call on the art of C. M. Russell at a time as propitious as this. We don't even have to brag about the rightness of such illustration. A Texan, J. Frank Dobie—the lovable, long-horn-mustang-rangeland-saga singer—without prodding, says of CMR: "The greatest artist of the West. He knew the range from working on it and yearned towards it with primal gusto. He had a genius burning inside him that hardly another American artist has felt. . . ." I'm sure Charlie Russell would be pleased to have his inimitable rangeland portraits in a volume depicting the Montana cattle industry, its history, and primary organization.

One other point, part of it implicit, some of it explicit in this book, but all of which I feel bears added emphasis here: Mari Sandoz says some of it in the introduction to her beautifully written book, *The Cattlemen:*

> . . . to most of the world the cattleman and his cowboys, good and bad, are not known for the significance of their beef production. Instead they are the dramatic, the romantic figures of a West, a Wild West that is largely imaginary. To some of the rest of us, however, the rancher is the encompassing, the continuous and enduring symbol of modern man on the Great Plains. His number has grown vast and varied through the long years since the first Spanish cows trailed their dust eastward from the Pecos, and his stories have become as numerous as the Longhorns that burgeoned in the new land. . . .

Maurice Frink sees another side of it in his searching book, *When Grass Was King:*

Grass never ruled supreme and alone. But some of the early cattlemen thought it did, and staked their fortunes on it. Before the throne of grass they built an empire—and then watched it wither away. . . . Droughts and blizzards played their part in the drama, as did ruthless economic trends before which the cattlemen could only bow as they bowed before the winds that seared their lonely plains. The swarming settlers play a part, with their plows and their fences. The despised sheepherder had a hand in it. So did railroad expansion. But the cattlemen's own avarice was a part of it, too. The founders of the industry expedited its collapse, by monopolizing what was not exclusively theirs, by using the land with little thought beyond immediate gain, by occasionally employing in their own interest a violence as ruthless as any of the economic or natural forces that warred upon them.

They shortened their day in the sun, but it would have been a brief day at best, for the open range methods . . . were wasteful and extravagant. It encouraged over-grazing; it led to losses of cattle due to their straying, and to the hazards of weather; it made proper care of the animals impossible and improvements of breeds difficult; it tolerated rough handling of cattle, with subsequent loss of weight; and it led to range disputes and controversies costly in time, money and life. . . . The days of the open range gave the cattlemen . . . a little while in which to make use of the wild land before it was tamed. If some of them developed their opportunity to the point of exploitation, they were not alone. Other interests in the growing young nation were doing the same. . . . There was political ferment, and industrial unrest. And in the thirty-year period of the rise and fall of the open range system . . . financial storm centers in cities far to the east sent their waves of depression rolling across the country to crumble the cliffs of the cattle empire. . . .

All this was possible because the pioneering cattlemen, who had great faults, also had great virtues. Stripped of their occupational trappings . . . they were essentially the same men who peopled our other frontiers as the United States grew from a cluster of colonies on the eastern seaboard to a nation crowding a continent. They were daring and durable. They were adventurous and on occasion lawless, for they were living in a land to which order had not yet come. . . . They were self-reliant. . . . Like the men of all frontiers . . . they were impatient of restraints and resentful of the encroachment of those who came after them along ways made easier by those who had gone ahead. They were independent, sometimes to the point of arrogance. They were visionary and often unrealistic, surprisingly slow at times to adapt to changing conditions. They were sometimes selfish. . . .

Both Mari Sandoz and Maurice Frink sketch a broad, multi-hued canvas, pertaining to all cattlemen in all the west; a task impossible to do without great generalization. Because generalizations have a way of establishing stereotypes and misconceptions, I am compelled to point out that Montana, from free grass to fences, enjoyed fundamental differences that are deeply vital and must be understood.

Cattle raising has been engaged in longer here on a major scale than in any other Northern Great Plains state. We Montanans are now well into the first quarter of the second cattle-raising century. Of all the range-cattle states, including the two greatest early ones, Texas and California, Montana has undergone the least change. What started here as a predominant industry has remained so, and there is nothing on the horizon to indicate that within the foreseeable future ranching will not continue to be a dominant Montana industry—perhaps *the* dominant one. Agriculture is as vital to Montana's economy in the twentieth century as it was in the nineteenth. Livestock is the heart beat of our agriculture.

The "throne of grass" never withered away here in Montana. The trauma of adjustment was more intelligent and orderly, less devastating, and better geared to meet changing conditions and times than elsewhere. In a century which saw terrible bloodletting between cattlemen and sheepmen, cattlemen and homesteaders, and cattle barons arrayed against small cattlemen and cowboys, Montana disclaims even a single such "war." Maybe nature was a fraction less harsh here in blizzard, drought, and the other frightful extremes, but I doubt it. Certainly such economic evils as national panics and hard financing were approximately equal in force. All the other hazards existed, but they always, somehow, were mitigated or better handled here.

There has been less avarice, better adaptability, more stability, better organization and leadership in Montana stockgrowing than elsewhere. Perhaps chauvinism overwhelms me in believing that this has always been *the* ideal cattle country, but I do believe it. I am convinced, too, that the quality of personal character of Montana cowmen has been a notch higher than elsewhere. I am also convinced that the continuity of several Montana stockgrowing generations has established a heritage, a spirit, a tenacity, and a know-how that cannot be equalled. Some of these intangibles are hard to express in words. They are important. Bob Fletcher states the case entertainingly, accurately, and well in the fascinating pages which follow.

MICHAEL KENNEDY
*Director, Historical Society of Montana*

# CONTENTS

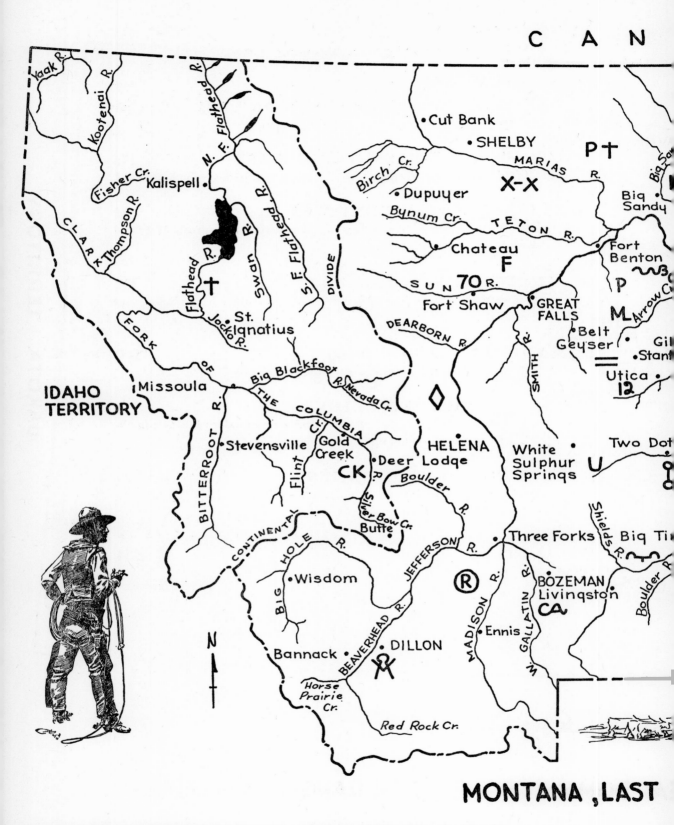

From the original map designed for this book by Robert Fletcher and Michael Kennedy; drawn by
C. Zuehlke, Assistant Curator, Historical Society of Montana. Line drawing by Charles M. Russell.

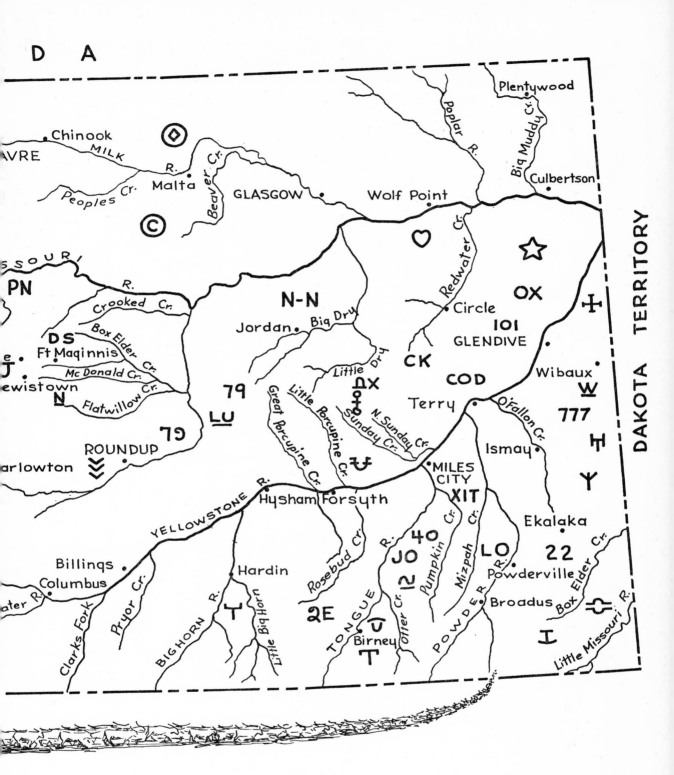

D A

Chinook
ꜹVRE
MILK
Peoples Cr.
Malta
GLASGOW
Wolf Point
Plentywood
Poplar R.
Big Muddy Cr.
Culbertson

⊙

©

♡

☆

OX

Circle

101
GLENDIVE

✝

Beaver Cr.
Redwater Cr.

SSOURI
R.
Crooked Cr.
PN

Box Elder Cr.
DS
Ft Maqinnis
J
McDonald Cr.
ewistown
N
Flatwillow Cr.

N-N
Jordan
Big Dry

Little Dry

Dry

CK

COD
Terry

Wibaux
W
777
H
Y

79

LU

79
ROUNDUP
ɑrlowton
≫

Great Porcupine Cr.
Little Porcupine Cr.
Sunday Cr.
N. Sunday Cr.

Ω⚬

U

MILES
CITY

Ismay

O'Fallon Cr.

XIT

Ekalaka

22

YELLOWSTONE R.
Hysham Forsyth

Billings
Columbus
ꜹter R.
Clarks Fork
Pryor Cr.
Hardin
BIGHORN R.
Little Bighorn

Rosebud Cr.

Tongue R.
2E
Birney
T
U

40
JO
2

Pumpkin Cr.
Mizpah Cr.

LO
POWDER R.
Powderville
Broadus

Box Elder Cr.
⚒
I
Little Missouri R.

Otter Cr.

DAKOTA TERRITORY

ꜰAT DOMAIN OF THE OPEN-RANGE CATTLEMEN

# ILLUSTRATIONS

Ox-team freighter at historic Fort Benton
H. K. Fast Freight terminal, Last Chance Gulch
Helena, 1868——Bale of Hay Saloon, Virginia City
Hangman's Tree, Last Chance Gulch, 1865
Johnny Grant's Deer Lodge Ranch. Drawing by Granville Stuart
Hungry Indians waiting for rations of beef

(between pages 68 and 69)

An early-day Montana ranch——Interior, Sawtell's ranch house
Conrad Kohrs——Nelson Story
*Texas Trail Boss,* by Charles M. Russell——T. C. Power
Power's trading post and freighter outfit
River-boat levees, Front Street, Fort Benton, 1878
Corrine, Utah Territory——Last Chance Gulch——Robert S. Ford
H. A. Milot's saloon and hotel, Sun River——Granville Stuart
Wolfer's shack——*The Surprise Attack,* by Charles M. Russell
Fort McGinnis in Indian Country——S. T. Hauser
Fort Keogh, 1878. Drawing by H. Steiffle
*The First Furrow,* by Charles M. Russell
*The Custer Massacre,* by Harold von Schmidt
CK cattle being trailed to Cheyenne

(between pages 108 and 109)

*I'm Scareder of Him Than of Injuns,* by Charles M. Russell
*A Fighting Chance,* by R. Farrington Elwell
A Montana beef herd on the way to market, 1900
A quiet gathering of ranch neighbors
Judith Basin roundup crew, 1885——Eating beans and beef at a roundup
Line camp of a cow outfit on Crow Indian land
An early southeastern Montana ranch
Coburn cowboys north of the Milk River, in the 1890's
Dining room, Old Grand Central Hotel, Fort Benton
Vigilante justice. Pen-and-ink drawing by Irving Shope
Facsimile of a pledge signed by early Sun River cattlemen
*The Herd Quitter,* by Charles M. Russell
Branding cattle on the Shonkin Range
White Sulphur Springs as a thriving cow town
*Settlers Braving the Blizzard,* by E. S. Paxson
*No Ketchum,* by Charles M. Russell
Early Northern Pacific cattle train——The Old Choteau House
Cowboys on the range between Havre and Shelby
Waiting for the next calf–Big Dry, 1904
James Fergus beef herd trailing to the railhead near Clagett, 1896

*All pictures not otherwise credited are from the collection of the Historical Society of Montana.*
*The Charles M. Russell drawings illustrating the text are from the same collection.*

*Free Grass to Fences*

Various phases of the western cattle story have been written often and well, but the history of the Montana Stockgrowers Association, which is an integral part of the tale—in fact, the actual core of the cattle industry in Montana—has never been compiled. Hence this book, in which a certain amount of frontier tradition and color is woven into the pattern of high hopes, bitter disappointments, and grim, hard work.

In the early days of Montana cattlemen's organizations, records were sketchy. The old-timers themselves have pulled stakes for the unfenced Elysian Fields. Their portion of the story must be pieced together from newspaper files, old letters, pictures, diaries, and the memories of their children and those others who were fortunate in knowing some of the pioneers and in seeing at least a part of the transition from free grass to fences.

R. H. F.

# 1. THE FUR TRADERS' WEST

When potential visitors look at a map of Montana, they suspect that the state is big, and when they travel it, they are convinced. Montanans have been known to send urgent appeals to friends back East, reading "Hurry out and help us look at the scenery—there is more than we can handle!" It is always "back" East because that is where most Treasure State residents or their forebears originated. "East" starts with Minnesota, Iowa, and Missouri.

You cannot know Montana by watching it stream past automobile and Pullman windows. You have to wander over it leisurely, taking time to do some traveling by foot or saddle horse, sometimes just sitting and looking. Though the two inseparables, settlement and fences, have altered appearances somewhat, it does not require a great deal of imagination to visualize the land in its primitive state.

There is an 11,000-foot vertical spread between Montana's high and low points, with the latter starting at around 1,850 feet above sea level. It is as far across the state by the looping highway, U.S. Route 10, as it is from

Chicago to Philadelphia. Because of this bigness in all directions, up and down as well as sideways, there is no monotony about Montana's climate, landscape, and people. They come in robust variety.

In the eastern part of the state shallow, narrow valleys stretch along the Missouri and Yellowstone Rivers. These elongated troughs and the bottom land of their tributaries are now fenced and irrigated. They are what the motorist sees when he follows the water grade of main highways. Between them, the airplane passenger looks down on breaks and badlands and on thousands of square miles of rolling benchland creased with coulees, stippled with buttes, and gouged by the stark channels of many dry creeks. Scrub conifers freckle wide areas, water holes are scarce, and it takes a lot of acres to graze a cow critter.

Montana's appearance changes with the seasons. When the young captains Lewis and Clark and their eager crew came questing up the far reaches of the Missouri in the spring of 1805, gaggles of wild geese were feeding on the flower-spangled prairie, cottonwoods were budding, and the wild cherry was in bloom. The willows and the ash along the river bottom were leafing, and currant, gooseberry, and "sarvis" berry bushes promised luscious fruit to come. Deer, elk, and antelope were abundant. Bighorn sheep scaled the cliffs and countless buffalo grazed as they slowly migrated, attended by lurking gray wolves. This was grass country. Much of it still is.

When June rains come, the fragile blooms of the prickly pear soften the severity of their spiny thrones and the gnarled sagebrush is fresher and more pungent. In the heat of summer the native grass cures on the stem and turns brown. White alkali patches mark dried water holes. Then the sage-tufted landscape may look bleak to unaccustomed eyes, but when you learn some of its secrets there is a lonely grandeur about the country that makes it akin to the more colorful primitive lands of the Southwest. What the stranger mistakes for an expanse of drab silence is really a region full of life and small noises. Down in the bottom of spring-fed coulees, Hereford cattle lie close to the cool seepage and chew their cuds while caressing their bald-faced progeny with mother-cow glances. Dusty streets of prairie dog towns resound to the chatter of their fat burghers, who sit with front paws drooped on paunch at the mounded portals of their homes. Sage hens and prairie chickens scuttle through the vegetation, quietly merging their protective coloring with the undergrowth. Antelope with insatiable curiosity stare at you until panic seizes them and they skim like wraiths in a wide circle, to halt and stare again. A band of range horses will spot you from afar and gallop out of sight over the first rise. Larks spring from underfoot, hawks soar overhead, magpies, looking like trig airplane models, cock a critical eye your way. The range country is not deserted.

This portion of Montana merges on the west with similar, but higher, ground that blankets the central portion from the Wyoming line to the

Canadian border. The immense domain is studded with isolated mountain ranges and flat-topped buttes that would be mesas in Arizona. The soft sandstones and shales of the plains have weathered to form characteristic rimrock escarpments which add to the confusion of surface contours. This region, too, was once unfenced range of pioneer cattle and sheep outfits. The Milk, Missouri, Musselshell, and Yellowstone Rivers cut it into big blocks, further subdivided by their tributaries. Each segment has its own lineaments and individuality. The lone mountain ranges are as picturesque as their names—the Crazies, Bear's Paw, Moccasin, Big and Little Snowies, Judith, Little Rockies, Highwoods, the Sweetgrass Hills. They are relics of the times when volcanic disturbances shook the West and raised festering blisters of molten lava.

The western third of the big state is a welter of interlocking mountain ranges, including the Continental Divide, mantled with ermine in winter and skirted with forest green the year around. In their fissures and crannies, and in the crevices of stream beds, Nature prodigally banked the ore that lured prospectors. The ranges encircle valleys or "holes," as the mountain men called them, and into these spacious basins, gulches pour clear, cold streams that unite to form rivers. Part of the water reaches the Pacific Ocean by the main stem of the Columbia River; most of the drainage on the east slope is gathered by the Missouri and flows to the Gulf of Mexico; a small portion reaches Hudson's Bay.

The mountain valleys sheltered Montana's first cattle herds and the tall-timbered labyrinths of the high places, now set aside as national forests, provide summer range for their successors. Lakes of exquisite beauty, cupped in cirques cut by montane glaciers, are surrounded by snowbanks that serve as supply reservoirs for the lowlands far into the summer. Montana was built to order for grazing cattle herds, but in repetition of man's ancient history, the hunter and trapper preceded the herdsman, who, in turn, was followed by the agrarian, with the Argonaut contributing cause and effect to the sequence.

When Louisiana was officially transferred in 1804, at St. Louis, from Spain to France, then to the United States, the American frontier along the Mississippi faced a new challenge to the west. Captains Meriwether Lewis and Billy Clark had hardly returned from their memorable journey to the mouth of the Columbia before eager businessmen and pioneers hastened to develop a fur trade in the Far West to compete with the British. St. Louis became the focal point of the urgent, restless movement that spread like a fan from Astoria to Santa Fe and lasted from 1807 to 1843—thirty-seven years of colorful adventure. This activity was inspired by the first of six great incentives that were to make an empire out of a wilderness—fur, faith, freedom, gold, grass, and grain.

The first few years would have discouraged less valiant adventurers. The St. Louis–Missouri Fur Company ran into difficulties with Indians on the upper Missouri River. John Jacob Astor was deprived of his foothold in Oregon by the War of 1812. The fur market collapsed. In 1822 it revived with a vengeance. General William H. Ashley and Major Andrew Henry organized a company in St. Louis, advertised for "enterprising young men," and got them. The Missouri River was the accepted way to the West and the first two Ashley–Henry expeditions followed it.

From a trapper's standpoint the Missouri–Yellowstone country still had disadvantages—most of them Blackfeet Indians. But it didn't take long for the enterprising young men to investigate the possibilities of other areas, and what they found was amazing. Activities were moved to the country lying northeast of the great salt lake. The region of the Green, Upper Snake, and Bear Rivers was a beaver bonanza.

Ashley instituted a new and popular trading scheme which prevailed for about ten years. A convenient gathering place was chosen in one of the mountain "holes," and a meeting time was selected for the early part of each summer. Trade goods were brought from St. Louis over a route along the Platte River, the Sweetwater, and across broad South Pass to the rendezvous. Trappers and tribes gathered there and when the caravan arrived, the packs were broken out, goods displayed, and trading began. It was a wild, picturesque bazaar in the mountains where old friends met and improvidently squandered the past year's profits on one grand bust. As soon as all the fur had been exchanged and accounts settled, the caravan packed up and headed east. The trappers, who had gathered like a colorful swirl of autumn leaves, were dispersed far and wide, blown by the same restless wind of adventure that had brought them together.

The fur furor did not create any lasting wealth or development for the country that furnished its product. It left no tangible mementos in Montana except crumbling adobe walls at Fort Benton and a few vagrant strains of white man's blood in Indian veins. But it was a prelude to settlement in which the explorations of the mountain men were helpful. There is significance in small items. In 1830 Bill Sublette brought covered wagons to the base of the Wind River Mountains and, later, to the Green River rendezvous. In 1833, his partner, Bob Campbell, brought supplies to a Rocky Mountain Fur Company rendezvous by pack string, and with the mules came two bulls and three cows—their eventual destination, the Yellowstone River. That year, and possibly three years earlier, cows were at American Fur Company's Fort Union near the junction of the Missouri and Yellowstone Rivers. These bovine curiosities in the West were not intended to be the foundation of beef herds. There was too much good meat running wild. Their primary function was to relieve the monotonous menu of the traders by providing them with the luxury of milk, cream, and butter, although for Christmas dinner at Fort Union in 1845, beef was the *pièce de résistance.* An 1850 inventory, taken at Fort Benton for Pierre Chouteau, Jr., and Company lists forty-two head of mixed cattle, appraised at from $5 to $25 per head. In 1851 there were twelve head at Fort Alexander on the Yellowstone, and the Fort Benton American Fur Company's journal, 1854–56, repeatedly mentions the presence of oxen.

Regardless of the inconsequential number of cattle that the fur trade brought to Montana, the part that the business played in the opening of the Oregon Trail had much to do with the future cattle industry of the territory and state. The Big Medicine Road of the Whites, which left the bent elbow of the Missouri River and persistently climbed to the broad saddle of South Pass, had dim beginnings as an artery of commerce when the mountain men discovered that it was the easy, natural route from St. Louis to the most productive beaver streams of the West. Robert Stuart, of the Astorians, had led a party eastward in 1812–13, roughly following the road's future course, and General Ashley's men had rolled a cannon through the pass in 1825. In 1832, two years after tall, blue-eyed Bill Sublette had pioneered a wagon route up the Platte, Captain Bonneville, on leave from the Army to take a flyer in the fur trade, put twenty wagons through to Green River with ox and mule teams.

Until 1834 there was no incentive for American fur traders to extend the overland trace to the vast, vague area called Oregon. Title to the Pacific Northwest was in dispute between the United States and Great Britain. The latter's claim was strengthened by domination of Hudson's Bay Company fur-trading posts, which were under the supervision of Dr. John McLoughlin whose headquarters were at Fort Vancouver on the Columbia. It was faith, not fur, that initiated the American settlement that made British traps succumb to American plows.

Early in the fur days, the Northwest Company of Montreal brought Iroquois Indians to the Rocky Mountains to teach the western tribes fur-trapping technique. Some of them became affiliated with the Salish (Flathead) and Nez Perce tribes. They had been taught Catholicism in the East and told their adopted tribesmen about it, their version being influenced by traditional Indian lore and their manner of interpreting the supernatural. Association with trappers had not been particularly edifying for the western Indians, either from a standpoint of business ethics or from a theological angle. Impressed by the Iroquois stories, the Salish and Nez Perce were anxious to secure white medicine men whose incantations might help them to prevail against their hereditary enemies, the Blackfeet of the plains. They sent emissaries—four different delegations of them—to St. Louis to petition for magi whose talismans and amulets were strong.

The first contingent traveled east, in 1831, with an American Fur Company brigade led by Lucien Fontenelle. Three Nez Perce and one Flathead reached St. Louis. Two of them succumbed to the complexities of civilization. The survivors, No-Horns-On-His-Head and Rabbit-Skin-Leggins, were bewildered, frightened, disappointed, and frustrated in their efforts to make known the intent of their mission. They were given an interview by the great red-headed captain, William Clark, now governor, who had passed through their tribal domains a quarter of a century before. He was sympathetic, but no zealous clergyman seemed to possess the requisite missionary fervor to swap the dubious comforts of the frontier settlements for a lonesome life in unknown country some two thousand miles away.

No-Horns-On-His-Head and Rabbit-Skin-Leggins managed to get passage the following spring on the steamboat "Yellowstone," bound for Fort Union. Both died, however, before they could complete the journey to the tribal range of their people and make a full report. Nevertheless, their errand had far-reaching results. Governor Clark told the story of their solicitation to William Walker, an educated Wyandot half-blood. Walker wrote to Mr. G. P. Disoway, of New York, wealthy secretary of the Methodist Board of Foreign Missions. At that time there was much interest in the Christianizing of heathen souls in faraway lands. Mr. Disoway wrote a letter for publication in the columns of his church's *Christian Advocate and Journal*. It got immediate and sympathetic response. Supplementary articles were journalistic feats of poetic license and touching appeal (although somewhat garbled as to fact) which revived any lagging ardor among the devout. The ingenuous petitioners were not to be forgotten.

The following year (1834), the American Methodist Episcopal Church liberally financed Reverend Jason Lee and a few helpers to answer the call. Big, extrovert Jason Lee met another Yankee in Boston, an ice-dealer turned fur trader. Nathaniel J. Wyeth, of Cambridge, starting with an academic knowledge of the fur trade, gathered from tales of Yankee skippers who had traded on the northwest coast, evolved a scheme of breaking into the highly competitive business. He would cut the cost of carrying trade goods overland by shipping them around the Horn, bringing back furs and salted salmon from the Columbia River.

In furtherance of his plan, for which he had been able to secure some financial backing, Nat Wyeth was pulling out of Independence, Missouri, in the spring of 1834, to deliver contracted trade goods to the Rocky Mountain Fur Company at their projected rendezvous on Ham's Fork of the Green River. Jason and his aides made arrangements to accompany the outfit. The pastor was no burden to the party. Jason Lee made a hand with the best of them. He did deplore Sunday traveling, but he was a practical man and bowed to necessity.

In due time, he met the Nez Perce and Flatheads—many of them—in the pandemonium of the rendezvous. The primitive braves were not prepossessing in that atmosphere of ribaldry, and they didn't appeal to the Reverend

Jason Lee as good missionary material. He preferred his parishioners proc-
essed by civilization to some degree—at least deodorized and less given to
debauchery. Also, lacking robes and ritual, he was a disappointing apostle
insofar as the panoply-loving redmen were concerned. Consequently, although the sanctification of Flatheads was his authorized mission, Jason Lee
and his helpers moved on to other fields.

Hall J. Kelley, fellow townsman of Nat Wyeth, was a long-distance,
fanatical lover of Oregon. Although he had not been there, he became obsessed with visions of commerce, settlement, national expansion, and the conversion of the Indians in that distant land. He founded the Oregon Colonization Company in 1832, and for a time Nat Wyeth was interested with him.
Jason Lee, no doubt, had been influenced by Kelley and by Wyeth, with
whom he had closely associated on his way west. After his unsatisfactory
contact with the Nez Perce and Salish, it is not hard to understand why
Oregon became his destination.

Finally the Lee party reached Fort Vancouver where the Hudson's Bay
Company's factor, genial Dr. McLoughlin, welcomed him and suggested that
he settle in the lush valley of the Willamette. It was a good arrangement for
all concerned. It put them south of the Columbia and far enough away from
the doctor's company interests to avoid any interference or friction, yet close
enough for the trading post to furnish them with supplies. Jason Lee could
establish his mission in a country of ample rainfall quite different from the
arid reaches he had traveled en route. He could combine conversion with
colonization, thereby gratifying both of his major urges.

The pastor hastened to build. He sent reports east that the Willamette
was "a broad, rich bottom many miles in length, well watered and supplied
with timber—oak, fir, cottonwood, white maple, and white ash scattered along
the borders of its grassy plains where hundreds of acres are ready for the
plough." Stories that would abash a modern Chamber of Commerce secretary
reached eastern ears. It was the type of travel promotion that gets tremendous
circulation. Oregon, in general, and the Willamette Valley, in particular, became lodestones that drew ambitious emigrants across the width of the continent.

In 1836 Dr. Marcus Whitman and his bride Narcissa, who were also
imbued with missionary fervor, drove their wagon through South Pass and
across the lava beds from Fort Hall to Fort Boise. Their four-wheeled vehicle
lasted to beyond Fort Hall, thereby setting a new endurance record. It was
then reduced to a two-wheeled cart which miraculously held together as far
as Fort Boise. Narcissa, evidently made of tougher fiber, got through without
breakdown to the journey's end on the Waiilatpu. There her husband built
his mission, just west of the present site of Walla Walla, Washington.

In 1839 a ship carried colonists around the Horn to Oregon. The next
year Joe Meek and his crony Doc Newell, fabulous characters known in

trapping circles from Santa Fe to California to the Athabaska, took frail wagons stuffed with Indian wives and kids through the Grande Ronde and over the Blue Mountains to the heart of Oregon. The fur trade was ebbing. New interests lured the nation's fidgety feet. In 1841 twenty-four westbound emigrants passed the Whitman mission. In 1842 there were over a hundred emigrants. The movement had started as a trickle; now the road to Oregon became a thoroughfare. In 1843 a caravan of 121 wagons and 1,000 persons made the trip, leaving Westport, Missouri, in June and reaching their destination in October. They had 698 head of oxen, 296 horses, and 973 head of loose cattle, most of the latter traveling in what they called the "cow column," under the care of Jesse Applegate. From then on, the number of ox-drawn prairie schooners increased each year.

It took from four to six months to cover the 2,000 miles from Missouri to Oregon, depending on the weather and the breaks. Oxen were favored as motive power. They were cheaper and more tractable than mules or horses, less coveted by the Indians, and complex harness was not required. They were not as easily stampeded and stayed closer to the wagons while grazing. As an added advantage, they could be converted into beef when occasion required. It has been estimated that at least 500,000 people followed the Big Medicine Road of the Whites and its various cut-offs. They packed their covered wagons with their household goods and garden tools and took off, singing "Oh, Susanna" while old Buck and Star laid into the yokes. They pushed along at the exhilarating pace of fifteen miles a day—some days. Babies were born in the prairie schooners and rocked to a lullaby of creaking leather and wagon wheels hollering for tar. Some of the starters were buried on the trail.

There were just a few, inadequate havens for rest, repairs, and purchase of supplies: Fort Laramie on the North Platte, built by Bill Sublette in 1834; Fort Bridger on the Black Fork of the Green River, built by "Old Gabe" and his partner Louis Vasquez when they saw the diminishing fur trade being superseded by opportunities for commerce with pilgrims bound for Oregon and California; Fort Hall on the Snake, which Nat Wyeth had built to stymie the American fur traders who had double-crossed him; Fort Boise, where Hudson's Bay's courtly Mr. Pierre Pambrun was in charge; finally, Fort Vancouver, presided over by hospitable Dr. McLoughlin, who, as American settlement thickened, had no illusions concerning the outcome of the international ownership dispute.

What a pageant it became! Organized wagon trains of hopeful home-makers; bullwhackers urging stolid oxen with whip, goad, and profanity; Mormons pushing and dragging hand carts, following their leaders with abiding faith to find sanctuary in Deseret; Forty-niners forking off to El Dorado; pony express riders breaking records by carrying Abe Lincoln's inaugural address from St. Joseph, Missouri, to Placerville, California, in

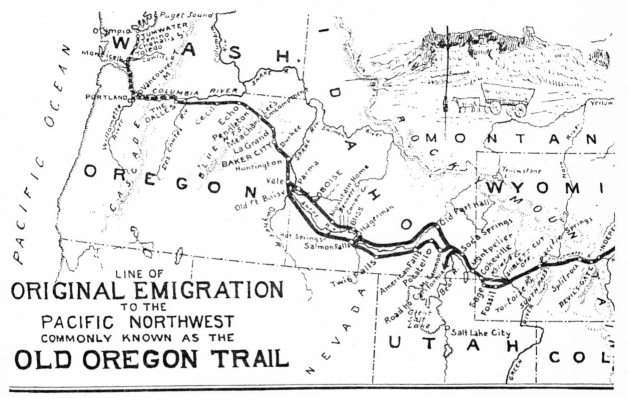

From the original Ezra Meek cartographic drawing of the Old Oregon Trail, Montana Historical Library.

seven days and seventeen hours; Ben Holladay's stage coaches; the freight outfits of Russell, Majors, and Waddell—6,250 wagons and 75,000 oxen transporting military supplies; and, finally, a crop of gold-seekers and settlers heading for the placer diggings and valleys of western Montana. No wonder the plains Indians clapped hand over mouth in the sign of amazement as the endless procession kept moving out of the east to disappear in the hazy blue of the west.

By August 14, 1850, the register at Fort Laramie had recorded the passing of 39,506 men and over 3,000 women and children so far that season, and since not more than 80 per cent registered, the total was probably close to 55,000. In their outfits were at least 9,000 wagons and 36,000 oxen, to say nothing of horses, mules, sheep, and milch cows. This was traffic made to order for any sort of roadside business—business that was not long in coming. The winter of 1849–50 overtook an Oregon-bound regiment of troops on the Trail. They were forced to camp on the Snake River near Fort Hall. With them was John Owen, sutler or storekeeper, who had accompanied the soldiers from St. Joseph. In the spring, his merchandising sense argued that it would be more profitable to sever his military connections and linger thereabouts to trade with the passing pilgrims than it would be to continue west.

That same season, Captain Richard Grant and his two sons came out of the north on similar business. The doughty captain, of Falstaffian proportions, was a former factor of the Hudson's Bay Company, having supervised a number of their trading posts, including Fort Hall, before his retirement to a life of independence. Though prone to wander in the interests of commerce, he maintained a log-cabin base in the upper end of Montana's Jefferson Valley, where the Stinking Water (now more elegantly named the Ruby River) flows into the Beaverhead.

Captain Dick was married to a convent-educated daughter of Red River mixed-bloods. Their sons, Johnny and James, lived with their own families in elkskin tepees near their parents, and the Grant community became the hub for the scattered homes of other mountain men. In the neighboring Deer Lodge Valley there was a tiny village of French breeds at the warm springs, whose salt-encrusted cone formed a lick that attracted the deer and gave the valley its name. There was a similar settlement at Cottonwood, now the city of Deer Lodge. The mountain valleys were good places for these people to winter. Game was fairly plentiful; they could be snug and comfortable in their cabins and lodges, consume bad trade-liquor on festive occasions, and visit back and forth while their squaws split the wood and did the cooking.

In the fall, the Grant men came home, driving a herd of cattle that they had accumulated by trading on the Mormon Trail between Fort Bridger and Salt Lake. John Owen also came north.

# 2. TRAIL TRADERS

Traffic reached such proportions on the Oregon Trail that grass along the route was at a premium. Work steers couldn't plod in the yoke day after day and do well on short rations. They grew footsore and gaunt. Many of them had to be abandoned when all they needed was rest and full bellies to put them in condition. The travel season was short, the way was long, and the emigrants couldn't take time out for rest. Former fur traders like the Grants and their neighbors, who had no particular place to go and were in no hurry to get there, camped beside the Trail and bartered. They found that the summer trade combined pleasure and profit.

The Grants, Delaware Jim, Bob Hereford, and others of the mountain valleys to the north had a system of exchanging trade goods and trinkets with the Salish Indians for horses, furs, and dressed skins, which were obtainable at bargain prices. The mountain men took the products of this trade to the Oregon Trail and swapped them for played-out cattle which they drove to the natural pastures in the Beaverhead and Deer Lodge Valleys. After a winter that put a layer of lard under their rinds, the cattle were hazed back to the Trail in time to meet the van of the next season's wagon trains. The traders then plied a brisk trade by exchanging one active, fat steer for two thin, trail-weary critters. Such profitable business attracted competition. White settlers had appeared in another big valley in the heart of the mountains and they, too, became interested in cattle.

Some years before, Father Pierre Jean De Smet, a young Jesuit priest of Belgian birth, had responded to the last of the Nez Perce and Flathead appeals for missionaries. At a preliminary meeting with them in 1840, he promised to return the following year prepared to establish a permanent center. True to his word, in 1841 he accompanied a party of Oregon-bound emigrants from St. Louis as far as Fort Hall. His small retinue of assistants was equipped with saddle horses, pack animals, four carts, and a wagon drawn by oxen. He was received by an expectant contingent of Flatheads, who conducted their new religious mentors to their ancestral home in the Bitterroot Valley.

Under Father De Smet's energetic guidance, the original St. Mary's Mission was built. During the next few years he and his aides accomplished much. They split rails and fenced a plot of ground where they planted wheat and potatoes with seeds brought from Hudson's Bay Company's Fort Colville, near Kettle Falls of the Columbia. They brought milch cows over travois trails from the same source. The mission flourished, but the unregenerate Blackfeet from the plains loved to harry the Flatheads. They were a perpetual menace. Also, white trappers and hunters formed the habit of wintering near the mission. Those hardy scalawags had an ungodly influence on the flock, according to Father Lawrence B. Palladino, who recorded that "amid the good seed sown by the Fathers, an enemy scattered cockle which seemed likely for a while to destroy the harvest of souls." The priests encountered other perplexing problems, and in 1850 decided to move farther west.

John Owen's arrival from the Oregon Trail was perfectly timed. He bought the mission improvements, found an industrious and comely squaw, and settled down to enjoy life in that fertile and scenic locality near the present town of Stevensville, Montana. He, too, fenced land and did a bit of farming. He rebuilt the saw and grist mills of the departed fathers and constructed an adobe stronghold that became known as Fort Owen. With the stock acquired from the priests as a nucleus, he developed a herd of cattle.

The fort became a gathering place and trading center for both Indians and whites. "Major" Owen catered to their wants with goods brought in by pack train from the Dalles on the Columbia. Settlers began to build homes in the neighborhood of the fort, where protection and supplies were close at hand. Some came over the Indian trails from the west; some, like the Grants, were former Hudson's Bay Company employees; others, like John Owen, had traded on the Oregon Road or had just drifted in. The major was a hospitable host who had accumulated a library of some three hundred volumes. His conviviality is indicated by his daily journal, which was salted with such laconic entries as "Old woman went fishing today," a reference to one of his squaw's foibles, and "Sundry nips last night," a reference to one of his own.

The decade of the 1850's was the first, and a prosperous, period in the cattle business of future Montanans. Many of these first stock dealers became leaders in subsequent industrial and political affairs of the territory. In 1851 Neil McArthur, in charge of Fort Hall, accompanied the Grant brothers to Salt Lake. There he met young Louis Maillet, fresh from the east and looking for employment. McArthur hired him, principally because he wanted Louis to teach him French. The winter of 1852–53 was extremely severe in parts of Oregon. The Columbia River in the vicinity of the Dalles was frozen for six weeks. Settlers in that area lost thousands of cattle. In the spring, McArthur made Maillet a partnership offer to buy stock on the Oregon Trail, drive them to the Bitterroot Valley for fattening, and then sell them in the settlements along the Columbia to replace the winter's losses. This idea started the two men on a horse and cattle trading career that kept them shuttling between the Bitterroot and Oregon. They ranged their stock in the Bitterroot, Grass, and Jocko Valleys and sold or traded them in Oregon, from Fort Colville to Fort Vancouver.

This was one of the earliest full-time cattle enterprises in what was to be Montana. The partnership was a success until 1859. Then, during Maillet's absence on a business trip to California, McArthur headed for the Fraser River gold excitement, leaving their financial affairs in a tangle. When they had last inventoried their joint property, it had figured at $150,000, a very comfortable stake for those days. When Maillet returned, he found that he was broke.

In 1851 Lieutenant Caleb E. Irvine was stationed at Fort Drum, a military post located at the Dalles. He met John Owen who was there after supplies for his trading post. The lieutenant resigned his commission in the U.S. Army and came to the Bitterroot with Owen. He spent the next five years trading on the Mullan Road and bringing cattle back to the valley. The transactions of these early cattlemen were not large, but as they moved back and forth between their home range and the markets of Utah, Idaho, and Oregon, each trip piled up a little more profit.

When General Isaac I. Stevens was appointed governor of the brand-new territory of Washington in 1853, he was interested in an expedition, outfitted at St. Paul, to make a reconnaissance that might determine the future of a northern railroad route to the Pacific. Lieutenant John Mullan, Second Artillery, U.S.A., was the ranking engineer of the party, which included Fred H. Burr, engineer, and Christopher P. Higgins, packer and wagon-freight expert. Congress was not as liberal with appropriations for public works in those days. It took a great deal of wheedling by proponents of the scheme to procure authorization of a very modest sum for locating and constructing a military road from Fort Benton, head of navigation on the Missouri, to Fort Walla Walla, Washington. The road was to serve as a precursor for steel rails.

Lieutenant Mullan began preliminary surveys from headquarters in the Bitterroot Valley and actual construction was started from the west end in 1859. That winter the engineers camped in a cantonment at St. Regis de Borgia, east of Lookout Pass, where they operated the first deep freeze in the Pacific Northwest. Beef cattle were driven in, slaughtered, frozen in the snowbanks, and they supplied the culinary department until spring. By 1862, Mullan had succeeded in constructing 624 miles of trail which an average wagon outfit could negotiate in forty-seven days. The road became of some importance in the moving of cattle from east and west. Both Fred Burr and Chris Higgins were to become cattlemen and prominent citizens in their new environment. In the fall of '58, Burr purchased 400 head of cattle in Salt Lake and drove them to the Bitterroot Valley. The young Irishman Chris Higgins, with his partner, Frank L. Worden, moved stock into the Hell Gate area, near the present Missoula, bringing them from Walla Walla in 1860.

Four years after the Jesuits sold their Bitterroot improvements to John Owen, Father Adrian Hoecken, originally of St. Mary's Mission, established the St. Ignatius Mission at the behest of the Kalispell and Pend d'Oreille clans of the Salish nation. The mission is located at the south end of Mission Valley, then called Sinielemen by the Indians, literally translated "surrounded." Twice a year the Flatheads were accustomed to leave the mountains to hunt buffalo on the plains. According to Father Palladino, "the Indians whilst on the great hunts, were a prey to the wildest excitement which left little if any room for religious instruction." There can be no doubt that those were mighty absorbing occasions, involving every member of the tribe. Unquestionably, the priests tried to discourage these hunts with all the diplomacy they could muster, which may account for the fact that four years after the Mission of St. Ignatius was built, the Indians, through the mission, owned 1,000 cattle, a docile, unexciting substitute for buffalo.

Robert Stuart, Virginian turned Forty-niner, left his wife and children in Iowa while he went gold-seeking in California. He evidently thought well of the opportunities out there for he came back to his family in the summer of 1851, tarried a few months, then returned to the gold fields, accompanied by two of his sons, James and Granville, aged twenty and seventeen, respectively. Robert himself stayed just a year, then returned to his Nancy. The boys lingered for four more years, with varying fortunes, before heading east with nine others. They reached Malad Creek in Utah in mid-July of 1857, and there Granville came down with "mountain fever." After delaying ten days, eight of the party went on, leaving the Stuart brothers and their close friend Reese Anderson at the camp of Jake Meek, trader and friend of the Grants.

At Salt Lake, Brigham Young had proclaimed the independent state of Deseret, an act that Congress construed as secession. When persuasion failed to alter the decision of the leader of the Latter Day Saints, a military expedition under General Albert Sidney Johnston was ordered out to bring Utah back into the Union. While Granville was convalescing, the Mormons became greatly perturbed over the approach of the troops, and their patrols blocked all roads and passes. Martial law was instituted insofar as traveling gentiles were concerned. The Stuarts could go neither east nor west, lest they be apprehended by Brigham Young's "Destroying Angels." When Jake Meek, their host, suggested that the three boys move north with him to a remote valley where they could wait for the "Mormon War" to blow over, they had little choice but to go.

They crossed the Continental Divide at present Monida in October and came down Red Rock Creek and the Beaverhead River to the mouth of Blacktail Creek where they holed up until Christmas, with the Bob Dempseys and the Antoine LeClairs their close neighbors. The Grants, the Tom Pambruns, John Powell, Louis Maillet, John Jacobs and family, the Bob Herefords, John Saunders, Antoine Pourrier, and several others were at their old stomping ground near the mouth of the Stinking Water, while Delaware Jim and his brother Ben held forth a mile down the Beaverhead. The Stuart boys and Reese Anderson soon became acquainted with the local citizens and fell into the routine of those traders and mixed-bloods.

Around New Year's Day of 1858, ten men who had enlisted as teamsters in General Johnston's army arrived from Fort Bridger, under the command of B. F. Ficklin. This detail had been given the assignment of buying beef cattle for the soldiers. By that time, Captain Grant had a herd of six hundred. Burr, McArthur, Maillet, and others were very much in the livestock business. In spite of the plentiful supply, Ficklin could not get all the cattle he wanted nor could he get them on terms that suited him. The mountaineers had heard exaggerated rumors of the Mormon situation. They were reluctant to sell stock to the Army lest they offend the Latter Day Saints, who, they feared, would retaliate by sending armed men to wipe them out. Some of them had even contemplated leaving for more remote places until the trouble was over. They refused to guarantee delivery of beef animals in Mormon territory under the existing conditions. Ficklin returned to Fort Bridger in the spring without beef, but he had set a record as the first cattle buyer coming to Montana.

The Stuarts had not lived the life of lotus eaters that winter, but still they were not eager to start for Iowa in the spring. They liked the country and the life they had fortuitously found, and decided to go trading on the

Road. This popular vocation was to engage their interest for two years. But before becoming traders, they made a cursory examination of alleged placer ground on Benetsee Creek, a tributary of Clark's Fork of the Columbia, west of Deer Lodge Valley.

Benetsee Finley, a Red River breed who had acquired some prospecting experience in California, had washed out about two ounces of gold dust there. He sold it to Angus McDonald, factor of the Hudson's Bay Company's Fort Connah on Post Creek of the Mission Valley. The gold proved to be high-grade, but Benetsee did nothing further about his prospect. Benetsee Creek (now Gold Creek) had fascinated the Stuarts ever since they had heard about the gold. They found colors but lacked equipment to do any serious development work; so off they went for the Oregon Trail with twenty head of trading horses.

Their excursions took them as far south as Camp Floyd, below Salt Lake, where General Johnston's invading army was encamped. From there, they went to Green River, favorite haunt of the mountain men in the fur days, and began buying and trading oxen in earnest. In the fall they drove the cattle they had acquired to the mouth of the Stinking Water. There the Indians pestered them by killing their stock, so they moved on to the mouth of Benetsee Creek, with the intention of developing their placer prospect. They switched from tepee to log cabin, wooed and won Indian helpmates, and in no time at all the new settlement of American Fork became a popular stopping point. Strangers, as well as old-timers, began dropping in. They came from the Oregon Trail and in from Fort Benton via the Mullan Road, and they found hospitality with the Stuarts. Most of them were en route to the Salmon River gold diggings, west of the Bitterroot Mountains. Some of them lingered awhile and sluiced out fair results in nearby Pioneer Gulch.

Mail deliveries were roundabout and uncertain at American Fork, but the Stuarts managed to keep in touch with their family back in Iowa and so learned that their brother Tom had turned Pike's Peaker. They got word to him that prospects looked good on Gold Creek. Tom may have told a friend, who told a friend. At any rate, gold-seekers soon came baying up the trail from Colorado. Two of them, Bill Eads and John White, wandered off the beaten trail and on July 28, 1862, struck pay dirt on Grasshopper Creek, originally named Willard's Creek by Lewis and Clark. Soon the little gulch was crowded to overflowing and the camp of Bannack came into existence. Other major discoveries followed: in 1863, fabulous Alder Gulch; in 1864, Last Chance Gulch. The hills swarmed with prospectors, and mining camps mushroomed wherever a strike was made. Suddenly there were thousands of hungry men to be fed in a corner of Idaho Territory that was soon to be southwestern Montana.

# 3. MEAT FOR MINERS

Not all the people who participate in a gold rush expect to mine, and so it was with the men who came hurrying to the gulches and canyons of Montana. Many of those whose fortunes and feelings had been disturbed by the war between the states were heading west in quest of new homes and careers. A Kentuckian (Samuel T. Hauser, afterwards territorial governor) wrote home from Deer Lodge in September, 1862, and said,

> Today my partner returned saying he had a claim that he thought by hard work would yield enough to buy grub with prospects of something better. Which has decided me to remain here for the winter and work with pick and shovel . . . rather a hard way to serve the Lord but better than living in the midst of the troubles at home, especially as my feelings and views are so entirely different from yours.

Those with special trades and talents set up shop and pursued the vocations they had followed at home. The barber continued to trim the hirsute, the merchant went to merchandising; the butcher, the baker, the candle-stick-maker—all dropped into their respective grooves. People of every description kept arriving at the Montana gold camps. All had the spirit of adventure and enterprise that takes men to new lands. The miners would produce the raw gold, but those who catered to their needs would have the full pokes when the diggings petered out. A local market of growing proportions was created in Montana, for Montana Territory itself had been created by act of Congress in the spring of 1864.

A hard-working miner, with appetite further whetted by youth, wanted meat as a major part of his diet and he didn't cavil about quality. He had no time to hunt game even if there had been enough to go around. Butcher shops displayed venison, mountain sheep, buffalo, elk, and moose meat as it was brought to them, but most of the men in the diggings preferred beef, even if fresh-killed and cut anywhere from shank to brisket, if it could be tossed in a skillet and fried in a hurry. But none of the early cattle traders—the Grants, for example—rose to the opportunity. Age, inertia, or other interests had overtaken them and they were succeeded by younger men whose names and deeds are now emblazoned in the records of western cow country.

There was Con Kohrs, twenty-six-year-old Danish rover who walked into the Deer Lodge Valley in 1862, after a kaleidoscopic career as cabin boy, grocery clerk, river raftsman, sausage salesman, California and Fraser River gold miner, with some experience as butcher and assistant in a brother-in-law's packing plant back in Davenport, Iowa. He was detouring through Montana with a small party of comrades intent on reaching the gold diggings of Florence and Elk City, in the Salmon River and Clearwater country of Idaho. They played out of cash and almost everything else before they got down the Deer Lodge River to American Fork where news of the big strike made by Eads and White on the Grasshopper started them backtracking. On the trail to Bannack, Con met Hank Crawford, who was looking for a butcher.

Crawford was Bannack's first, and rather temporary, sheriff, who had decided to supplement his sheriff duties with meat selling. He needed an experienced helper who knew a sirloin from a pot roast. He hired Con at $25 a month and found Con was a little short of tools, but he did have a skinning knife and managed to borrow a scales and a carpenter's saw. He whetted down a bowie knife to serve as a steak cutter. Then all he had to do was to herd three refractory heifers for 120 miles on foot to the site of the proposed enterprise. Hank built a shack with a brush roof, rustled a butcher block, erected a scaffold, and the abattoir, plus retail shop, was ready to go.

The shop was next to Cy Skinner's saloon—an appropriate location since Cy's place was itself something of a slaughterhouse at times. Before long, sinister Henry Plummer gunned his erstwhile pal Jack Cleveland into eternity at the very door of the meat shop, and Con dragged him in to die among the T-bones. This complicated matters for Hank Crawford because it started a feud with Plummer over Cleveland's death. Plummer suspected that Cleveland had divulged incriminating evidence concerning their lurid past history before he died. Thenceforth Plummer made things so disagreeable for Hank, particularly after the latter had taken a semi-official pot shot at Henry with a rifle, that Crawford left posthaste aboard a saddle horse for Fort Benton. He caught the first Mackinaw boat downstream, thereby leaving his sheriff's job for Plummer to inherit and the meat business to Con Kohrs. Con's legacy turned out to be the best bet. He parlayed the butcher shop into a cattle kingdom. Plummer was hanged.

The following year (1863), a small party of ragged prospectors eased into Bannack after a brief absence. Their manner was filled with mystery, their pokes with nuggets and gold dust. They had made a strike, and also a pact to maintain secrecy, but when they pulled out to return to their rich discovery, laden with supplies, the citizens of Bannack accompanied them en masse. The strike was on Alder Creek, a tributary of the Ruby River, sixty-odd miles east of Grasshopper Creek.

Mining camps burgeoned along Alder Gulch and soon there were 10,000 people, or practically the entire white population of Montana Territory, strung out along twelve miles of stream bed. The territorial capital was moved from Bannack to flourishing Virginia City. Con moved, too. Over there, most any worn-down ox that came in with wagon trains from the Oregon Trail would bring $100 on the hoof when sold at auction. Con and Ben Peel went into partnership in the beef business, on borrowed money and credit, at the camp of Summit.

They delivered meat from their brush wickiup shop on two burros. Their cattle came from the Bitterroot, from down Utah way, from Oregon, and from the States, the latter cattle arriving with emigrants. Miners had neither the inclination nor the "savvy" to butcher, and they had no way of keeping meat fresh for any length of time. They couldn't be bothered with boiling or roasting meat—it had to be steaks. But Ben and Con were frugal operators. They cut steaks to order and everything else went into sausage. The tallow was made into candles that sold for a dollar or more a pound. They developed good will by giving the hides to miners, who used them as rugs on their dirt floors.

It wasn't long before the partners were trading in cattle on a sizable scale. Con was the outside man while Ben ran the shop. They wholesaled to other shops and prospered in spite of the fact that much of the retail business was on credit, with the debtors likely to leave for the next new strike without bothering to settle their accounts. The year 1864 was a record one for emigrant arrivals. The newcomers were glad to sell their work cattle to the firm of "Con and Peel," who bought about 400 at $40 a head. No one seemed to know that Con's last name was Kohrs, and he didn't think it important enough to inform them. That fall, the two men bought 1,000 head for $12,000, borrowed at the rate of 5 per cent per month.

Last Chance Gulch, which became the main street of Helena, the territory's third capital, stole the limelight as a gold camp in 1864, and in '65 the partners invaded the new diggings with a big shop called the Highland City Meat Market and supplemented it with the Bull's Head. They also bought the Racetrack Ranch in the Deer Lodge Valley and picked up cattle at St. Ignatius, in the Bitterroot, and around Fort Benton. In August of that year, Kohrs bought the Johnny Grant Ranch and its mixed herd—the ranch on the edge of the city of Deer Lodge now operated by his grandson, Con Warren, past president of the Montana Stockgrowers Association.

There are many ramifications to the story of Conrad Kohrs. He was a tireless worker with the ability to call the turn on future trends in the cattle market. His interests were wide and, unquestionably, he dominated the cattle trade in the western valleys of Montana Territory for many years. His honesty was legend and his judgment respected. He is said to have had 90,000 cattle at one time and to have shipped thirty trainloads to Chicago one fall.

The first herds in western Montana were branded, usually with the initials of the owners. Even before the gold discoveries, Bob Dempsey's stock carried the RD brand and Tom Levatta's were decorated with a TL iron. Brand No. 1 in the official records of Montana Territory is the Square and Compass, and it belonged to Poindexter and Orr. Tom Poindexter left Virginia for California in his early twenties. The year was 1856, and gold mining was still attracting young men from far away. Tom met Bill Orr who hailed from Ireland but had reached the west coast via Arkansas. Poindexter was tall, handsome, and courtly; Orr was tall, tough, and practical. They possessed an exceptional combination of business talents.

They went into the cattle business in Siskiyou County and furnished beef to California miners. When the Idaho and Montana diggings opened, they extended their trade to the new discoveries. In the fall of 1865, Billy Orr brought 400 steers from the Shasta Valley to southwestern Montana and sold them to Con Kohrs. He wintered on Blacktail Creek and filed on a piece of land. Enthralled by the territory's broad mountain valleys, the partners continued trailing their cattle into the Beaverhead country for the next two years until they had located their entire stock business there and along Blacktail Creek, where it expanded prodigiously under their expert management. Portions of their properties out of Dillon operated under their names for over seventy years.

D. A. G. Flowerree (and if you are an old-timer, you will pronounce it "Flurry") was born in Missouri in 1835. When he was seventeen he went to California where he lived for the next five years. There is a gossamer tale that he next joined a troupe of ambitious adventurers (the Walker expedition to Nicaragua) intent on fomenting a revolution in a small Central American country, with the idea of taking it over and living regally thereafter. At least one biographer laconically and noncommittally states that Flowerree spent a year in Nicaragua. (He was lucky not to have remained there permanently.) The story, perhaps apocryphal, relates that the scheme met with disaster. The champions of the revolting peons were corralled by the barefooted loyalists, who lined them up against a 'dobe wall. However, so the legend goes, handsome Dan had captured the affections of a sloe-eyed senorita who, with a combination of Latin intrigue and Indian cunning, helped him to escape. Whether true or not, in the first year of Last Chance Gulch (1864), Daniel turned up hale and hearty and became the respected co-owner of an establishment perhaps less resplendent but proportionately as remunerative as the glittering casinos that now line the Las Vegas "Strip" in Nevada.

Dan Flowerree was widely known as a square dealer, a loyal friend, and a good citizen. He invested in cattle as a business that was subject to as much, if not more, risk as in his former pursuits. He brought a herd from Missouri in 1865. In 1870, he got 1,500 from Texas and repeated in 1873. He acquired range in Lewis and Clark, Teton, and Cascade Counties. It has been said that he could drive his stock from the Canadian border to Idaho and bed them down on his own ground every night. In 1883 he brought horses from Oregon and, the record states, a "mammoth" herd of cattle from the same source. In 1878 he brought 1,000 head from Oregon to Sun River and then began stocking that range on a large scale.

In his patriarchal days he was affectionately called Uncle Dan. By way of demonstrating his business versatility and acumen, he purchased grapefruit orchards in Florida and marketed the citrus gems in Montana when it was hard to convince people that they were edible. In his later years he once gazed across the Prickly Pear Valley from the elevation of Helena, where he made his home, and wistfully remarked, "When I came here that valley was entirely cohabited by antelope." Of course, like the Indians, the antelope have been driven out of the area by white settlement and now cohabit elsewhere, but the memory of Uncle Dan Flowerree remains green with the few remaining old-timers who knew him.

Still another youngster, Robert S. Ford, came west when he was about seventeen. He was born in Kentucky in 1842. His family, like many others of the Bluegrass State, moved to Missouri in 1855. Bob started his western career as a bullwhacker with famed Uncle Dick Wooton on the Santa Fe Trail, and then on the Oregon Trail, between Nebraska City and Fort Laramie. He must have displayed talents beyond the capacity of the average bullwhacker because he was made assistant wagonboss the next year and was master-in-charge of a train the year following. In 1863 he was captain of a train of sixteen ox-powered freight wagons loaded with merchandise that came to the Deer Lodge Valley; the next year he skippered a similar fleet of prairie schooners to Sun River.

Big Bob Ford liked Montana and found work with the Diamond R Transportation Company, freighting from Fort Benton and Cow Island on the Missouri River to the mining camps farther west. In the summer of 1867, he was foreman of a haying crew for T. C. Power, who had a contract to cut native grass and put up hay for cavalry troops stationed at Cow Island, a point of debarkation for river steamboats when low water would not permit their reaching Fort Benton, the head of navigation. Next year, Ford put in a bid of his own and got the haying contract at $65 a ton, which surprised him. He had set the high figure because he took into consideration the possible contingencies of bad weather and a poor grass crop, in which case he would have had to cut hay at distant points and haul it to Cow Island. As it was, everything went well; in fact, the tonnage called for was doubled by the Army when the Indians went on the warpath. Bob netted $12,000 on the deal, which gave him capital to buy his first cattle.

Ford went to Colorado in the fall of that year and bought 300 head of Texas cattle, wintering them at Fort Lupton. He started them for the Sun River in the spring of 1869, but was given such a good offer on his way through the Beaverhead Valley that he sold them then and there. In 1870 back he went to Colorado and raised the ante to 1,412 head, paying an average price of $15. By fall, he had them on the Sun River, branded 70 on the ribs in token of the year they arrived in Montana. This was the first herd to be trailed to the north side of the Missouri. Bob followed them with drives in each of the next two years and had a hard time keeping them from consorting with the buffalo when turned out on the Sun River range. In 1872 he located a ranch and built a home near the Sun River Crossing of the Fort Benton–Last Chance Gulch stage road, the ranch where his son Lee now lives. Tom Dunn then became his partner.

Bob Ford, who stood six feet two-and-a-half inches and weighed 225 pounds—all bone and muscle—was to be one of Montana's foremost pioneer builders, a leader in Montana's legislative, cattle, industrial, and financial affairs. His early cattle range was proportioned to a man of his size. It extended from the Sun River north to the Sweet Grass Hills, just south of the Canadian border.

Although some of the Territory's early citizens were foot-loose, restless prodigals, every wagon train brought settlers whose hopes and plans promised stability. Any way of getting to the gold country faster was worth looking into. So when old-timer Jim Bridger and newcomer John Bozeman each proposed a short cut from the big bend of the North Platte to the Yellowstone River, and thence to Virginia City in Alder Gulch, Montana Territory, they found prospective clients for their travel promotion schemes.

The cut-offs were discussed pro and con while emigrants tarried at Fort

Laramie. "Why, anyone who knows the first thing about the lay of the land can see that it will shorten the regular route by several hundred miles and save a month in time!" There would be no crossing the Continental Divide twice; plenty of good grass and water; game along the way, too—or so they claimed. Prairie schooners were built to take abuse, but there is a limit to the endurance of hickory, oak, and rawhide. Miles saved were valuable, so why not take the Bridger Cut-off, Bozeman Road, Bonanza Trail, or whatever you wanted to call them? Why dally away weeks on a roundabout course when you could save a month which could be put to better use washing out a bushel or so of nuggets? However, there was one serious obstacle—Indians!

Of course, there were no roads at all. They existed only in the minds of John Bozeman and Jim Bridger, but hopeful, ardent emigrants signed up nevertheless, and the first wagon trains left "Reshaw's" bridge over the North Platte and rolled away to probe forbidden land. Young Red Cloud, warrior, orator, and organizer of the Ogallalas and their Sioux tribal brethren, was decidedly opposed to permitting gross trespass on hunting grounds solemnly accorded the Indians by their last treaty with the whites. When the lurching caravans began crawling up and down over the foothills like elongated caterpillars, Red Cloud went to considerable pains to discourage them.

Early in the summer of 1864, Colonel H. B. Carrington was sent to build "forts" for the protection of whites using the new cut-off. Three were built and inadequately garrisoned. The Indians harried the military at every opportunity, and with every favorite ruse and others that they invented on the spot. They kept the soldiers holed-up and on the defensive. It was even inviting disaster to send details to the neighboring hills for timber and firewood. There were three little, undermanned "forts" to protect over 300 miles of trail. Red Cloud's star was in the ascendancy. His medicine was strong.

That same year, armchair strategists decided on a war of extermination. General Alfred Sully led an elaborately equipped expedition (4,000 cavalry, 800 mounted infantry, 3,000 teams, 12 pieces of artillery, 15 steamboats) into the badlands of the Little Missouri River to rub out the estimated 8,000 Sioux who were supposed to be haunting the area where Wyoming, the Dakotas, and Montana corner. The soldiers killed a few—just enough to irritate and consolidate the hostile tribes. It was reported a military success, but as a job of thorough erasure it was a mere smudge.

Under the circumstances, it took supreme guts and gall for Nelson Story to bring the first drive of Texas cattle into Montana in 1866. Born in Ohio in 1838, Story, like many another young buck of his day, headed west about the time he attained his majority. He was a rolling stone that gathered both moss and polish in the next few years. He tried all of the prevalent western trades—mining, logging, wagon freighting, merchandising—and made them pay. He reached the Alder Gulch mines soon after their discovery, acquired a claim above Virginia City, and hired a crew of men who sluiced out a sizable stake in a remarkably short time. He also found time to help jerk the drygoods box out from under road agent George Ives after a miners' court had sentenced Ives to be hanged, thereby assisting that infamous outlaw to reach the end of his rope in a hurry.

Story didn't allow his capital to remain idle, nor did he squander it. He betook himself to Texas where he bought 600 head of longhorns and headed them north. That was in 1866. Kansans didn't roll out the red carpet for trail herds at that time; the longhorns were alleged to bring Texas, or tick, fever with them. So when the Story herd was intercepted by determined Jayhawkers near Keosho, Story detoured via the Santa Fe Trail past Topeka to the vicinity of Leavenworth. There he bought fifteen wagons, piled them high with merchandise, attached 150 head of oxen to them as motive power, and with fifteen saddle horses and a posse of twenty-two men, struck out for Montana Territory on July 10, herding the loose stock.

After passing Fort Laramie, the resourceful young man took the short cut for the Yellowstone. The natives of that hornets' nest buzzed with resentment. Near Barrel Springs at the Dry Fork of the Powder River, shooting Indians raised Cain with the outfit, killed half-a-dozen cattle, and punctured one man with a pair of arrows that had to be removed with pliers. Story, who was a two-gun man, shot lead from his twin side arms so fast and effectively that he discouraged the attackers and succeeded in getting his outfit bedded down near Fort Reno, one of the government's protecting citadels.

In the morning, a herder came into camp with the announcement that his partner had been killed and the stock stampeded by Indians. Not to be deprived of his investment so easily, Nelson Story didn't wait to saddle; he forked a bareback horse and with a Colt persuader in each hand stormed across the Powder River in pursuit. His men joined the sortie and after running the Indians for about fifteen miles, they managed to get back to camp by midnight with practically all of the kidnapped stock.

As an added annoyance, the commanding officer not only objected to the Story herd depleting the grass close to the fort, but he decided that the drive was inimical to friendly relations with the Sioux, who were far from friendly, and who had been howling against such invasions. He forbade Story to pass. As each of the Story party was packing a new Remington breechloader that could reach out and detain an Indian a long way off, Story was not much impressed. He bypassed the fort at night and reached Fort C. F. Smith on the Big Horn River without further trouble. His herd was stampeded that night but recovered the next day. His party then crossed the Yellowstone and on December 3, 1866, reached the Gallatin Valley, having been on the trail since spring.

Story's difficulty with the Indians on the Bozeman Road was not unique. In December, 1864, Colonel J. M. Chivington had led Colorado troops to massacre a village of Cheyenne women and children. This unsavory foray, combined with the Sully campaign of that year, had started the tom-toms beating until the West was on the warpath from the South Platte to the Yellowstone. The spring of 1865 found more undaunted, or perhaps fool-hardy, drivers of bull teams taking the cut-offs. Every train was attacked. The troops in the three little forts were helpless. It was not that they lacked courage and fortitude—far from it. They had been ordered into an untenable situation with insufficient manpower to accomplish their assignment. As for Red Cloud, although suffering terrible losses on many occasions, his refusal to compromise finally brought about an official closure of the roads in 1868. The forts were abandoned and troops withdrawn from that area.

A new treaty was drawn, stipulating that no whites were to settle, or even pass through, the country recognized as the hunting grounds of the Sioux and Cheyennes, without their consent. Again the vast, vague region, including the Powder, Tongue, and Rosebud River valleys of southeastern Montana, was designated as a place where the Sioux and Cheyennes could roam and hunt unmolested as long as there were buffalo to supply them with meat and robes.

# 4. POPULATION PRESSURE

I was raised on the land where the sun rises—now I come from where the sun sets. Whose voice was first sounded on this land? The voice of the red people, who had but bows and arrows. The Great Father says he is good and kind to us. I don't think so. I am good to his white people. —My face is red; yours is white. The Great Spirit has made you to read and write, but not me. I have not learned. —When we first had this land we were strong, now we are melting like snow on the hillside, while you are grown like spring grass. . . . When the white man comes to my country he leaves a trail of blood behind him. Tell the Great Father to move Fort Fetterman away and we will have no more trouble. . . .

—*Red Cloud, before Secretary of the Interior Cox,*
*Washington, June 3, 1870.*

As the yield of old placer claims and the discovery of new ones dwindled in western Montana, there was growing interest and confidence in quartz mining possibilities, although hardrock operators were handicapped by shortage of capital, skilled labor, and adequate transportation. Covered wagons continued to come and the immigrants claimed so much arable land that stockmen, in many instances, were being forced to graze their cattle on the benches and foothills. But this was no great hardship and stockgrowers increased as public opinion crystallized into the conviction that Montana's future would be more than a golden flash in a prospector's pan. Rail service would give Montana a chance to compete in eastern markets. Everyone was looking forward to the time when railroads would solve their industrial problems.

Although mining continued to be the dominating industry of western Montana, it had settled down to a routine after the first sensational discoveries. Miners and freighters who had saved a stake went into the cattle business. A doctor used MD as his brand, a lawyer changed from clients to cows, and even the captain of the vigilantes, Jim Williams, went to ranching. It was all done without fanfare and usually a modest beginning grew to bigger, better things.

Bill Ennis gave up wagon freighting between Corinne, Utah, and Virginia City, Montana Territory, after he had brought his wife and baby daughter out from the States. He built a cabin in the Madison Valley, just over the hump from Alder Gulch, and started his ranching with a few chickens and milch cows. He sold wild hay, butter, and eggs to the mining camps across the hill. He accumulated beef cattle and horses, stamping them with a hot muleshoe before he adopted the Rising Sun brand, which is still used in southwestern Montana. By 1876, he was shipping cattle to an eastern market. He built a store and a fifteen-room frame house and, by 1881, rated a post office, over which he presided as postmaster. He left his name to the famous trout-fishing town on the Madison.

W. D. Jeffers also abandoned freighting and brought 1,000 head of Texans into the Madison in 1869, the drive taking six months. In 1870 he brought in 1,000 more and doubled that number the following year. The valley settled rapidly with stockmen who built substantial homes and acquired land by homesteading and purchase from the railroads. The slopes of the Madison, Tobacco Root, and Gravelly mountain ranges furnished good forage. Over to the west, on the Ruby, the Beaverhead, Jefferson, and Big Hole Rivers, the same thing was happening during the seventies, and some of the cattlemen were old-timers by then.

In 1863, the year of the Alder Gulch discovery, Dr. Leander W. Frary, of the MD iron, ran an ad in *Wonderland Illustrated,* a book published in Virginia City, that read:

Jessamine Stock Ranch, Madison County, Montana. Breeder and dealer in Thoroughbred and Graded Shorthorn Durham Cattle. Choicest breeds of thoroughbred Fowls. Stock bought and sold.

That Doc Frary was not a lone wolf in the stock business at that early date is attested by part of another advertisement in the same book:

> Our Thoroughbred stock are selected from the best herds in Kentucky and our common stock are the best in the Territory. We intend to make Thoroughbred stock raising a specialty and guarantee that everything is as represented. Our ranch is one of the best and we have fitted up our stable, corrals, and pastures in the best style.

That modest statement was sponsored by Messrs. Sedman and McGregor, who had purchased their base stock from the J. B. Snapp Home Park Ranch on Willow Creek, a tributary of the Ruby River.

In October, 1868, a Salt Lake firm bought cattle in the Jefferson Valley from Patrick Largey, agent for Ed Creighton who built the first telegraph line reaching into Montana. They were driven to Utah to fill meat contracts for construction crews along the Union Pacific right-of-way. Later in the fall, Jerry Mann drove a mixed herd south and disposed of them to a railroad grading contractor. It was not all one-way traffic. In the summer of 1870, L. E. Graham and J. B. Taylor brought 450 heifers and five purebred Durham bulls to the Deer Lodge Valley, shipping them by rail from Omaha to Ogden, Utah, and then driving north.

By the end of the sixties, Poindexter and Orr were well established on their ranches in Beaverhead County. Their place along Blacktail Creek, not far from Dillon, was noted for its dairy products. Many of the ranchers in the western valleys combined dairying with their beef cattle operations. One such enterprise churned three and one-half to four and one-half tons of butter a season. Under the able management of the partners, their holdings became an institution that employed thirty to forty men the year around. Their stock business was diversified. They ran fine Durham cattle, bred Clydesdale, Norman, and Percheron work horses, and sheared bands of Cotswold-Merino sheep. In 1876, they drove large herds of range cattle to summer in the high Centennial Valley on the Idaho border. Mrs. Orr named the valley to commemorate the Centennial Exposition then being held in Philadelphia. Cattle have grazed there ever since, sharing forage along the foothills of the Continental Divide with moose, deer, elk, and antelope.

Up Horse Prairie Creek, where Lewis and Clark first met the Shoshone Indians in 1805, on Bloody Dick Creek, in the Big Hole Basin, up Red Rock Creek, down the Deer Lodge Valley, over on Flint Creek and Nevada Creek, wherever grass grew and water ran, cattle were turned loose to do the harvesting. Dave Metlin, from Illinois, former Union soldier and gold miner, sluiced out enough dust and nuggets on his placer claim near Bannack to purchase 100 head of Texas cattle in Salt Lake. He expanded this small herd to 7,500 and owned 15,000 acres at one time. In 1863, Irishman Martin Barrett came in from Colorado with 200 horses and cattle. He began a dairy business to provide Bannack with butter at $1.25 per pound and sold wild hay to freighters at $40 a load. French, Swiss, Irish, Dane, Swede, Yankee—they came from foreign lands and a score of different states to make the southwest corner of the Territory the cradle of Montana's cattle industry.

Giving encouragement and financial assistance to the pioneer cattlemen of that area was Ben F. White, a unique character who started an adventurous career in 1854, at the age of sixteen, by sailing before the mast out of Boston to China and back. His second trip took him to the Golden Gate, and he lingered in California for several years before reaching Montana via Idaho. Not a dull moment occurred in any of those years. His occupations varied from fiddling in a honkytonk to fruit farming, studying law, politics, salt mining, freighting, and real estate. He was an organizer and a money-maker so it was quite natural for him to become a partner in the banking firm of Sebree, Ferris, and White, that founded Dillon's first bank. In the capacity of cashier, he was the active manager of the institution, since President Sebree's other extensive interests kept him in Idaho most of the time.

Ben White had confidence in the cattle business and, although some of his banking methods were unorthodox, the bank prospered. Like other old-school bankers, he loaned as much money on character as he did on security. He knew the capacity of the country and its people. His unconventional tobacco-chewing proclivities didn't hamper his personal popularity. His vocabulary was a composite of highlights gleaned from the lingo of sailors, miners, and bullwhackers, and he had a free-wheeling style of expectoration to punctuate his conversation. He considered cuspidors unnecessary refinements in office furnishings and was known to comment that if people didn't keep the damned things out of his way he would be tempted to spit in one of them.

He was elected to the Territorial Council, now called the Senate, in 1882, on the Republican ticket and was immediately recognized by other sections of the Territory as an outstanding leader. In 1889 President Benjamin Harrison appointed him Montana's territorial governor. To his liberal banking policies, justified by the integrity of his customers and the superb resources of southwestern Montana, may be credited a large measure of the development of that world-famous cattle country where cowmen are still doing business in a large way.

The national panic of 1873 raised hob everywhere. Even faraway Montana felt the effect of depressed prices. Cattlemen had been making drives to Ogden, Utah, to Granger and Cheyenne, Wyoming, and even to Bismarck and Fargo, North Dakota. It was a sixty-day hike to Granger and the feed en route was nothing to cheer about. This system of trying to find a market in hard times was not too popular, especially when the shipped cattle did not always pay freight and expenses. It is hard to square these conditions with a newspaper story that appeared in the Helena *Weekly Herald* of October 16, 1873. Under the heading "MONTANA BEEF CATTLE," it read:

> A Madison County stockgrower—Welch, we believe, is the name—drove to Ogden and shipped thence to Chicago over the U.P. and C. &. N.W.R.R.s, 1,000 head of Montana three and four year old bunch-grass fatted cattle. This band was started south in August, if we are not mistaken, and was put aboard the cars the latter part of September. The price delivered at Ogden was $45 per head—or $45,000 for the herd. Let us see what encouragement there is for Montana stockgrowers in this transaction. It is estimated by such prominent cattlemen as Poindexter, Swett, Kohrs, Frary, and others, that a four-year-old steer can be grown in Montana at a cost of $9. Accepting this as a basis, 1,000 head of four-year-old beef cattle can be raised here for $9,000. The expense of driving a herd of this number to the railroad is liberally estimated at $1,000. Ten thousand dollars, then, is the real cost, or more than the cost, of Welch's herd of 1,000 three- and four-year-olds at Ogden, for which he received $45,000—a net profit of $35,000. It is safe to say that 1,000 head, all four-year-olds conditioned as such cattle grown on our bunch grass ranges invariably are, and costing the stockman the moderate sum of $10,000—driving expenses included—will realize $50,000 at Ogden, or a net profit of $40,000.
>
> Isolated as Montana is, and obliged to seek a market 500 miles away, from whence this grand source of our wealth seeks transportation by rail 1,500 miles east to Chicago, it is satisfactorily demonstrated that cattle growing is one of the most profitable kinds of business in which our people can engage.

The intrigued reporter, by a stroke of his pen, raised the net profit on 1,000 head by $5,000 and left his readers wondering why such a financial wizard did not abandon his position in the fourth estate for the more lucrative career of stockgrowing. Regardless of what drover Welch may or may not have made selling his herd in Ogden, the cattle census of western Montana became top-heavy. In May, 1874, the Deer Lodge newspaper, *The New Northwest,* estimated that there were 17,000 cattle in excess of local needs— chiefly four- and five-year-olds. That age was then considered youthful. Down in Texas some of the mossy horns were in their teens. When some eastern buyers did find their way into the Deer Lodge and Beaverhead Valleys that year, they were welcomed. They bought cattle for Chicago at from $18.00 to $22.50 per head, prices that spoke well for the quality and weight of the steers that Montana was producing. In 1875, the market back East was still poor but, at that, the average value of a beef critter in Montana topped Wyoming, New Mexico, and Texas prices, even though it was only $20.00.

Incidentally, 1874 marked the beginning of the large-scale manufacture of barbed wire, which was to be both boon and bane to western stockmen.

It was during this period of the middle seventies that Con Kohrs, Bob Ford, Dan Flowerree, and others got a toe hold on the western fringe of the last, wild, Indian-occupied West, from which settlers were excluded. They put cattle on the Sun River, Marias River, Smith River, and Upper Musselshell ranges. All land north of the Marias and Missouri Rivers in Montana and south of the Yellowstone was Indian reservation. The Sioux and Cheyennes down around the Powder River country in southeastern Montana were no menace to these ranchers, but plenty of Bloods, Piegans, Gros Ventres, Assinniboines, Crows, and Crees prowled the central and western plains, ignoring reservation boundaries and restrictions when intent on their favorite pastimes. They hunted buffalo, stole horses, and organized hair-raising expeditions that kept things in a turmoil.

Early miners and ranchers in western Montana were never much concerned about possible Indian attacks on an organized basis. In 1867, there were rumors of a Blackfeet plot for a general foray and that, plus stories that Sioux and their allies were sun-dancing along the Powder before taking to the warpath, did make some of the timid citizens apprehensive. Mounted militia units were enlisted and military-minded civilians were egged on by an obsessed acting governor whose histrionic talents made the title particularly appropriate. The scare fizzled out with no casualties except the loss of the acting governor, Gen. T. F. Meagher, who fell, or was pushed, off a steamboat moored at the Fort Benton levee.

That year, two military posts were built on the eastern frontier as protection against the alleged threat. Fort Shaw, on the Sun River, was to safeguard settlers and the freight and stage road from Fort Benton to Last Chance Gulch; Fort Ellis, in the Gallatin Valley, was to hold the Bozeman and Bridger Passes against the breech-clouted hordes. Three years later, Camp Baker, afterwards known as Fort Logan, was installed in the Smith River Valley. The major for whom the camp was named wrote to Department Headquarters, ". . . in my opinion, there is no more necessity for a company at Camp Baker than there is in front of the headquarters of the Commanding General of the Department."

The Indians, meanwhile, were having a gala time out on the plains, according to their own standards of amusement, and had no thought of concerted attack on settlers in the mountains. Maybe the "forts" had a psychological effect on both Indians and whites, and at least the garrisons increased the market for beef, so they were not a total loss. By 1877, much of the range north of the Sun River was occupied by militant stockmen who did not need much outside protection. They were willing to look after themselves. The following is preserved in Bob Ford's handwriting:

SECTION 1. We the undersigned pledge ourselves as men to strictly adhere to the following by-laws and regulations of the "Sun River Rangers" and in the event of failing to comply with their demands, will pay all fines imposed on us.

SECTION 2. The object of this organization is to protect our lives and property against all marauding Indians and other outlaws.

SECTION 3. This organization shall be under the command of one Captain and two Lieutenants who shall hold office for six months unless sooner removed by a majority of the Company.

SECTION 4. There shall be a secretary elected who shall also act as treasurer. It shall be his duty to keep the minutes of the meetings and a strict account of all moneys collected and expended.

SECTION 5. The Captain shall preside at all meetings and in his absence the next officer present shall preside.

SECTION 6. It shall be the duty of each member to notify the Captain of the Company when they discover any Indians in this vicinity and if in the judgment of the Captain and members said Indians need looking after, the Captain shall immediately dispatch messengers to notify all the members whose duty it shall be to make all possible haste to attend.

SECTION 7. The Captain shall call a meeting at any time or place he may deem necessary and we as members of this organization do solemnly pledge ourselves to attend all calls of danger to our homes, our families, our lives, and our property.

SECTION 8. There shall be a meeting of this organization on the first Saturday of each month at the school house at 7 o'clock. It is the duty of all members to be present.

SECTION 9. When any member is called upon for duty, he shall immediately attend with such arms as are in his possession.

SECTION 10. When any prairie fire is discovered south of the Teton River or north of the Missouri River, the Captain shall summon all members of the Company whose duty it shall be to attend and render assistance in putting out the same.

This martial document was signed by fifteen men. The minutes of the Sun River Ranger meeting, held August 25, 1877, at the Largeant Hotel of Sun River, are terse and convey little clue as to matters discussed. They close with the succinct statement, "Adjourned to first Monday in September with instructions for every member to bring his arms."

By 1876 the pessimism created by the depression was waning. General conditions were encouraging. W. A. Clark, of Butte mining fame, gave an address at the Philadelphia Centennial Exposition, in which he said of Montana:

> The winters are unusually mild with little snowfall in the valleys, often not exceeding two or three inches at a time. Cattle, horses, and sheep subsist on the ranges every winter with no other feed than that provided by nature and appear in the spring in excellent condition and the percentage of loss is inconsiderable. There are occasional seasons of unusual severity when the loss is much greater and prudence dictates to the thoughtful stock raiser to provide for such seasons by driving his mower a few days in the natural meadows abounding everywhere.

It must be remembered that Clark's interests were all in western Montana and he and few others were familiar with the plains country and its extremes of temperature. Clark placed the population estimate of Montana Territory for 1875 at 30,000. He stated that in that year there were 20,000 acres of wheat and the same of oats in cultivation. He then went on to say:

> No portion of the great West is better adapted to the profitable growth of animals than this Territory. There are about 40,000 sheep and 145,000 cattle grazing on the wide range of bunch grass and they require but little care. Cattle are now driven 1,000 miles to Cheyenne on the Union Pacific Railroad for shipment east and yet pay handsomely on the capital invested, the cost of production being only nominal.
>
> She [Montana] invites capitalists to assist in opening her mountains of treasure, to engage in all the varied industries which her resources of mine and forest, water and soil suggest and give promise of satisfactory reward. Millions of capital now swelling the vaults of our eastern cities to plethoric fullness, or dragging in the unprofitable grooves of a depressed trade, might find, under judicious management, in the gold and silver fields of this Territory, such remunerative employment as would satisfy the most exacting cupidity. She invites the laborer, the miner, the mechanic, the farmer, the stock raiser, promising that in the development of her mines, the building of her cities, the cultivation of her soil, and the watching of her herds, they shall obtain an abundant recompense for their toil.

Allowing for sectional loyalty in some of W. A. Clark's descriptions and predictions, the following conditions actually existed in Montana at that time. Helena, Butte, Bozeman, Deer Lodge, Dillon, and Missoula gave some indication of growth and future importance. Other cities did not exist. Placer mining on the grand scale had been played out. The hills resounded to the noise of blasting and the thump of stamp mills at quartz mines. Although the copper deposits of Butte had not yet been uncovered, the camp had achieved international reputation as a producer of silver. The mountain valleys were being rapidly settled by farmers and small ranchers, who milked dairy cows. The owners of large herds of beef cattle had moved to the border of the Indian and open-range country.

Fort Benton was the point of transfer from steamboat to freight wagon and stagecoach and was far from losing its prestige as an inland port. Twenty-one steamboats arrived in 1876, forty-six in 1878. The Mullan Road gave access to the mining towns from Fort Benton on the east and Walla Walla on the west. The only other road to the settled areas was from the south over Monida Pass. The Union Pacific and Central Pacific had joined rails in Utah. Montana railroad service for cattlemen was several years in the offing. The Northern Pacific was stymied at Bismarck. All the plains country covering the eastern two-thirds of the Territory belonged to the Indians by inheritance, conquest, custom, and right of treaty. It was an isolated island of the original wild West.

For years, there was little or no controversy over the value and purpose of the Great American Desert that early cartographers showed on their maps as extending from the frontier settlements along the lower Missouri to and beyond the mountains of the Far West. It was generally conceded to be a useless expanse, but perhaps God-given to solve the current Indian problem. Recalcitrant eastern tribes could be deposited in this wasteland and left to shift for themselves. People who should have known better—trappers, traders, explorers—had no kind words for the wide prairie. They had no interest in crops, and folks back East, where it rained oftener than sometimes, did not look with favor on the agricultural possibilities of land west of the 100th meridian, where the average annual precipitation was less than twenty inches.

In the Southwest there were cacti, mesquite, chaparral, but on the broad plains to the north there was nutritious buffalo grass. No other grass had its food values. The curly, matted stuff grew close to the ground. It was inured to heat and cold. Drouth couldn't kill it. It endured, and even thrived, under the trampling of countless hooves. For centuries before the white men came, hordes of bison had grazed on it. And there was the taller blue joint with wheatlike head. So let the buffalo and Indians have the buffalo grass. The grass would support the buffalo, and the buffalo would support the Indians and keep them out of the white folks' way.

Even when the migration started for Oregon, the great plains represented just an obstacle and an aggravation—a long, weary stretch of monotonous travel to be suffered, benign or menacing as its mood changed with the weather. The emigrants cherished no thought of lingering in such an unprepossessing environment. With their eyes and hearts set on a more promising land beyond the western horizon, their passage was marked by a narrow pattern of wheel ruts in the sod.

When the young captains Lewis and Clark stood with their eager expedition on the ramparts of the wide Missouri in the spring of 1805, they saw a land that was God's great pasture, teeming with wildlife—the free grasslands of the vast northern Great Plains. Here by the millions ranged that shaggy ruminant the beady-eyed buffalo, staff of life of the wild Plains Indians, unaware that another half-century would usher in the white man's third bonanza, infinitely richer than beaver pelts or gold.

*Lewis and Clark, by Dean Cornwall*

*Assiniboine Breaking Up Camp, by Karl Bodmer (Fort Union, 1833)*

Following the Lewis and Clark explorations, fur traders converged into the region. Key fur-trading posts brought in the first cattle to provide the luxury of dairy products, as at Fort Union (*above*). As the beaver trade waned, Major John Owen built his fort (*below*), the first permanent stock ranch in the vast region, to bridge the gap between the Oregon Trail and the roving bands of ex-Mountain Men, now trading mountain cattle and oxen with the passing emigrants.

**Fort Owen, by E. S. Paxson**

*White Man's Buffalo, by Charles M. Russell*

Except for the Indians around Fort Owen, the Plains tribesmen were startled and perplexed by the first appearance of "the white man's buffalo." In the two-decade span between the end of the fur period and the discovery of gold in Montana—despite the sizeable livestock holdings of Johnny Grant and the Jesuit missions (St. Mary's and, later, St. Ignatius)—the total population of cattle in Montana Territory was infinitely less than the number of grizzly bear.

*Father Ravalli Among the Flatheads, by E. S. Paxson*

In the quiet meadows where Mountain Men had moved their cattle and in the stream beds where they had plucked the beaver, men now uncovered an incredible wealth: raw, free placer gold easily mined in places like Confederate Gulch, near Helena (*below*). In 1862 hard-bitten miners, worldly adventurers, and cold-eyed killers rushed to Bannack and its diggings along Grasshopper Creek. Next year came rich Virginia City on Alder Gulch (*bottom*), followed by the frenzied fever of Last Chance Gulch. Teeming camps sprang up overnight. Meat became not only a luxury but a necessity. For beef on the hoof, cattlemen got baskets of gold!

Hungry, sweat-soaked miners, some filthy rich, demanded the best of everything—banks, bagnios and bawdy houses, oysters and opera, tenderloins noisily swilled with champagne. *Left:* Bridge (now State) Street, Helena, 1865. *Below:* Virginia City, 1864. *Bottom:* Con Kohrs' meat market, Last Chance Gulch, Spring, 1868.

Dan Dutro photo

Word of the Montana gold strikes reached "civilization," and ox teams and mule- and horse-freight outfits toiled ceaselessly between the mining camps in the mountains and Fort Benton on the Missouri, where the river boats from St. Louis, now on triple shift, discharged their passengers and cargoes. Shown (*top*) is a Diamond R mule train in Prickly Pear Canyon between early Helena and Fort Benton. *Bottom:* an ox-team freighter at historic Fort Benton.

In the winter the river boats were ice-locked and bloody "food riots"—mostly over sugar, coffee, tea, and flour—developed. But there was always whiskey and beef for those who could buy them, even though sugar and spice were in short ration. *Above:* H. K. Fast Freight terminal, Last Chance Gulch, Helena. *Right:* Helena, Fall, 1868. *Below:* Bale of Hay Saloon in Virginia City, restored.

Honest men finally tired of brazen robbery, plunder, and murder. The Vigilantes speedily hanged every known rascal—including Sheriff Henry Plummer. Con Kohrs, who started as a butcher boy at Bannack, now owned the fine Johnny Grant ranch near Deer Lodge and was on his way to becoming Montana's first cattle king. *Left:* Hangman's Tree, Last Chance Gulch, 1865. *Below:* Granville Stuart's drawing of Johnny Grant's Deer Lodge Ranch.

In the Indian country buffalo herds were vanishing and the red men, becoming restive and hungry, were often held at bay only by soothing rations of beef and the businesslike guns of watchful United States troops.

The signing of the Homestead Act in 1862 created revised and differing opinions about the Great American Desert; how to make use of it became the subject of acrimonious debate among the whites. The opinion of the Indians did not change. They liked buffalo and the buffalo grass. Today you can still get into an argument about the economic worth, the efficient use, and the proper administration of the remaining acres of public domain.

When the rectangular system of land survey was officially adopted in 1785, land offices were established, where a prospective settler could buy 640 acres at $1.00 an acre. This was changed in 1800 to permit the purchase of 320 acres at $2.00 an acre, one-quarter down, and the balance in three annual payments. Twenty years later, 80 acres could be bought at $1.25 an acre, and by the Preemption Act of 1841 a land-hungry citizen could stake a claim on unsurveyed land and buy it later at the minimum price after section corners had been established. Although permissible acreage per person was reduced, the trend was for more and more liberal purchase requirements.

The Homestead Act went further. As the old story goes, Uncle Sam bet the homesteader a title to 160 acres of land against a filing fee that he couldn't live on the land for five years. If the settler showed good faith, as evidenced by cultivation and improvements, he could make final proof and gain title, or, after six months, he could get title upon the payment of $1.25 an acre—a method known as commuting.

Prior to the Homestead Act, there had been much land speculation throughout the Middle West. Greatly increased population created demand for farm products, with a consequent rise in farm land values. Industrialization lured labor to the cities. To replace the loss of manpower, inventive genius developed farm machinery that permitted the cultivation of more land with less effort. Extension of railroads afforded wider marketing opportunities for grangers. Land was in demand, especially cheap land. When it could be acquired for no cash payment other than filing fees, a different kind of western movement was started—a broad, creeping front of permanent settlement, plowed fields, and fences across Kansas and Nebraska—that accelerated after the close of the Civil War. Veterans were encouraged to take up land. Their term of service in the Union Army could be credited on the required five-year period of homestead occupancy then in effect. Immigration from Europe, represented in main by Germans and Scandinavians, was of unprecedented volume and it gobbled up free land with an insatiable appetite.

Much of the phenomenal filling-in of this central frontier was promoted by the railroads. To encourage the building of transcontinental railroads, Congress gave the companies huge land grants—every other section in a checkerboard strip on either side of the right-of-way—in Territories, this was twenty square miles for each linear mile of main-line railroad construction. This subsidy did not seem too munificent at the time. The idea of the Great

American Desert still persisted to some extent. When the panic of the early seventies threatened to check the integration of East and West by rail, the management of the lines resorted to advertising campaigns that got results. They promoted settlements of land along their rights-of-way and platted town-sites where prairie-dog towns had flourished before. They painted pictures of prosperous farms that sold their surplus land; they settled government sections, built up freight traffic, and closed the gap between the old jumping-off border and the arid foothills east of the Rockies.

Within twenty years after the passage of the Homestead Act, the population of Kansas swelled from 100,000 to 1,000,000 and that of Nebraska from 28,000 to 500,000. The central frontier was gone—but not before the inexorable advance had collided and conflicted with northbound Texas cattle headed for the extending railheads and the short-grass, free range beyond. An ever-narrowing belt of semi-arid land stretched over the great plains from Texas to the Canadian border, a strip that went through a spectacular phase, for those were the days of the Texas Trail and its branches, which cut athwart former lines of travel. These were to continue in use until the fences of the settlers overwhelmed them.

The history of the Texas Trail and the Long Drive that later broomed out on the plains of eastern Montana has furnished an unlimited supply of real and legendary material for song and story. When the Texas men and boys came home to their wide-open spaces after the war, the economic outlook was discouraging, to understate matters. Barring countless—well, at least millions of homely, spooky, long-horned cow critters with the speed of a scared jack rabbit, their assets were very slender. The evil-eyed beasts had been running unhampered during their absence at war. They had increased prodigiously and their nondescript progeny had gone unbranded. As adjuncts of the Texas landscape, they were worthless and there were no shipping facilities to get them to market.

The supply of beef cattle did not equal the demand after the war. The ninth census indicated that while the national population had increased 20 per cent between 1860 and 1870, cattle had decreased 7 per cent. In Kansas, Missouri, and Iowa, there were corn and pasture to spare. Enterprising "brush poppers" organized cow hunts and rounded up sizable herds of the vagrant Texas bovines that had escaped the census tally. They headed them north, to start the drives that persisted into the early nineties.

The first herds that were driven north in search of buyers in settled communities were threatened and harassed almost from start to finish, first by the Nations of Indian Territory, who exacted toll for crossing their tribal lands, and then by irate homesteaders in Kansas, who stoutly demonstrated their dislike for trespassers with buckshot-loaded scatterguns that made the most intrepid cowhands hesitate. The next considerable movement of the herds (in 1867) was to the new railhead of the Kansas Pacific at Abilene, 200 miles west of Kansas City. Then, as the trail was gradually forced west by encroaching settlement, Dodge City became the terminal, to be superseded by Ogallala, Nebraska. The Texas panhandle and eastern Colorado finally formed the narrowing corridor to northern ranges. Until the late seventies, it was blocked at the North Platte River by the Indian hunting grounds beyond. By that time, thousands of longhorn stockers were roaming the range in Colorado and southern Wyoming.

The Texas Trail has usurped the center of the stage in cowland's lore and fiction. Gun-slinging bad men, frosty-eyed marshals to copper their bets, and other stock material of the TV and woodpulp westerns are its by-products, but to the beef industry of Wyoming and Montana, the cattle movement over the Oregon Trail in reverse was more important. Regardless of the constant influx of Texas cattle, the herds of northern Colorado and southern Wyoming were not built up with longhorns. Long before they came, owners had started their business with stock abandoned along the Overland and Oregon Trails by emigrants and gold-seekers, with cattle obtained from wagon-freight outfits, and with Westerns brought back from Oregon.

With the coming of the settlers in the wake of Jason Lee, it did not take long for the Oregon ranges to be stocked with the good grade of combination beef and milch cattle that they brought with them out of the East. And these were not the first. In 1838 Dr. John McLoughlin had approximately 1,000 Shorthorns at Fort Vancouver, started with a few cows bred to Durham bulls brought from England. There was another herd at Fort Colville. The stock was prolific and thrived in the Oregon environment. David Guthrie brought in some notable Durhams in 1846, and the next year others arrived with choice products from the renowned Henry Clay herd.

As settlement made inroads on the free range in Oregon, growers began looking for an outlet for the third- and fourth-generation progeny of pioneer-family cows. They were the get of husky Shorthorn and Devon bulls—quite different from the composite breed coming north from Texas, and from the Spanish cattle of the haciendas of the dons and of the padres' missions in California. Western Montana and southern Wyoming stockmen liked them. The so-called Westerns, because of their physical attributes, developed by environment and inherited traits, were better suited to the northern ranges of the great plains than were southern imports. When moved to Montana, they did not have to become acclimated. They knew how to rustle in winter, and they had the stamina and instinct to assume more than perfunctory responsibility for their calves when it came to fighting off predators. The choice herds of early Montana cattle got their start with Westerns, not alone due to the comparative nearness of the source of supply, but because it obviously cost no more to raise a good beef critter that would top the market than an inferior type that hardly paid its freight. Cowboys were sent to Oregon by stagecoach to trail cattle east. They took their saddles and bridles along and rode prized Oregon horses back.

Baker, Oregon, became the gathering center and point of departure for herds that were to backtrack on their great-grandparents' trail to stock the grass country along the North and South Platte and the western valleys of Montana. By the late seventies some claimed that these areas were over-stocked. People along the Platte wanted new range to the north. Cattle growers in western Montana wanted rail transportation and new range to the east. Railroad officials in the East were anxious to expand westward. All turned avid eyes and pressure on the Wyoming and Montana short-grass country. Since the closure of the Bozeman Road, there had been scarcely a lull in the chorus of white agitation to throw open the buffalo country. Thus, the Indians were caught in a squeeze play from three sides.

In 1874, in direct violation of a treaty, a military expedition commanded by Lieutenant Colonel George Custer was sent to the Black Hills of South Dakota, ostensibly to explore. In the same year, Gallatin Valley settlers organized an elaborate outfit which they called the Yellowstone Wagon Road and Prospecting Expedition, designed to reconnoiter a proposed wagon route to a fanciful head of navigation on the Yellowstone at the mouth of the Tongue River, the present site of Miles City. It was quite an affair, aided and abetted by the governor of the Territory, who supplied guns and ammunition. At the end of three months and 600 miles of rough travel, and after four fights with Indians, the members of the expedition returned, not too sure about steam-boating possibilities but very positive that there were plenty of redskins on the prod. Wild ones.

Alarmed by these invasions, the Indians voiced objections which were disregarded in Washington. Many of them had never accepted the treaty of '68 and now others began joining the recalcitrants in the Rosebud country of southeastern Montana, where they were being incited to action by the Hunkpapa medicine man and chief, Sitting Bull. The brooding Sioux were no longer equipped with the bows and arrows and indifferent guns that they had used in the battles along the Bozeman Trail. They had repeating rifles, heavy Colt revolvers, and the confidence that accompanies efficient arma-ment. So when the Department of the Interior threatened to send troops against them unless they checked in at their reservations by February 1, 1876, the redskins ignored the mandate. The Army was thereupon instructed to subdue them.

It took much fighting to get the stubborn red men rounded up, but it was finally accomplished. The military campaign of 1876 that brought about the disastrous Battle of the Little Big Horn has been told over and over. It eventually culminated in humiliation and subjugation for the Sioux and Cheyenne warriors, who were forced to accept reservations that seemed very meager and futile to the defeated braves. George Custer, hero or Hotspur, has had staunch admirers and bitter critics. A stone monument has been placed where he fell. An unimpressive little monument marks another battlefield, lonely and neglected, on a byway south of Chinook, Montana. There gallant Chief Joseph and his band of Nez Perce, intent only on finding sanctuary in Canada, were overtaken by troops north of the Bear's Paw Mountains where, after a hopeless defense, they surrendered to Colonel Nelson A. Miles on October 5, 1877. Our record of Indian treatment is not one that deserves monuments.

The Crows, whose alleged friendship for the whites was inspired more by expediency than admiration, retained their excellent reservation, but with the years it shrank in size. The Blackfeet reservation line had receded from the Sun River to the Marias within the first year of its designation (1873).

In fairness, the Indian side of the situation should receive some explanation, if not defense. The Indians had endured the familiar sequence of the white man's maneuvering—trespassing, contempt of tribal rights and customs, unavailing appeals to a far-distant authority, farcical councils, further white encroachment, arbitrary regulations, ultimatums, corruption in agency administration, and finally violence. They cherished the notion that the virgin prairie covered with native grass and buffalo was a pleasing sight and that it belonged to them. They hadn't been sold on the beauty and utility of barbed wire and canned goods. They couldn't see that overalls were more practical and picturesque than a pair of buckskin leggins trimmed with scalp locks; following a plow didn't seem to hold the same thrill as forking a pinto pony on a high lope. All in all, it looked as though the Great White Father's repeated promise of a more abundant life was going to cramp their style. They were right. It did!

With the Sioux and Cheyennes corralled, the next chore was clearing the range of buffalo. The culture, religion, and the very existence of the hunting Indians of the plains were built about the buffalo herds. The bison were their cattle and the virtual extermination of the herds, encouraged by the government as a deliberate means of breaking the Indians' spirits, was a gut-shot from which the tribes never fully recovered. Thousands and thousands of tons of choice meat running wild on critters that couldn't be corralled, herded, tallied, branded, or shipped; that is a story of shameful but inevitable slaughter. With the brown hordes disposed of down to the last bleached bone, the range was clear for the coming of the cattle.

Some inkling of what happened can be gleaned from the railroad and steamboat shipping records of the time. In 1876, 80,000 hides went down the Missouri River from Fort Benton; in 1881, 50,000 hides went east via the Northern Pacific Railway. Robes from the northern herds brought two to three times as much as those from the southern plains. In 1882, some 5,000 riflemen and skinners went to work on the northern herds and 200,000 hides were hauled out by the Northern Pacific. The rail shipment dropped to 40,000 in 1883 and to a mere 300 in 1884, with none leaving Fort Benton.

Several small herds of bison are preserved under fence in Montana today, notably the Montana National Bison Range herd on the Flathead Indian Reservation and the Crow Indians' tribal herd on their reservation.

# 5. THE WEST MOVES EAST

In 1879 a booklet was published and circulated by direction of the Montana legislature, entitled *The Resources of Montana Territory and Attractions of Yellowstone Park.* The cover proclaimed that the contents were

> Facts and Experiences on the Farming, Stock Raising, Mining, Lumbering, and Other Industries of Montana and Notes on the Climate, Scenery, Game, Fish, and Mineral Springs, with Full and Reliable Data on Routes, Distances, Rates of Fare, Expenses of Living, Wages, School and Church Privileges, Society, Means of Acquiring Homes, and Other Valuable Information Applicable to the Wants of the Capitalist, Homeseeker, or Tourist.

It is easy to see that the booklet was a fairly comprehensive presentation of why angels should leave Paradise for Montana Territory. The author was Robert E. Strahorn.

This modest brochure, now on file at the Historical Society of Montana Library in Helena, went into considerable detail. The section entitled "Cattle Growing" was particularly designed to set men's feet and palms itching. Mr. Strahorn stated that "oxen . . . thousands of head, worked hard in the season, are turned out to forage in December until April, none ever having tasted a mouthful of hay or grain." He estimated the expense of caring for cattle in herds of 1,000 or more to be about 60 cents per head per annum, including taxes, which made a five-year-old steer cost $3 for care and feed. He stated that beef steer commanded $20 to $28, and that "most of the cattle in the territory are from good American grades . . . there is not a full-blooded Texan, I believe, in the Territory . . . and are being rapidly improved by the introduction of the best shorthorn sires money can buy. The beeves are eagerly sought by outside buyers . . . three year olds dress from 750 to 900 pounds. . . ."

The enthusiastic author then wrote: ". . . in this vast free pasturage, no one need really own an acre of land and thus far, few have cared to." He explained that a ranch usually consisted of a plain log cabin and a large corral for branding and that to "what extent the boundless grass-lands surrounding are utilized by the owner, depends entirely upon the size of his herd and his inclination to let cattle roam and care for themselves."

This master of publicity assured the reader that ranch improvements need not cost more than $250 and that if the owner did his own herding, the additional expense, including cost of living, would be from $250 to $400 a year. He said that one man could easily care for 1,000 cattle, except at roundup twice a year. During roundup, which lasted about two weeks, he would have to spread himself for two to four extra hands. Strahorn said that loss from all causes had not been over 2 per cent per annum, even though some quite severe winters had been experienced; and that the average profit realized could, without a doubt, be placed at 2 per cent per month on money invested in cattle in Montana. In support of this statement, he cited Con Kohrs as owning some 8,000 head and marketing about $40,000 worth of beeves annually. He quoted tall, Lincolnesque Con as saying, "I often find it profitable to borrow large amounts to invest in cattle at 2 per cent per month."

Strahorn got the following statement from Sam T. Hauser, who at the time was president of Helena's First National Bank:

> We loan at 1½ to 2% a month and we know their [stockmen's] profits are often larger than ours. We know all a man has to do is to brand his cattle and go to sleep; he needn't wake up for a year and still his ability to pay will be unquestioned.
>
> Of probably a hundred men who borrow money here at these high rates

of interest to go into the cattle business, we know of none who are not on a short and sure road to fortune. Room? Why, we have hardly more than a cow for every square mile of pasture in the Territory and you can ride a whole day over some of our best ranges and hardly see an animal. Risk? There is almost none.

There will be some 20,000 head exported this year and this is just a beginning, for our largest dealers have only been in business a few years so that three- and four-year-old cattle, until recently, have been very scarce. Next year these exportations must be tripled and quadrupled and so on in the future. We, who had a little money a dozen years ago, were short-sighted not to take hold of the stock business but are a good deal worse if we don't take hold now.

As additional gratuitous information, Strahorn's brochure related that in 1878, the year before its publication, there were an estimated 250,000 head of cattle in Montana, and of these probably not more than 1,000 had ever tasted hay or grain or seen a shed. The principal route to market was down the Yellowstone to Fort Custer on the Big Horn, thence along the general route of the Bozeman Trail to Pine Bluff, a station on the Union Pacific fifty miles east of Cheyenne. There was excellent grass and water en route so that the stock arrived in good condition after a two-month drive.

On first reading, the Strahorn presentation seems to be a fantastic pipe-dream, but upon analysis there is more than a little truth in it, the times considered. In the spring of 1879, Con Kohrs had branded about 4,900 calves in his Sun River herd. It was just such rosy descriptions, published or circulated orally, that started the cattle boom of the eighties—one of those fabulous movements that grip the public imagination and make gamblers of the habitually cautious. Fortunes were made—and lost.

How much fuel the official Montana booklet added to the flame of speculation cannot be measured, but about a year after it appeared a book was published for general circulation, entitled *The Beef Bonanza or How To Get Rich on the Plains*. Its author was General James S. Brisbin, of the United States Army, whose military title naturally added an aura of authenticity to the book. The general was no amateur author, having written a number of other volumes. In *The Beef Bonanza* he gave Texas, Colorado, and Wyoming full treatment, going into great detail regarding costs and profits in the range-cattle industry.

When the general got to Montana, his statements were fully as glowing as those of Robert Strahorn. He estimated profits on herds at from 26 per cent to 48 per cent per annum. One interesting item for today's Montanans is a tabulation of herd owners in 1879, from which the following list of proprietors of over 1,000 head is taken:

| SUN RIVER RANGE | | GALLATIN RANGE | |
|---|---|---|---|
| Clarke and Elin | 10,000 | Nelson Story | 1,300 |
| Con Kohrs | 6,000 | Martin & Myers | 1,300 |
| Flowerree & Cox | 6,000 | | |
| Robert S. Ford | 3,000 | On South Side of Missouri | 20,000 |
| O. H. Churchill | 6,000 | Flat Creek and Dearborn | 10,000 |
| T. J. Stocking | 3,000 | On smaller streams | 2,000 |
| Lepley & Austin | 2,000 | | |

The General wrote, "Poindexter and Orr have a fine herd of thorough-bred cattle . . . which they imported from Canada." He quoted Mr. Orr as speaking for his firm:

> We are of the opinion that blooded-stock breeding will eventually be one of the greatest interests in Montana. With the healthiest stock climate in the world, the purest water, and the best feed, there is nothing to prevent Montana from taking the front rank in production of fine stock. We have been in stock raising for more than twenty years in California, Oregon, and Montana, and hold Montana as best.

The general certainly did his bit to promote outside interest in Montana cattle-raising, but he forgot to mention the hazards. Montanans themselves needed no propaganda to convince them that the business was profitable.

Late in 1879, Sam T. Hauser and Granville Stuart, with A. J. Davis, Butte banker, who, with his brother Ervin Davis, of New York City, took one-third of the co-partnership, organized the outfit that came to be known as the DHS (Davis, Hauser, Stuart). By the first of the following year, Stuart, as active manager, had contracts for the purchase of 2,000 American cattle in Montana and Oregon at from $14 to $17 a head, with calves thrown in. Early that spring (1880), he set out from Helena to scout the eastern country for a ranch site. At that time he just about had his choice of locations. The DHS was never the largest spread on the range but many of its operations were typical, and Granville Stuart, in *Forty Years on the Frontier,* has left more in the way of narration than in any other available source. His descriptions of the areas traversed on that spring reconnaisance and his story of subsequent events give a vivid picture of the cow country and some of its dramatic events.

As Granville journeyed across the Bozeman Pass to follow the course of the Yellowstone River, he was particularly observant of range conditions. He was not too impressed by the upper Yellowstone from the mouth of the Shields River to the Stillwater, but the Big Horn country of the Crows looked very good to him. The drawback was that it would require a lease to run stock on the reservation. He commented on the rotting carcasses of buffalo and the piles of hides stacked high between the Porcupine and the Tongue, and estimated the hunters' winter kill in that area as at least 10,000. In the Rosebud district, there were still herds of the hulking beasts, but very few cattle and fewer settlers were to be seen.

He could afford to be choosey and, after a leisurely and thorough examination, picked as ideal a location on Ford Creek at the base of the Judith Mountains in central Montana. He liked it because there was good timber and spring water handy; magnificent grass country stretched for a hundred miles in every direction; there was plenty of brush shelter—plum thickets, chokecherry trees, bullberry bushes, soil that would grow anything, and no sheep. The pine in the mountains furnished house logs and corral poles. The mining camps of Maiden and Gilt Edge and a drab settlement called Fort Reed, later to become Lewistown, were not far away—if they could be claimed as advantages.

Stuart located 1,000 acres of hay land and got title to 400 acres by using soldiers' scrip. The bulk of his range was unsurveyed and no title could be obtained. Then, unexpectedly, the Army moved in and built Fort Maginnis in the upper end of his cherished hay meadow, calmly taking half of it as a military reservation. Cowhands and soldiers never did fraternize. This was to be no exception. By fall, Mr. Stuart had built a home, had put 5,000 head of cattle on the range, owned 60 horses, sold a few head of beef cattle to the commandant of the fort for $45 a head, and the DHS was in business.

Several significant things happened in that year of 1880 that did not get much notice from the local cowmen. Eighty million pounds of barbed wire were sold; L. A. Huffman, a young photographer, was developing his wet plates at Miles City; Frederic Remington and a youth named Charles Marion Russell came west.

In the fall of 1879, 2,000 head of steers arrived in Bismarck, driven from Montana; that same autumn the Northern Pacific crossed the Missouri there and started laying track westward. The railroad was the answer to the cattlemen's prayers. As it crept across the Dakota prairie, it was met by other herds, token of freight traffic to come.

When the first trains left Mandan, North Dakota, for the Montana border in 1881, almost every passenger was equipped with a firearm of some sort. Jack rabbits, badgers, deer, antelope, and coyotes were never out of sight, and the travelers amused themselves by taking running shots at them. The accommodating conductor instructed them to stop the train by pulling the bell rope in case they downed anything worth taking aboard. A great barrage was laid down and each passenger bragged about his marksmanship —but no one pulled the cord.

In November of that year, the Northern Pacific rails reached Miles City and were met by Nick Bielenberg with 6,000 sheep ready to ship. Guthrie and Ming, of Helena, had the distinction of shipping the first beef cattle from Custer County, but not by rail. Their cattle wintered on Pumpkin Creek and to fill a contract for supplying stock to Fort Buford, Dakota Territory, they were shipped down the Yellowstone by boat in June, 1881. Symbolic of the changing times, the Chief Rain-in-the-Face band of Sioux, sullen braves and wailing squaws under military guard, also left Miles City by steamboat for their reservation—shipped down the river.

On the Dearborn, Sun River, Teton, and Smith River ranges, pioneer Montanans were running cattle. True, the hard winter of 1880–81 was a set-back. The snow was deep and the temperatures were low. There was a big loss of cows and calves in February. The Robert S. Ford records show that he lost 750 cows and 250 steers. By spring, the coulees were dotted with dead critters and skinners were peeling them for their hides, often without regard for ownership. A few mild winters followed; calf crops were large, so everyone accepted the hard winter's losses without a great deal of complaint.

There was a developing market in Canada that offered great possibilities. About 500 Northwest Mounted Police had to be fed by the government, also Blood, Stony, Piegan, and other Indians in the vicinity of Fort McLeod. The Canadian Pacific was to build through, and a big immigration was expected from northern Europe. Bob Ford met Major John Stewart, a member of the Canadian Parliament. Stewart, who possessed very desirable talents and connections, admired Ford's ability as a cattleman. He wondered why Ford hadn't bid on the Canadian government contracts for beef. When told that it was because the stockman lacked funds to finance such a large deal, the major offered to stake Ford on a fifty-fifty basis. They made a killing.

Bob Ford was kept on the move to fulfill the contracts. He did not have enough stock of his own and so had to buy constantly from others. The business kept him traveling back and forth between Sun River, Fort McLeod, and other Canadian points. Because the Indians en route were not to be trusted, he broke two fast saddle horses to harness and drove them to a light rig. He traveled at night and hid out in the daytime. In an emergency, he could get away in a hurry by riding one of the team. The major kept urging him to sell out in Montana and move to the prairies north of the border, where their combined abilities would win even greater rewards. Bob Ford made no serious mistake by declining. Besides other income, his notebook shows that in 1888 he collected $23,601 in interest on personal loans made to prominent Montana citizens on a hip-pocket banking basis.

Con Kohrs also profited by the Canadian situation. In 1882 he sold 1,500 head of what he called "the Territory's finest cattle" to Charley Conrad and I. G. Baker & Co., who had a large contract for beef to feed Canadian Pacific construction crews. Poindexter and Orr sold 4,000 head to the Cochrane Ranch Company of Canada and trailed them to just south of Calgary. Orr commented that they were cutting down their herd because the Dillon area was getting overstocked.

During the early eighties, central Montana, north of the Yellowstone and east and south of the Missouri, was filling up with the cattle of Montana owners. The Judith Cattle Company, consisting of T. C. Power, his brother John, J. H. McKnight, and H. P. Brooks, was the first in the Judith Basin. Brooks was the active manager and bought their cattle in the Gallatin Valley. He wintered them en route to the Judith and in 1879 reached the Basin, where he built cabins and corrals and established a ranch. He was followed by James Fergus and his son, who located on Armell's Creek. Con Kohrs and his half-brother, Nick Bielenberg, moved Oregon stock onto the Flatwillow near the Big Snowy Mountains; Robert Coburn and Henry Sieben both had cattle on the Flatwillow; John Dovenspeck picked Elk Creek, and John T. Murphy, of the Montana Cattle Company, ran his stock from the east side of the Crazy Mountains to Lake Basin. Others were the Pioneer Cattle Company (DHS); the Bay State Cattle Company, managed by Tom McShane; Kaufman and Stadler; Charley Price; "Doc" Frields; and the IJ outfit, a famous horse ranch on the headwaters of Donald Creek. Dave Hilger jeopardized his popularity by trailing sheep from near Helena, to winter them on Salt Creek in the Judith Basin.

Cattlemen resented the intrusion of sheep on range that they had arrogated to themselves. The attitude is traditional. Even today, newsstands are ablaze with western pulp magazines whose covers depict the art of wrangling ringy cow critters. But if a sheepherder appears in the picture at all, some gaudy cowhand is exhorting him with a six-gun to "get the hell out of here with them damn woolies."

The bias of cattlemen is understandable. Sheep nibble close, and even in those days of sketchy cow-outfit gear, they didn't require the investment in equipment and personnel necessary for a sizable cattle operation. A lone herder and a couple of smart sheep dogs could keep a band of sheep cutting grass like a lawn mower. These nomads ruined range for cattle. So there were bound to be clashes, some of them accompanied by violence.

Despite such prejudice, sheep are an inseparable part of the western landscape and rate as important commercial items where owners go in for mass production. John Burgess, California sheepman, brought the first of them to eastern Montana. He had heard about the gold discoveries in the Black Hills of Dakota. In the spring of 1875 he and his son pointed a band of the blatting beasts towards that El Dorado. He wintered them in the Prickley Pear Valley, just north of Helena, and in the spring of 1876 hit the trail again. His route took him down the north side of the Yellowstone to the Tongue River, where he arrived in October.

The sheep were ferried across the river and, as the Indians were still on the prod between there and Deadwood, Colonel Nelson A. Miles, commander at the Army cantonment, advised him to stay put and even gave him permission to winter the band on the military reservation. In the spring, Burgess sold his sheep to Captain F. D. Baldwin and George W. Miles, a nephew of the colonel, for $2 a head, the tally coming to 1,007, with Burgess tossing in the odd seven for good luck. The partners shipped the clip from this band to Sioux City by boat for the next few years until the railroad reached Miles City.

Sheep and cattle don't mix well. Cattlemen often expressed, or demonstrated their displeasure at what they believed to be unwarranted encroachment by sheep, although some owners ran both sheep and cattle—and still do. Robert S. Ford expressed the feelings of many early cowmen when he prepared this pointed resolution on the subject:

Sun River, M.T.
Decr. 10th, 1879

Whereas, we the pioneers of this Sun River Valley having established ourselves here at an early day and prior to all others in the cattle and horse growing business, taking our chances with the Indians and all other outlaws, and built for ourselves and families good, comfortable, and costly homes;

And whereas, If we quietly submit to sheep raisers to graze upon our occupied and long established cattle and horse ranges, our occupation will soon be gone;

And whereas, There are millions upon millions of acres of unoccupied grazing lands that await the occupancy of cattle, horses, and sheep raisers where they will not trespass, interfere, or render useless the occupation of anyone;

And whereas, Certain parties are trespassing upon our prior rights to certain portions of the public domain;

And whereas, In the absence of any and all laws as to the vested rights of American citizens to the public domain;

Resolved, That we, the undersigned cattle and horse raisers of Sun River Valley feel it our duty to our God, our families, and ourselves to oppose to the bitter end all parties owning sheep to locate and graze upon any portion of our long-occupied cattle and horse ranges, and we do hereby pledge our all, our property, and our lives, if need be, to the accomplishment of this end.

You can see with half an eye that Bob Ford did not want sheep around, but he does not seem to have found any signers for his protest. The "certain parties" may have included Paris Gibson, founding father of Great Falls, since he had sheep on Belt Creek at the time.

If they had been given a chance, the Indians probably would have sub-scribed to a similar document had the word "cattle" been substituted for "sheep" and "buffalo" for "cattle and horses."

# 6. THE GREAT RUSH FOR THE OPEN RANGE

Western Montana cattlemen who had moved to central Montana on the heels of the vanishing buffalo were well-established on choice portions of the open range before herds from the south surged into eastern Montana. There appeared to be ample room to accommodate all comers, a fallacy that it did not take long to dispel after the southern invaders were joined by waves of cattle from the East, supplemented by more herds from Oregon. Down the Powder River plodded longhorns, "through" cattle from Texas, with alkali dust hanging heavy in the wake of the drag; out from the East rolled trainloads of pilgrims—pampered barnyard stock from the farms used to being fed by hand. There was free grass for the taking. Short buffalo grass curled and cured on ridges swept bare of snow by winter winds; there was ripening blue joint, often stirrup-deep, whose wheatlike heads were almost as good as corn to fatten cattle.

Such simple equipment as a few saddle horses, a log ranch house, and a branding iron put men on the high road to fortune—sometimes just the branding iron—for the big beef boom that was seething in Texas, Colorado, and southern Wyoming had broken the barrier at the North Platte and reached Montana in the short-grass country, the last holdout of the open range. The fever had spread to England, Scotland, and France. Big outfits were organized and financed abroad and back East. Little outfits clung to their flanks and were so handy with a long rope and a running iron that their cows frequently and miraculously had twins and even triplets. It was the beginning of cowboy classics in Montana.

First arrival of Texas cattle was in the fall of 1881, when an English company drove 5,000 head to the mouth of Otter Creek, tributary of the Tongue River in Custer County. They arrived late in the season, tired and gaunt from the long hike. The winter wiped them out. It was not an auspicious start; nevertheless the northern range became a wonderful outlet for Texans. Ranchers down there found out that their yearlings would weigh 200 pounds more at maturity on short grass than if left on their native range.

The extended Texas Trail was now known as the Long Drive. By the fall of 1883, there were big outfits along the Montana–Dakota line in southeastern Montana. One of the first was the Hashknife of the Continental Land and Cattle Company. The brand was owned by Hughes and Simpson, of Texas, who also had the HS brand on thousands of horses. They were cowmen in the early seventies on the Brazos River, west of Fort Worth. Colonel John M. Simpson, an attorney, managed the company. He picked the northern range in 1879 and built cow camps the next spring to receive the trail herds. They were the first southerners to locate north of the Black Hills, and although their main ranch was in Wyoming, their stock ran across the line into Montana in the vicinity of Alzada. The Mill Iron trailed the Hashknife into the area where South Dakota, Wyoming, and Montana meet.

Brands, stockmen, and cowpunchers, whose names became legend, made the Long Drive—the XIT, or Ten-in-Texas; the Turkey Track; the OX of W. A. Towers and Gudgell, ramrodded by Johnny Goodhall; the Three Sevens (777) of the Berry, Boice Cattle Company; the Neimmela outfit, financed by Sir John Prender, of England, and Commodore H. H. Gorringe, U. S. Navy. Carpenter and Robinson brought in 3,000 head of stockers from Nebraska and put them on the Rosebud; the Niobrara Cattle Company (N Bar) drove in 10,000 Oregon cattle to range along the Powder River; Scott and Hanks, of the SH brand, with Joe Scott as range manager, located on the Little Powder with a herd from Nevada; bands of sheep arrived from Texas and New Mexico. Speculation in range cattle was taking the country by storm.

The DeHart Land and Cattle Company located on Rosebud Creek with 8,000 cattle, and the Griffin Brothers and Ward drove in 3,000 and settled on the Yellowstone. J. M. Holt, of the LO, who had handled cattle for

Nelson Story, brought 3,000 head to Cabin Creek. Tusler and Kempton put three herds of 3,000 each on the Musselshell in central Montana, and the Green Mountain Cattle Company drove in a couple of thousand and stopped on Emmel's Creek. The Pioneer Cattle Company, successor to the DHS, brought in another 3,000 to Sun River, and other outfits concentrated in the same area.

The East made contributions. A. C. Huidekoper, of Pennsylvania, who first came to the Little Missouri in 1881 to hunt buffalo with Howard and Alden Eaton, returned two years later to become their partner in the Custer Trail Ranch. In 1882 Huidekoper had bought railroad land along the Little Missouri at $2 an acre. The next year, he and Eaton began their cattle career with 1,000 head of Minnesota cows, bought at $16 a head, and a carload of blooded Shorthorn bulls.

Theodore Roosevelt came to western Dakota in the fall of 1883 in quest of health and buffalo. He was a little late for the latter but, by dint of assiduous scouting, he finally found and downed a lone bull. He became intrigued with western scenes and bought into the cattle business in a small way, without acquiring title to any land. His initial investment was allegedly $14,000, and in the brief span of his role as a cowman he absorbed enough Wild West lore to permit him to talk and write impressively about his melodramatic adventures on the frontier.

Down in the badlands of the Yellowstone below Glendive, Frank and Henry Fletcher turned loose a few carloads of States' cattle, in expectation of tremendous future profits that never came. By October, 1883, an estimated 600,000 cattle were on the range with enough sheep and horses in addition to crowd the safety point, in the opinion of the firstcomers. Half of them were in the area around Miles City, where they ranged along the Tongue, Powder, Rosebud, and their tributaries, and across the Yellowstone in the Little Porcupine country. From 1880 to 1885, it was not unusual for western cattle companies to claim 50,000 to 100,000 head. The Prairie Land and Cattle Company was supposed to run 124,000 head at one time, with the Swan Land & Cattle Co. Ltd., of Wyoming, tallying just a few hundred head less.

Padded figures were the rule of the day, and the book count customarily accepted by British and Scotch companies was apt to be far in excess of actual range count. In 1885 the secretary of the Wyoming Stockgrowers Association proudly reported that in its first twelve years of existence the Association's membership had grown from ten members, who owned 20,000 head of cattle valued at $350,000, to 435 members, who owned 2,000,000 cattle worth $100,000,000. The boom was one of those phenomenal whirlwinds of speculation that draw conservative Americans, Englishmen, and canny Scots into its vortex every so often. Right at that time, refrigeration for ships and railroad cars was initiated and packing plants began shipping dressed beef. It was the popular notion that the market would expand indefinitely.

It all happened very fast in Montana—too fast. The range-cattle industry suddenly represented a huge investment in wandering, irresponsible critters, most of them new to their surroundings, and anything might happen to them. They were turned loose on public domain and, theoretically, one owner had just as much right to the free grass as another. If the range became overstocked and overgrazed, all would suffer; but who was to determine when range capacity had been reached, especially since the grass crop fluctuated from year to year? And if the range was fully stocked, who had authority to deny room to the next comer?

When the buffalo were gone, cattle became the substitute on the menus of wolves and Indians. No single man could cope with the wolves or carry sufficient weight to receive consideration from the Commissioner of Indian Affairs. The policies of the men in Washington were often at variance with the ideas of stockmen. Indian agents were political appointees and no special knowledge of Indian mores and psychology was required of them. The plains Indians of Montana were not accustomed to being cooped-up on reservations, and they didn't like any part of the diets, costumes, and regulations dealt out to them by a paternalistic government bureau. They were in the habit of visiting or battling their neighbors as the spirit moved them, and they thought beef a poor substitute for hump meat. They were prone to take off without bothering to get the agent's permission and, as the white men had eliminated their dietary *pièce de résistance,* they considered it only just to return the gesture by killing cattle—the alibi, hunger.

Not only did the Montana Indians raise hell, but Crees and Bloods from Canada found it very sporting to make forays across the border, to harass stock, and then to retire from pursuit and retribution by loping back to their own stomping grounds. The Canadian government had a practice of paying their Indian annuities in September, and the recipients would gather by the thousands at Fort McLeod and Fort Walsh to receive their money. They would then head for the cattle country south of the border to buy whiskey as long as the cash held out. After that, they spent the winter living on range beef and stealing horses. Stockmen's opinions of them coincided with that of the Army officer who filled in a discharge for Little Eagle, a Cheyenne scout, when his enlistment expired. In the space headed "Character," he wrote: "Dangerous when drunk; worthless when sober." Little Eagle, who could not read, proudly displayed the document to all, even permitting Casey Barthelmess, of Miles City, to photograph it.

Trouble with the Canadian Indians became a source of international irritation. The Mounties were cooperative but the border was a long stretch to patrol. Moreover, the laws and powers of enforcement on our side of the line offered no reciprocity. This created a delicate diplomatic situation and certain scofflaws in the Territory took advantage of it. Appeals to Indian agents and to the Commissioner of Indian Affairs got the protests of individual cattlemen nowhere, and the military were no help. Concerted action was needed.

The Indians were bad enough when left to their own devices, but aiding and abetting them were nests of unsavory characters who had holed-up in abandoned wood yards along the Missouri River. The Indians, in view of their hereditary customs, plus incompetent supervision, might be excused, but not the white outlaws. They were the remnant of three trades that were fast becoming obsolete—wood chopping, wolfing, and buffalo hunting.

During the flush days of steamboating on the upper Missouri, the occupation of woodhawk developed. The wood-burning packets had to fuel at yards along the shore line. In timbered areas, wood choppers worked prodigiously during the winter to cut and cord up firewood close to the river bank, where it could be taken aboard with a minimum of time and effort after navigation opened in the spring. The life was hard and dangerous. So were the men who worked at it. When river traffic slackened, many of them were obliged to find other means of earning a living. They turned to peddling whiskey to the Indians, under the guise of running legitimate trading posts.

They were joined in that occupation by other renegades, professional buffalo hunters who had shot themselves out of revenue, and wolfers, whose life had its perils and hardships, too. These gentry came to the conclusion that rustling, and stimulating Indians to do the same, was no more dangerous than their former occupations, certainly less arduous, and possibly more lucrative. Not that the redskins needed encouragement to pursue an activity that combined business and pleasure. They gladly traded other people's horses for firewater and didn't care on which side of the international boundary line they picked up such steeds.

Another serious loss to cattlemen was from animal predators. The wolves that were the constant escorts of buffalo herds were the chief offenders. The big, yellow-eyed fellows ran in packs under the able direction of leaders whose brains and brawn had brought them to the front. They were prolific breeders. They whelped in April, and when the pups were only a few months old the parents began training them to hunt. As the buffalo herds dwindled under the relentless sharpshooting of hide hunters, the wolves were deprived of their regular rations. They were elusive as ghosts but far more substantial, weighing from 125 to 150 pounds. Downing buffalo was routine work for them, so killing cattle was easy. Buffalo bulls would form a living corral around cows and calves and stand off the gray predators. Cattle, especially stock new to range life, were helpless against the attack of wolves. Sometimes it seemed as though the wolves killed merely for sport.

The toll of range cattle that wolves levied ran into appreciable figures, which were augmented in certain areas by the kill chargeable to mountain lions and the new-born calf take of coyotes. In the first year of DHS operations, Granville Stuart figured a 13 per cent loss, crediting 5 per cent to Indians, 5 per cent to predators, and 3 per cent to bad weather. It was further estimated that during the winter of 1880–81, at least 3,000 head of cattle were killed by Indians in Meagher and Chouteau Counties, but as it was an unusually tough winter weatherwise, it could very well be that prejudice attributed loss to Indians that should have been charged to snow and temperature.

Western Montana cattlemen became interested in grading-up their herds as soon as they switched from trading cattle to raising them. They got rid of culls and bought registered bulls and some purebred she-stuff. Con Kohrs, during his long and successful range life, repeatedly bought fine stock in Iowa and went as far afield as Toronto to better the grade of his cattle. This practice spread to eastern Montana, but on the open range, where herds were intermingled, what assurance could an owner have that his top bulls were not contributing to the betterment of another brand rather than his own? An owner of stock with a broad streak of plebeian lineage could acquire some aristocratic calves with the compliments of a neighbor's philandering imported sire.

On the open range, duplication of brands could, and did, lead to dispute, litigation, and enmity, but without an established system and recognized authority to guard against this, who was to say which owner should relinquish his right to such a brand? There was also the vexing question of maverick ownership. Obviously, the doctrine that maverick calves found on the "accustomed range" of a stockman belonged to him would not hold water when applied to a country that had so recently been the accustomed range of buffalo and was now occupied by dozens of irons. When the spring calf crop began arriving, it was always a temptation for certain avaricious owners to get out on the range with a branding iron ahead of the others. It just might lead to the acquisition of a few extra calves. It also didn't do cattle much good to be disturbed by half-a-dozen different roundup crews. This could be controlled in only one way—mutual agreement and self-regulation.

What constituted an estray? Half-wild range cattle couldn't recognize a county line if it were visible. If a steer with the travel urge should be spotted a hundred miles from his brand-mates in another county, did anyone have the right to impound him at the county seat and sell him on the theory that he was lost? The use of brands that could be easily blotched or altered was inviting the attention of the unscrupulous. The subject of marks and brands, although given cursory attention in the early legislative proceedings of the Territory, certainly demanded serious thought, as did protection from disease.

With all these problems in mind, the need for cooperation through organization was plain, and the industry had no lack of rugged characters to

take the initiative. On January 23, 1879, a group of stockmen met informally
in Helena, and James Fergus advocated the formation of a central association with which smaller, local organizations could affiliate. Those present
decided to adopt the rather all-inclusive name of The Legislative Farmers',
Stockgrowers', and Miners' Club, and E. G. Brooke, of Whitehall, was elected
president. Under the heading "MEETING OF THE LEGISLATIVE CLUB," the
February 13, 1879, edition of the Helena *Daily Herald* carried this item:
"The regular meeting of the above club comes off at the hall of the House
this evening, at which time a permanent organization of the Stockgrowers'
Association will be effected. Let all those interested be there. . . ."

On the following day, the *Herald* reported as follows, under the heading "LEGISLATIVE FARMERS' CLUB":

> W. F. Wheeler was called to the chair and W. H. Sutherlin was appointed
> secretary. Mr. Ford of Sun River, chairman of the committee to draft a con-
> stitution and by-laws for a Stock Growers' Association for the Territory, said
> he had telegraphed to Colorado and had also written for similar documents
> but they had not arrived. He thought if the committee had another day they
> might draft a constitution and by-laws that would be satisfactory. . . .

It is evident that such a move had been contemplated for some time, with
Colorado setting a precedent.

On February 19, 1879, another meeting of the group was held in the
Legislative Hall in Helena. R. S. Ford, who was chairman, presented a constitution that was read and adopted section by section, and a committee of
five was named to draft by-laws. There were twenty-five signers as founding
members. Robert S. Ford was elected president; E. G. Brooke, vice-president;
Ross Deegan, secretary; and John N. Ming, treasurer. J. H. Freeser, H. H.
Mood, Dr. A. H. Mitchell, Martin Barrett, and H. M. Cooper were elected
members of the executive committee.

Through the newspapers and by correspondence, the new association
urged all cattlemen to organize locally and also to join the parent body. The
response was good. There were soon local associations in Madison County,
on the Sun River range, in Lewis and Clark, Gallatin, and Deer Lodge
Counties, in the Shonkin district near the Highwood Mountains, and in the
Smith River area. That just about covered the portion of Montana where
native herds had developed since the gold discovery days. Central and eastern
Montana were still not a part of cowland.

Bob Ford's leadership in effecting an organization of the Sun River
district may be judged by his address to his neighbors:

> The object of this meeting is to organize a stockgrowers association to be a
> branch of the Territorial Association and to send delegates to the Territorial

Stockgrowers Association which meets in Helena the 3rd of March next. We are all young in the stockgrowing business and do not know our wants. Every stockgrower heretofore has been on his own footing. We do not propose to deprive you of any of your former rights by organizing, but rather wish to increase those rights.

We want to get together and consult upon this important subject, prove all things, and hold fast to that which is good. If we organize we can come to some understanding as to our wants and have such general laws passed as will prove the greatest good to the greatest number.

The narrow gauge railroad [the Union Pacific branch from the south] will soon penetrate our borders. The Northern Pacific will be built to the Yellowstone the present year. [Ford was two years premature in his prophecy.] Many rough characters are coming to our Territory, besides we already have quite a sufficiency. The stealing of cattle and horses is becoming a common occurence and by organizing and all of us becoming detectives as it were, we can the easier put a stop to this thieving business. As it is now, if a man steals thirty or forty head of cattle from you or me and gets off with them, the chances are we will never exert ourselves to catch him because the cost is too great and we will say, "Let him go." But if we organize and bear our pro rata of the expense, the thief will be hunted down and punished and it will cost each of us but little.

Besides, these branch associations can make certain regulations in regard to roundups, the management of their ranges, can settle the maverick question, the number of bulls that each stockman should be required to furnish for each hundred head of she stock, and various other things that it is not necessary to mention here. In fact we do not know our wants. Let us then organize and find them out.

The sentiments expressed are no doubt typical of those stated at similar meetings in other districts. Bob Ford was elected president of the branch association that included Lewis and Clark, Choteau, and Meagher Counties. It was an up-and-going concern with headquarters at Sun River. Among the membership were Henry Sieben, who branded his stock with a Diamond on the left ribs and ranged them on the lower Smith River; Carroll and Myers, who ranged in the Teton Valley out of "Old Agency," now the town of Choteau; and W. A. Hedges, O. H. Churchill, D. A. G. Flowerree, the Bielenberg brothers, Jesse Taylor, Dave Auchard, W. C. Swett, and a long list of equally salty characters.

The local organizations got into action fast. The slaughter of cattle by Indians had become so flagrant that Milton E. Milner, secretary of the Shonkin Stock Association, issued a summons to the stockmen of the Shonkin, Highwood, and Belt districts to meet in Fort Benton, August 15, 1881, for the purpose of organizing a stock protective association. It was agreed that the association's committee should select one cattleman living in Fort Benton to go with Sheriff J. J. Healey on all trips that he made in their behalf. A reward of $100 was posted for the apprehension and conviction of anyone selling, bartering, or giving whiskey to Indians on Association range, and this included half-breeds. A reward of $500 was offered for convictive evidence against anyone who maliciously or negligently set fire to the range.[1] The stockmen also decided to hire men to ride the range to keep an eye on stray Indians and to intercept Crees and other "visiting" Indians at the Canadian border.

At this meeting, the exasperated stockmen were advised by Montana's territorial delegate to Congress, Major Martin Maginnis, that if the Government refused to protect its citizens, they had no recourse but to protect their own property and should do so. The major, who had come across the plains from St. Paul to Last Chance Gulch in 1866, was a fairly rugged individual.

Association measures brought a storm of protests which were supported, if not initiated, by the whiskey peddlers. The protesting element affirmed that high-handed cattlemen were putting the run on innocent settlers and confiscating their property. They dolefully predicted a breach in international relations if the wanderings of the Crees were restricted, and some newspapers even headlined such guff. Major Maginnis had many close friends interested in cattle and he tried to do his best for them in Washington. He endeavored to have them compensated for depredations of the Indians, but Congress refused to authorize funds to pay for the misdeeds of the Government's wards.

The idea of concerted action by the stockmen of a given district was not entirely new in the Territory. In December, 1873, a few of them had gotten together at Virginia City and framed an invitation to the stockmen of Madison County to meet with them on January 18, 1874. At the meeting, a chairman was elected and a legislative committee appointed to draft a bill pertaining to grazing regulations, the disposition of estrays, branding rules, and protection from rustlers. The territorial assembly was then in session and the bill was presented. That was the sole objective of the meeting and, having achieved it, the group dissolved, leaving further action up to the legislators. The needs for legal or cooperative controls were not as dire or complex as they would be a few years later.

The assembly did pass "A Bill for an Act concerning the management of livestock and the better to protect the interest of stockgrowers in the Territory of Montana," which was a start in the right direction.

The Montana Stockgrowers Association, as organized in Helena in 1879, met several times and, pursuant to Bob Ford's explanation of association

---

1 Warring tribes of Indians used to set fire to the hunting range of their enemies. In the fall of 1881, prairie fires burned five hundred square miles of grass country in Montana.

aims, "came to some understanding of its members' wants," and set about
to "have such general laws passed as would prove the greatest good to the
greatest number."

# 7. THE GAVEL BANGS

With the spreading out of the cattle industry in the Territory, there had been no great shift in the center of population. It remained in the more heavily settled western portion where mining interests predominated. The majority of the voting public were therefore apathetic about the troubles of cowmen and, with such a situation, stockmen's bills had not always fared too well in the legislative hopper. That had been one of the major factors in starting a central association. The larger the membership of such an association, the more influence it could wield.

A fair number of influential stockmen were elected to the thirteenth legislative assembly, held in 1883. Granville Stuart was president of the Council, as the senate was then called. The cattlemen had not had any luck appealing for federal help in controlling the roving red men, but they did manage to persuade the assembly to sponsor a memorial to Congress. It read:

To the Honorable, the Senate and House of Representatives of the United States of America in Congress Assembled.

Your memorialists, the council and house of representatives comprising the legislative assembly of the Territory of Montana, respectfully represent to your honorable bodies that the tribe of Indians known as Piegans comprising a portion of the Blackfeet nation whose agency is located on Badger Creek in this Territory, have been continuously, for years, stealing horses, killing cattle, and committing divers other depredations upon the rights and property of citizens of this Territory; that where heretofore game was plentiful on their accustomed hunting ground, little or none can now be found; that the subsistence furnished at the agency is utterly insufficient to supply the demands of necessity, and these Indians are frequently driven to such desperate rigor as to be compelled to resort to these means to avert starvation;

That by reason of the causes aforesaid, the depredations of said Indians, instead of diminishing have been increasing until they have become so frequent of late that the lives and pursuit of industry, particularly that of stock raising, of the white settlers in their vicinity, have been greatly endangered and seriously jeopardized;

While it is a well known fact to the citizens of the vicinity of said agency, that these raids have been occasioned by reasons of extreme necessity, yet it is a conceded fact that unless some action is taken to avert these aggressions in the future, a collision between these Indians and the whites must inevitably ensue;

Your memorialists would most respectfully further represent that frequent complaints have been made and petitions presented to the Indian Department at Washington, the agent of said tribe, and the military in this Territory, setting forth the wrongs and grievances aforesaid, and requesting that said tribe be kept upon their reservation, all of which has been ineffectual until your memorialists have despaired of any relief save the interposition of your honorable bodies.

Your memorialists would also most respectfully represent that said Piegan tribe of the Blackfeet nation, would readily adapt themselves to the pursuits of husbandry and, in a great measure if not entirely, become self-supporting, thereby averting the evils aforesaid, and relieving the government of great inconvenience and expense, if their supplies for subsistence are made commensurate with their actual wants at the present, and they are furnished with the humbler implements employed in the ordinary pursuits of agriculture; that in this way they can be made to remain contented upon their reservations, their valuable tillable lands made available for some useful and beneficial purpose, and their complications with the white settlers ultimately terminated.

Wherefore, your memorialists respectfully request that such action be taken in the premises by your honorable bodies as shall be deemed expedient and proper to meet the emergency, and satisfy the demands of justice; and your memorialists will, as in duty bound, ever pray.

GRANVILLE STUART, President of the Council
ALEXANDER E. MAYHEW, Speaker of the House of Representatives.

Stripped of its rhetorical trimmings, what the cowmen wanted was for Uncle Sam to ride closer herd on his wards, keep them at home, and issue them more steer meat. The memorial had a double-barreled intent. If heeded, it might reduce the loss of maliciously killed cattle on the range and develop an additional market for beef. All in all, the wording of the communication showed considerable diplomatic restraint.

Another memorial to Congress expressed alarm over contagious pleuropneumonia which was prevalent among cattle in some of the far eastern states—a disease that seemed difficult, if not impossible, to cure. The infected area was far from Montana; nevertheless, the memorialists considered the danger of importing diseased cattle and explained that the nature of the range industry would make introduction of disease a disaster that would be uncontrollable if it ever started. They said it was of national import and, hence, deserving of immediate attention by Congress.

The sponsors of the memorial were not unduly alarmed nor overzealous. The possibility of disease among cattle becoming a national catastrophe was recognized by stockmen everywhere. That fall, action was taken in Chicago, at a meeting of cattlemen from far and wide, that resulted in the sending of a delegation to Congress and the subsequent founding of the federal Bureau of Animal Industry.

When the Montana Territorial Assembly passed a bill to create a Board of Stock Commissioners, the cowmen were jubilant. The board was authorized to employ cattle inspectors and detectives. Taxable property in the Territory was to be assessed one-half mill per annum to pay the expenses. There was much opposition from those who had no interest in cattle. The antagonism was particularly strong in Silver Bow County, which was populous, vocal, and devoted to mining. In Butte, beef on the hoof was not accorded much attention. The only time it received acclaim was when it appeared baked in a Cousin Jack pasty or as a "bucket steak" that fitted snugly in a miner's lunch pail. When newly-appointed Governor John S. Crosby vetoed the measure, it was a blow to cowland aspirations.

Denied the legal machinery that would have been made operative by a Board of Stock Commissioners, there seemed to be no remedy for an intolerable situation, except direct action. After the spring roundup of 1884 in the Judith Basin country, a few stockmen met at DHS headquarters. They had information concerning some of the more active and better organized rustlers and decided to do something about it. They enlisted the services of Floppin' Bill Cantrell.

Big Bill Cantrell was a gangling, overgrown kid of twenty when he reached the upper Missouri from the hills of Arkansas in the late 1860's. His father had been one of Quantrell's guerillas during the war. Bill lingered in the vicinity of the Mouse River in Dakota for some time before moving farther west where he took an Assinniboine bride and went into business as a wood yard owner on one of the timbered points of the Missouri near Fort Peck. He had a peculiar technique with an axe, which he described as "a kind of floppin' motion" of the arms, that gave him his sobriquet of Floppin' Bill. The locale of Bill's operations, which came to include trapping and wolving, with Mr. Pike Landusky as a partner, gave him acquaintance with most of the rapscallions who infested that part of the country.

Just why, when, and how he hooked up with the cattlemen around Fort Maginnis, instead of with the rustlers, is a trifle obscure, but Bill became Montana's first stock detective. Raconteurs of the period seem agreed that Bill's choice was not dictated by ethics, but by the prospect of compensation. At any rate, he became a hired defender of property rights, and he executed his assignments—as well as his quarry—with thoroughness and dispatch.

Young Jack Stringer, better known as "Stringer Jack," was a former buffalo hunter—handsome, adventurous, and a companion of marauding stock thieves. He was, in fact, the leader of a notorious gang, whose hangout was Bates' Point, about fifteen miles down the Missouri from the mouth of the Musselshell. As a result of the affiliation of Floppin' Bill and the stock-growers who had met at the DHS, a self-appointed vigilance committee called on Stringer's gang that summer and found Old Man James, his two sons, Frank Hanson, Bill Williams, Stringer Jack, Paddy Rose, Swift Bill, Dixie Burr, Orvil Edwards, and Si Nickerson at home. There are many speculative tales and conflicting accounts of what followed. Omitting sanguinary details, in a short time most of the gentlemen named could be referred to in the past tense, their spirits having been wafted to the Sand Hills on a cloud of gun smoke. Their survivors were inclined to be taciturn and the others could not be interviewed except through the unreliable medium of a ouiji board.

There was considerable public and private comment, pro and con, concerning both the principles and the principals behind the affair. Dixie Burr was the son of a highly respected pioneer and the nephew of another. There were well-known citizens in the posse. That summer, a chartered train picked up another band of avengers and their horses at a secluded siding near Miles City. It stopped at intervals between Billings and Medora. The train crew waited until the passengers had returned from missions to the hinterland. Nemesis rode with them packing a hair rope. It is alleged that the tally credited to this and similar forays totaled sixty-three. Rustling subsided for awhile.

It might be argued that this drastic action lacked legality and so was not to be condoned, but it did make clear the need for central, respected, regulatory authority, properly equipped to enforce its mandates, especially in the eastern portion of the Territory.

The western area (Sun River, Madison, etc.) cattlemen had organized after some groping and had set a militant example. On the east range the need grew more compelling in direct ratio to the increase in the cattle census. If lawlessness approaching chaos was to be avoided, something had to be done about it fast. The men of that area were familiar with the accomplishments of Colorado, Texas, and Wyoming cattlemen associations; in fact, some of them were members.

On the evening of October 12, 1883, E. S. Newman, E. H. Cowles, Joseph Leighton, Colonel T. J. Bryan, Henry Tusler, J. W. Strevell, E. C. Graham, J. M. Holt, W. A. Cotant, J. J. Mann, and M. C. Conners met at the Palace Restaurant in Miles City and reached a decision to form the Eastern Montana Stockgrowers Association and to adopt the by-laws of the Wyoming Stockgrowers Association in their entirety. The initiation fee was set at $15 and annual dues at $10. There were diplomats among these gentlemen for they immediately made W. D. Knight, of the *Yellowstone Journal,* an honorary member. History is indeed indebted to him for detailed accounts of the Montana Stockgrowers Association meetings from 1890 through 1917, the secretary having stopped his longhand recording of minutes after 1889.

Seventy attended the second meeting, including twenty-nine applicants for membership. They met March 21, 1884, in the Custer County Court House at Miles City and immediately got down to business. They petitioned the Secretary of the Interior to give the Cheyenne Indians sufficient rations to keep them from killing cattle for their underfed families; they picked E. S. Newman, W. Harmon, H. H. Fletcher, Judge J. W. Strevell, and Matt Ryan as delegates to attend the national stockmen's convention being promoted by the Texans; they appointed a roundup committee with duties to designate districts, select captains, and suggest the time for spring roundup; and they directed that bulls be taken off the range from December 1 to July 1. The executive committee was given the responsibility of compiling a brand book. Their problems and objectives were no different than those of all range-cattle operators.

By the third meeting, in September, 1884, there were 107 members of the Association. Clearly, there were advantages in organization, and leading members began to wonder if Wyoming's idea of a territorial association was not applicable to Montana. True, Wyoming's sole interest was cattle, whereas Montana's interests were divided between livestock and mining. Perhaps that was even more reason for forming a strong association to battle for stock-men's needs.

It so happened that Con Kohrs had called a meeting of cattlemen in Helena that spring to consider measures for preventing a threatened epidemic of foot-and-mouth disease. The men he summoned met in the First National Bank building to reorganize and revitalize the Montana Stock-growers Association. Con Kohrs, John A. Ming, and O. R. Allen were selected as a special committee to give the matter thought and to make recommendations. They sent out the following bulletin:

GENTLEMEN:

WHEREAS, at a meeting of a number of stockmen held at Helena, Montana, the 21st of April, 1884, it was resolved that the time had arrived when a more complete and thorough understanding of the wants of the vast live-stock interests of this Territory should be arrived at, and an unanimity of action be decided upon among the different branches of this industry.

The stock interests of this Territory last year amounted to about one-third of the total assessed valuation,[1] and will this year be largely augmented by the immense number of horses, sheep, and cattle that will be driven in.

The time is at hand when the Stockmen must band together for the pro-curing of such legislation as will protect and foster this great industry, which is so vital to the welfare of this Territory.

In order that this matter may be reached in a proper manner, it is desired that a meeting of all those engaged in stock raising in this Territory be held at Helena, July 28th, 1884, for the purpose of devising ways and means by which the better protection of the stock interests may be obtained. It is suggested that all who are engaged in the business of stock raising hold meet-ings in their various districts and send delegates to this convention. It is also desired that as many stock owners, outside of delegates, as can possibly be present, be here, as this is a matter of utmost importance to all.

In connection with this matter we would call your attention to an extract from the report of the Executive Committee and Secretary Sturgis, of the Wyoming Stockgrowers Association at its last meeting:

In reviewing the history of the last twelve months, your Committee find that their labors upon matters of interest to the Association have been directed to a large number of subjects and those of greater im-portance than have been forced upon them in any previous year. The time has come when our business can no longer be done by the old rule of thumb method. In former days, we had only to brand our

---

[1] The signers of the bulletin were modest. Actually, livestock plus ranchland was valued at $21,542,774, or nearly half of the $44,698,461 assessed valuation of taxable property in the Territory.

calves when dropped, and ship our beeves when fat. The calf tally would be notched on a shingle and the checkbook was the only book kept, and the balance or overdraft at the bank showed the whole business.

Times are changed. The man who would win and win permanently, must look ahead and read the signs of the future. He must introduce system, economy, and judgment in his business. He must buy where he can buy cheapest, both of cattle and provisions. He must sell where he can transport the cheapest and realize the most. He must anticipate the measures necessary to prevent disease. He must provide that his grazing facilities remain uninterrupted. It is a famous saying that "Eternal Vigilance is the price of Liberty." Eternal Vigilance in anticipating coming danger is to be the price, henceforth, of successful stock raising in the West.

O. R. ALLEN, Secretary        W. B. HUNDLEY, Chairman.

In response to the call, forty-two cattlemen were present, representing eleven of the Territory's fourteen counties, including Custer County members of the Eastern Montana Stockgrowers Association. There was a thorough threshing-out of the various opinions that were advanced. There were those who advocated the formation of a federation of local associations. They were afraid an over-all association would commandeer local association authority, and might grow into a domineering, dictatorial body that would totally eclipse the smaller groups. In the end, it was concluded that a territorial association to which stockmen would belong as individuals would be preferable to a federation type of union with delegates representing each local at the meetings. In short, the town-meeting principle defeated the representative plan. Every member in attendance at a territorial association meeting would have a vote.

On the second day, Granville Stuart was elected president of the rejuvenated western association, with former Governor B. F. Potts as vice president, Russell B. Harrison,[2] as secretary, and J. P. Woolman, territorial auditor, as treasurer. The delegates from Custer County displayed some reluctance about committing the Eastern Montana Stockgrowers Association to a merger, until it was agreed that the plan for consolidation should be presented to that association at its regular spring meeting in Miles City.

The July meeting was a shot in the arm for the western association,

2 Russell B. Harrison was the only son of Benjamin Harrison. He came to Montana in 1880, at the age of twenty-six, to join the personnel of the U.S. Assay Office in Helena. He became interested in cattle ranching and in 1885 managed the Montana Cattle Company. He served as Secretary of the Montana Stockgrowers Association until 1890, when he returned to the East. His father was elected President of the United States in the fall of 1888. Benjamin Harrison was distressed by his son's western "speculations" and seeming indifference to incurring debts.

Photographs by W. H. Jackson (Hayden Survey Party of 1869–71)

*An early-day Montana ranch*

Moving the perimeter ever outward, bold cowmen drove their herds into the Beaverhead, Madison, and Gallatin Valleys. Soon they occupied the Sun River and Marias country, pushing the buffalo and angered Blackfeet before them. Shortly, cattle rushed into the lush grasslands of the Judith Basin, Smith River, and the Upper Musselshell. Ranch houses were crude but functional and sturdy— each an island and a fortress—the ever-present firearms constituting personal arsenals of defense against Indians and renegade whites.

*Interior, Sawtell's ranch house*

Conrad Kohrs (*right*) started as a butcher boy at Bannack, bought out Johnny Grant's ranch to stock his markets with beef, and soon his profits pyramided into new herds and many new ranges. One man, Nelson Story (*below*), was a decade ahead of his time. With gold dug at Alder Gulch, he purchased 1,000 longhorns and trailed them from Texas in 1866—twice as far as any other cowman had pushed a trail herd. His profits

—close to $100,000—speedily made him another of the new cattle kings. *Below:* "Texas Trail Boss," a major water color (1918) by Charles M. Russell, depicts the epic era of the great cattle rush to Montana Territory. His similar pen-and-ink sketch of this subject will become famous as the central design for the new (1961) U.S. 4-cent Range Conservation stamp. This version has been reproduced on the dedication page.

Fort Benton flourished as the economic heart of a lavish trade area extending from Utah to the Whoop-Up region in Canada. With profits pouring in from trading, transport, mining, and banking, many Montanans started to invest in ranching, too. Among them was T. C. Power (*left, below*), whose trading post and freighter outfit are also shown. *Bottom:* River-boat levees, Front Street, Fort Benton, 1878.

As the mining camps boomed, Helena became the financial stronghold of the Territory, with a slice of every melon cut from Fort Macleod to Corrine (*top*), southern terminus of the vast region south of Canada. Soon Helena would boast of more millionaires per capita than any city in the world, with fortunes gained from ranches, mining, freighting, and other frontier enterprises. Shown below is an early, rare lithograph of Last Chance Gulch, at the peak of this period.

*Robert S. Ford*

By the 1870's there were two classes of stockgrowers: the "entrepreneurs," such as Stadler & Kaufman, Sam Hauser, A. J. Davis, Charles Anceney, J. H. McKnight, Russell Harrison (only son of Benjamin Harrison), B. F. Potts—even Con Kohrs and Nelson Story, who now operated largely from the cities—and the "rawhiders," who lived on their isolated ranches, worked daily with their cowboys, and resisted city life. Robert ("Bob") S. Ford (*above*) was a typical rawhider, a true frontiersman, seasoned as a freighter on the tough runs to Santa Fe, Fort Laramie, and the Montana mines. From 1869 on he brought in four successive annual drives of Texas longhorns to open the new range on the Sun River. Like countless new cow towns, Sun River burst suddenly into existence, with H. A. Milot's saloon and hotel (*below*) among its key edifices.

*Wolfer's shack*

L. A. Huffman photograph, courtesy Ruth Huffman Scott

*Granville Stuart*

Water color by C. M. Russell (1898)

*The Surprise Attack*

With the Sun River range quickly occupied, the veteran frontiersman Granville Stuart, backed by Davis & Hauser money, established the famed DHS Ranch in the heart of the Indian country. Their huge range was ringed with fortress-like line cabins (*top, left*). Despite the building of nearby Fort Maginnis (*below*), the soldiers too frequently were caught grooming horses while the cowboys held the line in lively forays against marauding Blackfeet, Gros Ventre, and Assiniboine, as pictured by cowboy-artist Charles Russell (*left*).

The astute S. T. Hauser (*below*), certain that the public would demand ever greater protection from the Indians, watched with pleasure the building of Forts Shaw, Ellis, C. F. Smith, Logan, Keogh, Custer, Assiniboine, and Maginnis, which ringed the rangeland. The last four named were built after the Custer battle. Fort Keogh, as seen by soldier-artist H. Steiffle in 1878, is pictured at the bottom of the page.

If Hauser had qualms, they came from the indication of a great influx of settlers and the fencing of the open range, symbolized by Charlie Russell when he painted "The First Furrow" (*above*), showing Bill Skelton breaking some of the first sod in the Judith Basin. This act foreshadowed the stockgrowers' next great dilemma—settlers and fences.

*The Custer Massacre, by Harold von Schmidt*

With the Battles of the Little Big Horn and the Bear's Paw over, the back of organized Indian resistance was broken. Building of the Northern Pacific railroad could be accelerated. Soon CK (Con Kohrs) cattle for the Eastern markets did not have to be trailed to Cheyenne for Union Pacific shipment (see *below*); Montana Territory had its own steel road connecting the rangelands with the beef-hungry millions in the East.

which had been suffering from inertia although its local affiliates had remained active. During the winter of 1884–85, the leaders of the revival discussed and perfected plans for the joint meeting with the eastern association. They also found time to campaign so effectively for stockmen candidates to the fourteenth territorial legislative assembly of 1885 that the session has gone down in history as the Cowboy Legislature. Proud of results obtained in the legislature, the president and the secretary of the association sent out the following report:

MONTANA STOCKGROWERS ASSOCIATION

Secretary's Office

HELENA, MONTANA, March 28, 1885

To The Members of The Montana Stockgrowers Association and the Stockmen of Montana:

DEAR SIR:

At the Convention of Stockmen from all parts of the Territory, held in Helena in July 1884, which resulted in the organization of the Montana Stock Growers, the unprotected and exposed condition of the livestock interests of the Territory from theft and disease were fully discussed and in pursuance of the resolutions adopted, the President of the Association called a meeting of the Executive Committee in Helena, January 12th, 1885, to which meeting Stockmen from all parts of the Territory were invited, the object being to secure the passage of better stock laws.

The Executive Committee was in session during the entire session of the Legislature, and while it was acknowledged by all that the stock interests needed protection from dangers, both present and prospective, yet it was unanimously determined that although a majority of both branches of the Legislature were favorably inclined toward this great and rapidly increasing industry, no legislation would be asked for except such as would commend itself, not only to stockmen generally, but to every citizen of the Territory. To the President and Secretary of the Association, assisted by such stockmen as could be present, was assigned the duty of preparing bills in accordance with these views. This was done with the following result.

A bill was passed and became a law authorizing the Governor to appoint a Territorial Veterinarian Surgeon whose duty it should be to examine and report upon all cases of disease among horses, cattle, and mules, and where said disease is generally fatal and liable to become epidemic, he shall have the diseased animals appraised and may order them killed and burned, the owner receiving two-thirds of the value thereof.

The Surgeon also has power to quarantine all stock shipped or driven into the Territory that are diseased or that he has reason to believe may be diseased. The necessity for this law becomes apparent when we consider the impossibility of arresting a disease of a contagious and fatal nature, when once started among cattle and horses roaming at will over large districts, the only safety in such cases being in using all possible precautions against any disease obtaining a foothold.

A law was also passed authorizing the Governor to appoint six Live Stock Commissioners, being one each for the counties of Dawson, Custer, Yellowstone, Meagher, Chouteau, and Lewis and Clark, who should in turn appoint and employ such inspectors and detectives as they may deem necessary to best protect the livestock interests of the Territory. Said Commissioners receive no pay or mileage and the inspectors and detectives employed by them are to be paid out of a special tax levy of one and one-half mills on the dollar, to be levied upon the cattle, horses, mules, and asses in the counties named. The other counties, being excepted from the provisions of the bill, have no inspectors.

This law is one of importance and is intended to put a stop to the stealing of livestock, which has grown to be an evil of great magnitude, and also to assist the Veterinarian Surgeon in finding and stamping out diseases of a contagious and fatal nature.

A law was also passed prohibiting the branding of cattle upon the public ranges during the month of August and from November 15th to May 15th, next succeeding; but the bill provides that any owner of stock may brand cattle on his own premises at any time if done in the presence of two responsible citizens. The exemptions from the provisions of this bill are the counties of Missoula, Deer Lodge, Silver Bow, Beaverhead, Madison, Jefferson, and all of Gallatin County lying west of the Belt or Bridger range of mountains.

A law was also passed to enable persons attaching or attempting in any other manner by legal process to take possession of livestock running at large on the public ranges of the Territory, to attach and hold the same, between the first of November and the next succeeding fifteenth day of May, by filing and recording with the County Clerk or Recorder of the County, wherein the property is roaming, a copy of such process, with a notice appended, giving the number, description, marks and brands of the animals. Such copy of the process, with the notice appended, after it has been so recorded, has the same effect as if the actual custody of the property had been taken. But the law requires that the *actual custody* of the property attached must be taken prior to the first day of August. This law applies in the same way and manner to the taking possession of the property under the foreclosure of a chattel mortgage on stock running at large on the public ranges. The intention of this law is to prevent the handling or collecting together of live stock on any range in winter because of the great injury and damage that would result, not only to the stock gathered, but to all other stock on the same range.

The enactment of these laws will go far towards preventing great losses from theft, disease, and other causes, hitherto sustained by the owners of livestock in this Territory, and we urge upon every citizen the necessity of aiding in their enforcement.

We prepared a bill in regard to the payment for stock killed or injured by railroads, which was in the main satisfactory to the stockmen and the representatives of the railroads, it being to a considerable extent a compromise measure, but owing to the long discussion over it in the endeavor to harmonize conflicting interests, it passed a short time before the close of the session, and to our great surprise the Governor held and thus prevented it from becoming a law, a result the more to be regretted because it was a law for the protection of the farmer and small stock owners along the lines of railroads, who are much greater sufferers from the loss of stock killed and injured than the large owners whose stock, being wild, are less liable to be run over and injured.

Stockmen can best serve their own interests, and at the same time secure greater protection and other advantages, by joining the Montana Stockgrowers Association and we most earnestly urge them to cooperate with us by doing so at once, if not already members of the Association. It costs but fifteen dollars ($15) to secure a membership, and the annual dues, after the first year, are ten dollars ($10).

Among the many advantages offered by the Association, one of the most important is the publication of a Brand Book each year, giving the brands, range, postoffice address, and other necessary information concerning members. Each member of the Association is entitled to one copy of the Brand Book and as many additional copies as are desired can be obtained at a nominal price. Application for membership in the Association should be sent to the Secretary accompanied by a check, draft, or P. O. order for fifteen dollars ($15), the initiation fees and annual dues for the first year.

Yours truly,

GRANVILLE STUART, President

R. B. HARRISON, Secretary, Montana Stockgrowers Association.

The scant paragraph given to the Board of Stock Commissioners in the foregoing report is no index to the importance that the board was to achieve in the livestock industry, nor did the terse reference to appointment of a territorial veterinarian surgeon give indication that such office was the forerunner of a Livestock Sanitary Board. Profiting by the experience in the legislature of 1883, the 1885 session bill creating the Board of Stock Commissioners did not call for a tax levy on all taxable property in the Territory. It confined the levy to the livestock in cow counties. The board was to consist of one member from each of those counties. It must be remembered that this was long before the days of "county busting," at a time when counties were few, as large as some eastern states,[3] and easily classified as to major industries.

The duties ascribed to the board were:

> . . . to exercise general supervision over, and, so far as may be, protect the stock interests of the Territory from theft and disease, and shall devise and recommend from time to time such legislation as in their judgment will foster this important industry. Said Board of Commissioners may take all lawful and necessary steps, procure all lawful and necessary process for attendance of witnesses, and employ any counsel they may deem proper to assist in the prosecution and conviction of any and all persons guilty of any of the crimes and misdemeanors against the laws of this Territory in feloniously branding or stealing any stock or any other crime or misdemeanor under any of the laws of this Territory for the protection of the rights and interests of stock owners.

The board was further authorized to appoint such inspectors and detectives as they deemed necessary, these men to be empowered to make arrests for any crimes or misdemeanors violating stock laws, and to be under the direct supervision of the board.

The Board of County Commissioners in each of the counties named was to levy a tax recommended by the stock commissioners, not to exceed one and one-half mills per dollar on the assessed valuation of all cattle, horses, mules, and asses in the respective counties. When collected, the money was to be paid to the territorial treasurer, to keep in a separate fund to be known as the Stock Inspector and Detective Fund, and to be used to defray expenses incurred under the provisions of the act and "for such other purposes as, in the judgment of said Stock Commissioners, shall best subserve the stock interests of the Territory."

Any owner of not more than ten cows and two horses or mules was exempt, and the board's expenditures were not to exceed the special tax levied for that year. The Territory was divided into two districts, with Dawson, Custer, and Yellowstone Counties in the first, and Meagher, Chouteau, and Lewis and Clark in the second. Inspectors and detectives were made district officers, each assigned to a district by the board. The six counties concerned covered the entire eastern two-thirds of the Territory, and,

---

[3] The original nine counties of Montana Territory were Missoula, Deer Lodge, Beaverhead, Jefferson, Edgerton (Lewis and Clark), Gallatin, Chouteau, Madison, and Big Horn. The boundaries of the first eight were defined when they were created, but Big Horn County was simply designated as "what was left." It was the largest county in the United States and was about the same size as the state of Missouri. On January 15, 1869, Dawson County was detached and, after the Battle of the Little Big Horn in 1876, the remaining 35,000 square miles became Custer County, with Miles City named as county seat. Later, Custer County was reduced to a mere sixty-by-seventy square miles.

although the board's duties and services did not extend to stockgrowers of the mountain valleys, the law was amended in 1887 to include other counties if the county commissioners thereof so desired, such counties to constitute a third district. Granville Stuart was the first president of the board and Russell B. Harrison the first secretary. Inspectors and detectives were given authority to summon posses and to make arrests, exercising the powers of a deputy sheriff, but they were to expect "no fee or emolument from either Territory or county."

The going was not easy for the first ten years. In 1887, and again in 1890, the board was forced to cut down on personnel because of a shortage of funds caused by the failure of certain counties to levy the special tax. In 1893 and 1894 several counties were delinquent and because of this the board threatened to quit. For many years, serving as a commissioner was a thankless chore with small honor and much grief. Naturally, there had been an interlocking of personnel between the board, which later became the Montana Livestock Commission, and the Montana Stockgrowers Association, the same secretary serving both bodies for many years.

# 8. MUTUAL PROTECTION

When the Eastern Montana Stockgrowers Association convened on April 3, 1885, in the Court House at Miles City, Granville Stuart, as president of the Montana Stockgrowers Association, was invited to the platform. The important question of the day was a proposed consolidation of the two associations. It was agreed that five members from each should constitute a committee to work out the details of such a merger. E. S. Newman, J. W. Strevell, J. N. Simpson, William Van Gaskin, and J. J. Thompson were chosen to represent the Eastern Montana group, and R. S. Hamilton, former Governor B. F. Potts, Granville Stuart, and R. P. Walker were selected as representatives of the western men, with Nelson Story named as an alternate.

While awaiting the report of the consolidation committee, the eastern association went about its regular business. Of the current membership of approximately 100, about two-thirds were present, and there were 54 applications pending. Among them was that of a young Harvard graduate, Theodore Roosevelt, who had the Maltese Cross and Elkhorn irons on the Little

Missouri, just across the Dakota line. His application had been submitted by the Marquis de Mores. Mr. Roosevelt's eligibility was not questioned. He was accepted and eventually became an active and extremely vocal member.

At the afternoon session, some controversy arose over the designation of roundup districts and the appointment of a roundup committee. Montana stockmen had the benefit of the experience of older associations in Texas and Wyoming in organizing and operating such districts. It is also evident that early laws of the territory, although repealed, had some influence on the roundup district system in effect on the open range in the eighties. The EMSGA had adopted a policy of deciding district boundaries, and then leaving the starting date of roundups and the selection of a foreman to the choice of the outfits occupying each district. There had been four districts in 1884, but with the expanded territory that would result from consolidation, more would be required, and there was no unanimity of opinion on how it should be divided. The matter was finally, and quite properly, left for the initial meeting of the new organization, at which twelve districts were decided upon. The association never had control over the designation of all roundup districts, or of their methods. Members were expected to comply with certain well-established and accepted principles, but arranged their operations to suit their convenience and local conditions. Routine in the mountain valleys never quite paralleled that of the plains. Well-defined natural barriers in the West served to simplify ranges.

Boundaries of districts, as agreed upon by association members, were published in the newspapers. The following is a typical description, taken from the April 24, 1886, issue of the *Weekly Yellowstone Journal and Livestock Reporter:*

District #4. Commences at Hocket's ranch, May 25, 1886, works down Powder River to the mouth of the Mizpah and splits. The first division works up Mizpah to its head, then meets the Tongue River roundup at the mouth of Pumpkin Creek and works back up Pumpkin Creek to its head. Second division works down Powder River to its mouth and then down the Yellowstone to Cabin Creek, up Cabin Creek to its head, thence to the head of Little Beaver and down Little Beaver to the lower Hashknife Ranch. E. P. Fletcher, Foreman.

At the evening session of the Eastern Montana Stockgrowers Association, the report of the consolidation committee was received and accepted as presented by the committee chairman, Governor Potts. The name of the new, combined organization was to be Montana Stockgrowers Association. As stated in the report, the object of this association was "to advance the interests of the stockgrowers of Montana and adjoining territories, and for the protection of same against frauds and swindles, and to prevent stealing, taking, and driving away cattle, horses, mules, and asses, from the rightful owners thereof, and to enforce the stock laws of Montana."

The Association did not hesitate to assume enforcement and, as the Board of Stock Commissioners was dedicated to that same laudable objective, it began to look as though violators were in for a rough time.

It was stipulated that there be semiannual meetings, the annual meeting to start on the third Tuesday in April, at Miles City, and the interim meeting to start on the third Monday in August, at Helena. The importance of cattle interests in each county represented can be deduced by the number of members per county allotted to the executive committee. Meagher and Chouteau Counties were to have three each; Lewis and Clark, Yellowstone, Dawson, and the Territory of Dakota were allowed two each; all other counties were accorded one member each.

Eligibility for membership was defined as follows:

> . . . a stockgrower, viz. a person owning or controlling cattle, horses, mules, or asses, and engaged in the business of breeding, growing, and raising the same for profit. To become a member all persons must be proposed by a member, each proposition must be accompanied by the fee of admission hereinafter specified, together with a statement of the number of cattle, horses, mules, and asses owned or controlled by such person, or his firm, or company, with all the brands and marks of such stock. The application is subject to examination and approval of a membership committee consisting of three men, the Executive Committee, and the Secretary-Treasurer of the Association.

Membership was a privilege and being denied it could hamper a cattleman's success.

Members were pledged not to divulge any Association discussion or action of a confidential nature, under threat of a hearing and possible expulsion. At most subsequent meetings, there were as many nonmembers present as there were members; there is no record of any executive sessions of the general membership being held. Members were required to notify the executive committee if they came by any knowledge of persons stealing or killing stock, the committee being empowered to "act in such manner as will, if possible, bring such person or persons to justice and recover said property." This gave the committee considerable latitude, especially if its collective conscience was elastic.

The first formal business meeting of the new Montana Stockgrowers Association got off to a flying start on the next morning, April 4, 1885. One of the first matters on the agenda concerned the publication of a brand book. Montana Territory's first legislative assembly recognized the importance of an official system of identification for livestock and for the recording of same. In 1872, Montana's first book of marks and brands was published and imprinted "Office of the Clerk of the Supreme Court and General Recorder of Brands for Montana Territory, Virginia City, M.T., August 1, 1872."

Two hundred and forty-one brands were recorded on forty-four pages, each description couched in formal phrase, e.g., "Be it remembered that Joe Dokes of Beaverhead County, Montana Territory, has adopted and claims the exclusive right to the following stock brand and marks, to-wit, etc. . . ." Supplementing the printed pages was a fourteen-page index with the brands hand-drawn in ink. This was adequate for the time and existing conditions, but it was incomplete and impractical when acres by the million and cattle by the hundreds of thousands became involved. In discussing the need for preparing a new book, the obvious was stated: "It is a matter of great importance to the Association to have an accurate brand book so that the men in the employ of Association members and others can become familiar with the brands and in that way do much towards protecting each other." Of course, the older Montana brands and many of those that came up from the south were already legend in the Territory's cowland, but there were many small owners whose stock could be lost unless listed in a properly distributed brand book.

Another thing that disturbed certain members was reported by a committee on bulls that was a holdover from the original Montana Stockgrowers Association. The committee's investigations showed that the calf crop from dairy herds ran as high as 90 per cent, while on the range 60 per cent was a fair average. The conclusion was that some form of range control applied to breeding would pay off, even though it would entail considerable expense. Theoretically, there might be no deficiency of bulls on the range, but the tendency of herds to break up into small bunches gave some of the cliques an undue proportion of sires while depriving others of adequate service. The solution seemed to be that each member be required to turn loose a surplus of bulls in proportion to his herd, and not to depend on the generosity of his neighbors.

The question of quality was deemed of great importance and the committee held that each bull should be "well-conditioned, vigorous, and virile" and "nothing less than half-blood [Texan]," and after five years, not less than three-quarters. It was further recommended that every bull should be condemned for use, and so marked, after five years of age, and at six, if not sooner, should be removed from the range—scrubs to be castrated or otherwise disposed of.

No stockman could find fault with the logic and benefits of such control but, as the committee reported, "The great American test applied to all proposed change is, 'Will it pay?' " In this case, the new expense would come from the further recommendation that all bulls be rounded up on November first of each year, and herded by themselves so that they could not rejoin the she-stuff until sometime in June, or, better yet, in July. Such a system might require well-fenced pasture and hay feeding. Cutting out the bulls, sorting, and delivering to their owners looked like a large and costly chore. To offset that, the increased effectiveness of each animal as a sire would show in an enlarged calf crop of better quality; there would be close control of calves; no more untimely dropping of puny calves by winter-weakened cows, with consequent losses of both due to the rigors of birth in bad weather.

Another advantage of this revolutionary proposal was that it gave the officials of the Association an opportunity to get an accurate check on the number of bulls owned by each member, their quality, their brands, their ages, the number of young bulls needed to make up owners' quotas in the spring, and whether disease existed. The committee on bulls then clinched its argument by declaring that "exact knowledge forestalls cheating and stimulates pride in improvement of breed animals." All owners did not have the facilities for wintering their bulls; so it was suggested that groups of owners combine and find a way to solve their localized problem of pasturage and hay-feeding. The report carried weight because it was signed by Con Kohrs, John T. Murphy, Azel Ames, Jr., Charley Anceny, John M. Holt, and William H. Martin. (Martin died before the report was presented.)

Resolutions were adopted, (1) authorizing the members of each roundup district to select the time and place for starting and to name the captain, (2) agreeing to place all men working on the roundup under absolute orders of the foreman as to duties and conduct, (3) requiring all owners to turn out on the range eight serviceable bulls for every hundred head of females one year old and upwards turned out on July 1 of each year, thereafter to supply the same proportion of bulls for all the cattle they own, (4) no cattle to be gathered between November 15 and the spring roundup without informing neighboring ranchers and giving them an opportunity to examine the cattle being driven off, (5) forbidding employment to anyone owning cattle on a range or who has or runs a brand separate from that of his employer. (This last resolution was rescinded at the fall meeting because it offered an obstacle to honest, frugal employees who were anxious to get a legitimate start on their own.)

Fifteen members of the executive committee also met on April 4 and did some resolving themselves. The first motion made and carried required all proceedings to be secret and members were honor-bound not to tell or publish the nature of any business transacted. They directed a resolution to the Secretary of the Interior, stating that the Cheyenne Indians were being issued inadequate provisions and were forced to go on cattle-killing expeditions to supplement their food supply. The committee, on behalf of the Association, wanted this situation corrected. It also protested the permitting of Indians on all reservations to leave at will, inasmuch as such departures always coincided with a surge in cattle killing and horse stealing. As agents refused to permit ordinary citizens or even duly commissioned inspectors and detectives of stock associations to enter the reserves to recover possession of stolen horses and mules, the committee requested authority for the legally appointed inspectors of the Territorial Board of Stock Commissioners to be admitted. If any stolen stock were found, the committee asked that the agent be instructed to take evidence as to the ownership and, if proof of theft were established, to give possession of the stolen animals to the board of commissioners, their detectives or inspectors, or to the rightful owners without unnecessary delay.

Another resolution forbade gambling on roundups and provided that roundup captains be so notified and made responsible for enforcement of the rule. It is doubtful if these members of the executive committee frowned on card games as corrupters of cowhand morals. They did regard roundups as times for earnest, undistracted effort—not as social sessions—and they didn't want the disruption of morale and discipline that might ensue after some disappointed optimist had bet into a one-card draw.

Soon after the consolidation meeting adjourned, members of the western association received the following notification:

MONTANA STOCKGROWERS ASSOCIATION
Secretary's Office

HELENA, MONTANA, April 15, 1885

DEAR SIR:

The Committee appointed from the Montana Stockgrowers Association to meet a similar committee from the Eastern Montana Stockgrowers Association, met at Miles City, Montana, April 4th and 5th, 1885, and would respectfully report that they succeeded in consolidating the two Associations into one to be called the "Montana Stockgrowers Association," and elected the following officers:

President,                                          First Vice-President,
    T. J. Bryan [1] of Miles City                       B. F. Potts [2] of Townsend

[1] Colonel Thomas J. Bryan, an Iowan, was a veteran of the Union Army. At the close of the Civil War he returned to Iowa and became a livestock dealer and feeder. He then came west and ran range cattle. In 1880, he and his wife reached Miles City, where they built a home.
[2] Benjamin F. Potts, of Ohio, was appointed governor of Montana Territory in 1870 and served in that office until 1883. He was a brevet major general in the Union Army when the Civil War ended. An able administrator and a good businessman, he established a large stock ranch near Helena. He died in 1887.

Second Vice-President,
   Wm. Harmon [3] of Miles City

Secretary and Treasurer,
   R. B. Harrison of Helena

### Executive Committee

*Beaverhead County,*
   Dr. Azel Ames, Jr.
*Chouteau County,*
   R. P. Walker
   Jno. Lepley
   Jesse Taylor
*Custer County,*
   Frank Robertson
   E. S. Newman
   Jos. Scott
   J. J. Thompson
*Dawson County,*
   J. S. Day
   David Hunter
*Deer Lodge County,*
   Conrad Kohrs
*Gallatin County,*
   Charles Anceny
*Jefferson County,*
   S. S. Huntley

*Lewis and Clark County,*
   R. S. Hamilton
   Jno. T. Murphy
*Madison County,*
   Alex Metzel
*Meagher County,*
   Granville Stuart
   Jno. H. Freezer
   S. S. Hobson
*Missoula County,*
   C. P. Higgins
*Silver Bow County,*
   Nicholas Bielenberg
*Yellowstone County,*
   A. A. Ellis
   Samuel Garvin
*Dakota Territory,*
   Marquis de Mores
   Jno. N. Simpson.

It was resolved that there should be two regular meetings of the Association each year, the spring meeting to be held in Miles City on the third Monday in April, and the fall meeting in Helena on the third Monday in August. Every member of the old associations was declared a member of the new one. It was also resolved that the annual dues of $10 from each member for the year beginning April 4, 1885, and ending April 21st, 1886, should be called for at once, and you will please remit the same to R. B. Harrison, Secy. and Treas. at Helena, by check or P. O. order. Your attention is especially called to this matter, as the brands for those in arrears for dues will not appear in the brand book of the Association, soon to be published.

The Committee would further report that they were guided in their action by a vote of the members of this Association—every vote cast being in favor of consolidation—and that they believe the new Association, being very much larger and stronger, can do more to assist and protect, as well as secure the best results to the stock interests of the Territory, than could be accom-

[3] Captain William Harmon was a Civil War veteran. He and a partner named Hale started the 22 Ranch on Little Beaver Creek, six miles southwest of Ekalaka. He was in on the rustler cleanup of 1884. He married Zoe Lulu Picotte in 1870. She was the daughter of Henri Picotte, a Pierre Chouteau partner, and a Sioux woman who had been educated in Chicago and St. Louis.

plished by the old Associations working separately and independently. We therefore urge every member of the Montana Stockgrowers Association to become a member of the consolidated Association at once.

R. B. Harrison, Secretary          Granville Stuart, President
R. P. Walker
B. F. Potts
R. S. Hamilton
*Committee on Consolidation on behalf of the
Montana Stockgrowers Association.*

Seventy members attended the fall meeting set for August 26, 1885, in Helena. Among them were many men who attained wealth and prominence in Montana ranching, mining, and mercantile businesses—such men as Charley Anceny, Nick Bielenberg, Harry Childs, Tommy Cruse, James Fergus, Dan Flowerree, Joe Gans, R. S. Hamilton, J. M. Holt, Con Kohrs, John T. Murphy, B. F. Potts, T. C. Power, A. J. Seligman, Nelson Story.

It was reported that recorded brands had reached a total of 3,236, the year before 800 having been recorded, and at least 1,000 expected in 1885 before the year expired. A committee was appointed to assist the overburdened territorial officials who were charged with the duty of keeping the records. There was complaint that the records were cluttered with duplications and with brands that seemed to be obsolete.[4] Owners had gone out of business, moved, or left the country without notifying the recorder or leaving a forwarding address. The books were becoming a mess.

This situation brought about a discussion of possible corrective measures through legislation, and the committee was given the further job of listing recommended legislation for the coming session of the territorial assembly. Dr. Ames was emphatic in his opinion as to the value of a brand. He said, "A brand is personal property and we have no right to appropriate it although it is obsolete. Some of the owner's representatives may still be in existence if he is dead and they have a right to these brands."

By resolution, the work of the comparatively new federal Bureau of Animal Industry was commended, and Congress was invited to pass additional legislation and to appropriate funds to compensate owners for the slaughter of cattle affected by contagious disease. Importuning Uncle Sam for financial assistance was in vogue even then.

Incorporation of the association had been suggested, but action was deferred since the majority believed the advantages were outweighed by the

4 The legislative assembly of 1911 passed a law requiring the re-recording of brands, a colossal task, the object of which was to eliminate obsolete brands that complicated the books. It was expected that at least 15,000 old brands, many of them exceptionally good ones, would be made available to those who cared to adopt them.

disadvantages. The editor of the *Miles City and Cheyenne Stockgrowers Journal* addressed the meeting. His speech bristled with indignation and invective because of attacks headlined by eastern newspapers against "the Monopolists of the Range." This was a favorite topic of eastern newswriters when other material ran low. The eloquent defender of the West declared that the western range damn-well supplied the effete East with high-protein viands, without which there would be famine back there. He asserted that the influence of those unscrupulous and uninformed defamers of the honest stockgrower had induced the President of the United States to issue orders for the tearing down of illegal fences on public domain. Perhaps they had. A long sequence of national trends had led up to it.

The Civil War disrupted the nation's economy, as do all wars, and in the postwar period drastic changes occurred in industry and agriculture. The abnormal wartime demand for foodstuffs and commodities, which had created feverish speculation, declined as the country's business and people tried to adjust to peace. Homesteaders, who had so eagerly gone into debt for livestock and equipment when the prices for farm produce soared, went broke when mortgages fell due. The rapid western agricultural expansion was a contributing factor to the Panic of 1873. Disillusioned have-nots looked for a place elsewhere on which to fix the blame. Corporations were fair targets. Thus, when industrialists organized "pools"—the forerunners of trusts—between 1873 and 1887, they were branded as monopolists. It was not hard to inflame public feeling against any group to which the slightest allegation of monopoly could be applied. "Monopoly" became a rabble-rousing word and, coupled with the phrase "greedy cattle barons," it was to haunt western stockmen for years. It did not increase their general popularity or strengthen their standing with Congress when controversial measures affecting range industry were introduced. In contrast, much romanticism and maudlin sympathy had been drummed-up for the sturdy homesteader, who was so gallantly making a home for the little woman and an ever-increasing bevy of offspring.

It had been discovered in the cow country that barbed wire could scratch both ways. Homesteaders stretched miles of it to keep cattle out; stockmen built more miles of it to fence government land in. Big cow outfits that leased or got title to alternate sections of railroad-grant land often ran a fence around a solid block that included government sections, and thereby discouraged homesteading inside what they implied was their pasture. As homesteaders were more numerous than cattlemen, their chorus in opposition to the practice swelled the loudest. They protested that "there ought to be a law," and directly there was one.

In February, 1885, Congress passed a law forbidding the fencing of public land even though a gate was provided. The President was given authority to use force, if necessary, to remove illegal fence. President Grover

Cleveland gave instructions to do that very thing. By 1887, illegal fences enclosing 135,000 acres had been removed in Montana, with action pending on as much more—small potatoes compared to what happened in other parts of the West. While the editor of the *Miles City and Cheyenne Stock-growers Journal* berated his eastern craftsmen, the Association members listened respectfully, and then adjourned.

# 9. THE DISASTROUS WINTER OF 1886–87

The law passed by the "Cowboy Legislature" of 1885 for the suppression and prevention of "disease among domestic animals and Texas cattle" was no idle gesture. Cattlemen were seriously concerned about the possible importation of diseased stock, especially from the East, and had urged that competent and thorough inspection be made at all rail entries to Montana for the discovery and control of disease among incoming cattle. Under the law, the governor, upon recommendation of the Board of Stock Commissioners, had to quarantine stock brought in from suspect areas at Montana ports of entry for rigid inspection. Such a proclamation was issued in 1886 and directed against cattle shipment from the East. There was laxity in the enforcement of the quarantine.

That fall the executive committee of the Association interviewed the governor and emphatically demanded that such shipments be held at Glendive while Territorial Veterinarian George H. Keefer, or a deputy, inspected them unless the shippers could produce proper and acceptable bills of health.

The committee accused Keefer of having been derelict, in fact criminally negligent, in his duties and so had jeopardized the cattle interests of the Territory.

Their contention had some foundation. One hundred and twenty head of cattle owned by Walter J. Etherington had been stopped near Mandan, Dakota, that fall and, upon examination by a competent veterinarian, were found to have pleuropneumonia. They were killed with the consent of the owner upon the assurance of the governor of Dakota Territory that he would be recompensed at the appraised value of $2,820. It required an act of the Dakota legislature to authorize the payment and by the time the next legislature met and approved such a course, a new governor vetoed it. This was most embarrassing.

Inasmuch as the Montana Stockgrowers Association included some prominent Dakota residents, the executive committee prepared an elaborate resolution commending the Dakota legislature for its fairness and Etherington for his generous cooperation. They had no kind words for the new governor, but did diplomatically suggest that he would see the light when the facts of the case were presented to him. Teddy Roosevelt had a hand in the preparation of the resolution. Having sent the neighborly epistle, the Montanans wanted to make sure that a similar situation could not arise with them.

The next Montana legislature (1887) amended the law concerning quarantine, and outlined in detail the duties of the governor, the territorial veterinarian, the stock owners, and custodians of incoming or disease-suspected stock so that there might be no excuse for misunderstanding or laxity in the law's enforcement. The series of episodes came to a happy ending with the legislative approval of the appointment of Deputy Herbert Holloway to replace Veterinarian Keefer. Satisfaction with the change was expressed: ". . . the stockmen of this territory can now congratulate themselves that they have a qualified, efficient, and honest officer in charge of that department . . . determined to bring to a close the loose and careless management which has hitherto characterized it."

After the Northern Pacific tapped the Yellowstone country, the Union Stockyards in Chicago became the primary market for Montana shippers. It was a long haul, with interruptions for feed and water and usually an aggravating delay for switching at the Minnesota Transfer between Minneapolis and St. Paul. It seemed that that inconvenience might be eliminated, and shipping costs lowered, if a market could be established at St. Paul. Granville Stuart was made chairman of a committee appointed to investigate the possibilities. He reported that the local consumption of beef in the Twin Cities was about 70,000 head per annum, coming largely from Kansas City and the southwest, whereas the natural source of supply should be Dakota, Montana, and northern Wyoming. He said that there was not a market north of Council Bluffs and Omaha and west of Milwaukee where a trainload of cattle could be sold. In the area tributary to Minneapolis and St. Paul, feeding for the market was unknown, although unusual facilities existed. The committee reached the conclusion that strong encouragement should be given businessmen in the Twin Cities to correct the deficiency, despite the pending construction of sheds and packing plant by the Marquis de Mores at Medora.

The year 1886 had opened auspiciously, weatherwise, with every section of Montana giving good reports on the condition of range cattle. It was announced in the Dillon *Tribune* (January 2, 1886) that "at no time within the past four years have the conditions been so favorable to carry the herds through winter with a minimum of loss. . . . We have had no very cold weather yet. Cattle are not simply in fine condition, but they are fat enough for beef with few exceptions."

By April, the hopes of continuing mildness had been justified but there was apprehension that alleged purchases of 100,000 head in Texas and 25,000 head on the west coast would seriously crowd the plains country of Montana unless some of the Indian reservations were reduced in size—wishful thinking that did not materialize. Word was received that the Hashknife Ranch of the Continental Cattle Company at Seymour, Texas, had engaged a veterinarian surgeon to spay several thousand heifers. The company would start two 3,000-head herds of them for their Montana ranch. During the summer, rumors became fact. Cattle did come in by thousands from east, west, south —sheep, too—coming to range that in mid-June got momentary relief from threatened drouth, only to dry out again. In August the burned-out grass country of the prairie and benchland was a sorry sight. Large streams went dry.

Theodore Roosevelt was not exactly an authority on the livestock business—neither did he work full time at it—but he was observant. He vibrated between New York and the Little Missouri. A Mandan reporter caught him en route after he had made a four-month sojourn at his Maltese Cross and Elkhorn Ranches. Mr. Roosevelt announced that where ranches were under efficient and honest management they were paying well, but not excessively. In his opinion, the rosy days were over as there were too many ranchers in the business. He stated that in certain areas the losses were enormous because of drouth and overstocking; that cattle were crowded on the plains beyond the range's capacity to sustain them, and cowmen were paying the penalty. Drouth, grasshoppers, and late spring frosts had devastated the grass.

It was all true. Nature was being uncooperative. Kohrs went to Canada and leased 100,000 acres of grassland in the Cypress Hills for the Pioneer Cattle Company. The Canadian Government, as an inducement for Montana cattlemen to utilize the grassland of the Northwest Territory, had set up a lease system whereby the holder paid from one to two cents an acre per annum; he could lease any number of acres, providing he stocked them with a specified number of cattle within a reasonable time. The customary duty of 20 per cent ad valorem levied on States' cattle crossing the border was waived, partially or *in toto*. A number of sizable Montana outfits took advantage of this attractive offer. The Pioneer Cattle Company planned to move its stock right after the fall roundup. They had missed a sale of their herds to eastern parties for a cool million dollars in a deal involving delivery of 33,000 head. Former Governor Potts had inspected the cattle for the prospective buyers and found them satisfactory, but he cannily advised them to postpone purchase unless rains came to insure a good growth of grass. That sage counsel and the death of the syndicate's agent stopped further negotiations. Bob Ford, convinced that the winter risk in running large herds of cattle in Montana was too great, sold out to Dan Flowerree just in time.

At the fall meeting of the Association in Helena, only twenty-seven members checked in at the Public Library building. Not finding the premises satisfactory, they moved to Harmony Hall on Park Street. The name was auspicious for a successful session. Secretary Harrison was a bit embarrassed when he had to report that the minutes of the last meeting could not be read; the stenographer employed to record the proceedings had not been able to read the notes he had taken.

The growing nuisance of grub-line riders came up for attention and drastic rules were adopted: (1) a register of the self-invited visitors, date of their arrival and departure to be kept at all ranches, (2) all arrivals to be required to pay road ranch prices for all accommodations, (3) foremen sending men on missions were to furnish each with a pass entitling them, while employed, to stop at other ranches, (4) foremen were directed to enforce these regulations, which were to be printed on cloth and posted at the ranches of all members. This put a crimp in the style of many a knight of the road.

The committee on bulls had reported at the spring meeting the need for immediate adoption of their recommendations made the year before. Their proposed plan had not yet been put into operation. They were earnestly interested in improving the grade of Montana cattle as a matter of pride as well as profit, and the project would need cooperation from everyone to be effective. As in all associations, the inertia of some was maddening to those who were aggressive.

As any Montanan of long residence will tell you, the only safe prediction about Montana weather is that it will be unpredictable. The state is so big and its topography so varied that while robin redbreasts may be turning blue from the cold in one section, bluebirds eighty miles away are turning red from the heat! Cattle shipped in the fall of 1886 were not in top condition. The drouth, causing a scarcity of grass, and overstocking had taken their toll. The bottom had dropped out of the market and cattle were selling at record lows. The poor quality of the shipments accelerated the drop. Stock remaining on the range were in no shape to endure a hard winter, and when it came, it brought misery.

The snow fell in late November and lay deep. All roads were blocked. The chinook came early in January and worried stockmen were encouraged, but their hopes were thrown into reverse when, at the end of the month, a blast of brittle cold came out of the north that changed the melted snow into a coat of crystal armor and then covered it with a soft, treacherous mantle. The slender blades that held the hope of life were locked against pawing horse hooves and nosing cattle muzzles. Starving and helpless, the famished stock drifted, piled up in coulees, stumbled over cutbanks, or just froze in their tracks. It was awful.

Kid Russell was wintering with Jesse Phelps on the Stadler–Kaufman ranch near Utica in the Judith Basin country. Jesse was range foreman for the outfit and Charlie Russell was the wrangler. There wasn't a thing they could do about the weather as the cold, stormy days dragged on. Charlie would while away part of the dismal monotony with the paints and brushes which he packed around in a sock. Range cattle were taking a terrific beating. A brindle Texas cow moped around the horse barn for what little protection it afforded, and by the time Jesse got a letter from "K" Kaufman asking how the cattle were doing, she was pretty gaunt and about done for.

After Phelps read the letter, he tossed it over to Russell and said, "I just haven't the heart to tell him. I don't know what to say." Next day Charlie made a sketch on the pasteboard cover of a collar-box and handed it to Jesse, who exclaimed, "Hell, that picture tells the story better than I can write it." Russell's drawing of a forlorn, emaciated cow, standing in the dreary, storm-swept prairie with three wolves awaiting the moment when her legs would buckle, is famous among Montana cattlemen as "Waiting for a Chinook." (The other title, "The Last of Five Thousand," was added later.) It started Charles Marion Russell on his way to artistic fame and fortune, and the old brindle cow was his model.

Louis Stadler and Louis Kaufman had a meat shop on Edwards Street in Helena at the time, and when the card was received, "K" Kaufman took it across the street to show Ben Roberts at his harness shop. Roberts knew young Russell and asked for the sketch. Kaufman gave it to him. It had no particular value at the time—just a clever drawing by a talented kid out on a ranch. Neglected, it became soiled, and it was in that condition that Wallis Huidekoper bought it for $125 in 1913.

Huidekoper had the sketch cleaned and framed by an expert, and took it to the Russell home in Great Falls where Charlie autographed it and added the words, "This is the real thing painted the winter of 1886 at the OH ranch." Huidekoper then had Kaufman autograph it. In the winter of 1942–43, Major Huidekoper presented the historic little card to the Montana

Stockgrowers Association and it hung on the wall of Secretary Ed Phillips' office until 1952, when it was placed on permanent loan for exhibit in the Russell Gallery of the Historical Society of Montana, at Helena.

The western valleys were more fortunate than the plains country. The Big Hole Herding Association worked the Red Rock, Horse Prairie, and Grasshopper ranges on the spring roundup of 1886 and handled about 12,000 head of cattle. They were well pleased with the fine calf crop. Almost from the beginning of the cattle business in the western part of the Territory, ranchers had made provision for winter feeding. Wild hay was plentiful and that summer the Big Hole Basin was one vast hay ranch, with the crop selling at $8 a ton in the fall. By February, 1887, hay was selling for $30 a ton in the neighboring Flint Creek Valley.

Everything was going smoothly until the night of January 31, 1887, when the howling van of a raging blizzard swept over southwestern Montana. The temperature dropped to thirty-two below, and stayed there for four days. Trains were late and in some instances abandoned. On February 9, a "little blizzard" appeared in the vicinity of Dillon and put the thermometer down to four below zero. People of the west end, however, seemed more concerned about what might be happening to their fellow stockmen to the east than they were about their own herds. Fort Benton was reported isolated and low on food and fuel, with sixty below prevailing. Crow Indians were said to be living on the meat of froze-to-death cattle.

First reports in the west end were exaggerated, just as they were along the Yellowstone. On the Red Rock Lake range (Centennial Valley), 250 head had been left in to winter as an experiment. Preparations had been made to feed them if necessary, but when the blizzard came, the weather was so bad that riders couldn't gather them and there was about a 12 per cent loss before the cattle could be driven to feed.

In the middle of February, a story was current that Con Kohrs had lost 800 head in the Big Hole, and that the two-foot blanket of snow between there and Anaconda would cause tremendous losses. A month later, it was determined that Kohrs had only 200 head in the Big Hole, out of which he lost one old cow. The total loss in the entire Basin was estimated at only 1 per cent. In fact, when things began to get back to normal and an accurate count could be made, the western valley losses were found to be extremely low in comparison with those in central and eastern Montana. Alex Metzel said his loss on the Upper Ruby did not exceed 2 per cent from all causes, and other cattlemen in that vicinity did equally as well. Light losses were tallied in Missoula County; in Nevada Valley, J. H. Helm was sure in early March that the 5,000 to 6,000 head of that area would pull through in excellent shape with hay left over, despite two feet of snow. One estimate of the loss in the Deer Lodge and Beaverhead Valleys placed it at 8 per cent. By mid-

March, even in the high Big Hole Basin, stock was being turned loose to rustle, as the snow was fast disappearing.

There has been a great variation in the estimates of losses during that hard winter, men of excellent judgment differing widely. Conrad Kohrs said the loss was 50 per cent; Nelson Story placed it at 66.66 per cent. Granville Stuart couldn't believe the loss was great until his spring roundup showed 900 calves branded, as compared with 8,000 the year before. It was bad enough everywhere, but some areas suffered much more than others. Many small outfits and a number of very sizable ones were wiped out. One spread went from assets of $1,000,000 to liabilities of $350,000. Teddy Roosevelt and the Marquis de Mores left for New York and India, respectively. It was a bitter dose to take, but it purged the industry of many bad practices.

Colonel Sam Gordon, editor of the *Yellowstone Journal,* who was an on-the-spot observer of the eastern range, as well as an intimate associate of cattlemen in that area, summed up the big debacle years later when he wrote:

From whatever source the inspiration came, it certainly was quickly and widely known that there was a great opening for profitable investment in the range cattle business in the valley of the Yellowstone, and by virtue of its central location and its trading and banking facilities, Miles City became the center of this new business. In a day, almost, we began to talk knowingly of range prospects and conditions and to be interested in the genus "cowboy," simon-pure specimens of which began to drop in on us from Texas and the Southwest.

The change wrought was sudden and complete; all business interests now catered to the new element, and well they might, for from 1881 to 1885 the wealth that was dumped in Custer County in the shape of range cattle requires no exaggeration to make it an interesting statement. It was not alone the experienced cowmen of the Southwest who had found and were eagerly taking advantage of a rich, virgin range, but eastern capitalists of the class who are always willing to take long chances for big returns, were falling over each other in their rush to get into the business. They had figured it out on a basis of one hundred percent of calves each year, all heifers, and reproduction on the same scope from these calves—not the first year—they did give them one year of maidenhood—but a "turn-off" each year of "threes" and "fours" at fancy prices of stock that had cost nothing but the ranch expenses.

As a majority of the "companies" and individuals knew nothing of the business, it was essential that there be at the head of each outfit a manager or superintendent to take charge of the technical part of it. These managers were usually cowboys who had become "top-hands" on the southwestern ranges and were absolutely competent to run herds, but were rarely good financial managers. Then there were other outfits that had for managers men who were interested in the ventures; men of good business repute at home and fully competent to run a store or factory or an enterprise fitted to well-established grooves, but as much out of place running a cow outfit as they would have been commanding an army—more so, probably.

Looking backward, it is a hard guess which method was most disastrous; the manager with "cow sense" but no idea of the value of money, or the thrifty financier who didn't know a branding iron from a poker. They were bad combinations, each of them. Things were generally run at high pressure. The cowboy manager, naturally improvident and reckless and feeling that he had good backing behind him, set the pace both in ranch and town expenditures for his more provident tenderfoot neighbor, and the latter being here to "learn the business" was not as slow in adopting his teacher's methods as he might have been in matters more within his ken.

The result was a lively gait both on the range and in town, and to make the stockholders or owners at home feel good, the spring reports from the range would be "Winter losses nominal—probably one or two percent." Now it may be said here, in passing, that experienced and conservative cowmen who have been in the business here in Montana for thirty years, hold that 10% is a normal yearly mortality. There are many ways of losing range stock aside from winter-killing. Wolves and spring miring are potential factors. New grass brings grief to quite a few and the rustler claims his percent with reasonable regularity. While 10% may be a little too conservative, it is easy to believe that a mortality of 5% could prevail year in and year out without any unusual disaster.

Well, after these "investment herds" had been run for four or five years and a couple of beef shipments had been made out of them, it became evident to the managers that the "book count," based on their reports of nominal losses, would have to be revised in some way. The roundups were not satisfactory and the owners were beginning to inquire why shipments were not larger. It is comforting to reflect on the number of reputations that were saved by the "hard winter" of 1886–87. It *was* a hard winter—the latter end of it—and the worst of it came when the cattle were weak and thin and unable to stand grief, but it never killed half the cattle that were charged to it. It came as a God-sent deliverance to the managers who had for four or five years past been reporting "one percent losses," and they seized the opportunity bravely, and comprehensively charged off in one lump the accumulated mortality of four or five years. Sixty percent loss was the popular estimate. Some had to run it up higher to get even, and it is told of one truthful manager in an adjoining county that he reported a loss of 125%, 50% steers and 75% cows. The actual loss in cattle was probably thirty to fifty percent, according to localities and conditions.

Of the 337 members of the Montana Stockgrowers Association, only 98 were present at the spring meeting in 1887. The secretary's report reflected their mood:

> Since we last met in annual meeting . . . the range business of the plains has had severe trials to pass through. 1st. The unprecedented drouth that prevailed last spring and summer causing a great shortage of food and making the cattle poor in flesh for the market and winter; 2nd. The low price of beef that ruled in Chicago during the fall, shrinking our profits materially; 3rd. The very severe winter which has just passed brought general loss, more or less severe depending upon circumstances, to every member of the Association and, in fact, to every stockman in the Northwest.
>
> These reverses were sufficient to try the patience and fortitude of everyone throughout the range country and, as you are aware, have demoralized the business and turned the tide of investment from us to other directions. That the trials through which we have passed were remarkable, not only for their severity, but particularly because they followed each other so closely, is universally admitted. A drouth without parallel; a market without a bottom; and a winter, the severest ever known in Montana, formed a combination testing the usefulness of our Association and proving its solidity.
>
> Thinking that these trials were not sufficient for our industry, Congress, in its wisdom, has added a fourth, the Interstate Commerce law which has seriously interfered with the attendance of this meeting owing to the difficulty of securing reduced transportation and which threatens to interfere seriously with the necessary rights and privileges of cattlemen of the far West in transporting their quota of the food supply of the nation to eastern markets for consumption.

Teddy Roosevelt wanted the criticism of the Interstate Commerce bill deleted in the secretary's report. The secretary stood pat. A compromise was finally arranged by bracketing the offending paragraph and appending a note to the secretary's report, stating that the Association declined to express an opinion concerning the merits of the bill and "does not sanction the insertion of the sentences of the report enclosed in brackets." The buck was thereby passed to the secretary and the objectionable sentences remained—bracketed. Everyone, even the secretary, was satisfied by this masterful handling of the delicate situation.

Having opened on this dolorous note, the meeting chirked up and voted to place stock inspectors at Deadwood and at the Standing Rock Agency in South Dakota, the expense to be divided between the Montana and Wyoming Associations. They also raised $1,000 by voluntary contributions to pay John Clay, Jr.'s moribund Consolidated Cattle Growers Association, of which the Montana association was a member. Its history was brief.

Since the last meeting, the secretary had prepared and issued the first brand book to be published by the Association, today a collector's item. There was an atmosphere of optimism despite the difficulties of the past year. Before the end of the eighties, there were more cattle on Montana ranges than ever before.

# 10. THE RAWHIDE ERA

Much of the technique of handling cattle on the northern open range came from the experience of Texas owners and the cowhands who had sifted into Montana with the long drives. A great deal of their knowledge had originated with the Mexicans who had been herding stock since the days of Cortes. They were superb horsemen and ropers. Many of the phrases that have become universal in cowland operations are of Spanish origin. Not only was personal skill required, but also efficient organization, especially where numerous outfits were occupying public range in common.

The spring roundup, usually starting the last of May or early June, followed the arrival of the bulk of the calf crop; the fall roundup, which began around September 1, was for the purpose of separating the beef animals for shipment—steers, dry cows, culls—and to brand late calves or any that had been overlooked in the spring. The calf roundup in the spring gave owners a field tally of increase; the beef roundup determined their income for the year. Both were equivalent to bank statements.

The foreman, or "ramrod," of a roundup was given autocratic authority. His word was law and any infraction or insubordination was not tolerated. He had to be fearless and impartial in enforcing his dictates as he was dealing with very independent and rugged employees. Any wavering on his part or the condoning of a violation could destroy morale and discipline in a hurry. He had to be so well trained in the cattle business and so thoroughly versed in the psychology of cows and cowboys that the latter, at least, would respect him. The reputation of such top hands became known throughout the range country. R. S. Ford, W. C. Burnett, and George Brewster were among the best.

Neighboring outfits using common range found it economical to combine their roundup activities into what was commonly called a pool. The number of riders and chuck and bed wagons to be furnished by each outfit was determined on an equitable basis. Day and night horse wranglers were hired and the custodian of the pots, pans, and dutch oven. "Reps," as representatives from other districts or outfits were called, rode with each roundup crew. They were usually favored in the work assignments as they had to be in a position to keep an eye out for their employers' brands. Just as important as the men were the saddle horses. To this day, no mechanical contrivance can quite replace them.

It took eight to ten horses to keep one rider in fresh mounts, so every roundup crew was accompanied by a herd of loose horses known as the *remuda,* or "cavvy." Day and night wranglers kept them from straying and brought them into camp when a change of mounts was in order. Depriving a cowhand of his horse could make things very inconvenient, even tragic, for him. Neither his boots nor his disposition were made for walking. The development and extension of range-land practice required a special type of saddle horse and the sagacious cow pony became an integral part of it. Sheep dogs are herders by instinct. Cow horses have to learn their trade through experience and schooling, but once initiated their ability is amazing and their intelligence phenomenal.

The horses that came up the Texas Trail with the herds, and the various bands of mares driven into southwestern Montana from California, were of the small, Spanish type that had retained the qualities of their Arab and Barb ancestors. They were alert and intelligent, with endurance and agility beyond the ordinary. "Cayuse" has become a disparaging term for any undersized, nondescript saddle horse. It should carry no opprobrium because, originally, cayuses were sturdy, little ponies bred by the Cayuse Indians from that same Arab stock brought to America by the Spaniards. They were far from being scrubs. Indian mares of Arab blood produced saddle ponies weighing 800 to 950 pounds when crossed with standard-breds and Morgans. They were intelligent and had great stamina.

Oregon horses were trailed into Montana for use on the range. They weighed between 1,000 and 1,500 pounds, had good feet, were tough and fast. The predominating strain was from their immediate ancestors who came over the Oregon Trail from the States. So, at first there were three types of cow ponies on Montana's open range—the cayuses or Indian ponies, the Spanish type, either California bronc or Texas mustang, and the so-called American horse, some of the latter being of Morgan or Steeldust descent. There was a subsequent merging that resulted in Montana-bred horses with superior physical qualities that were attributed to the water, grass, and altitude.

Individual cow horses became specialists. Circle horses had to have long legs and stamina to cover much ground in a day; a cutting horse must outguess and outmaneuver its dodging quarry with little or no direction from the rider; a good rope horse has perfect timing and knows just what to do after a loop has been dabbed on a calf or steer. Night horses were not easily "spooked" and were credited with having uncanny, nocturnal eyesight. Mountain horses were sure-footed on the narrow trails. There were strong-swimming "river horses," valuable for pushing herds across streams on a long drive. The unpopular equine performer was the shifty-eyed jughead who specialized in unloading his man when such antics were least expected.

Many cowhands had a horse or two of their own on whom they lavished much care and affection. Certain horses became great pets and were pampered by indulgent cowboys who slipped them piecrust and biscuits when the cook's roving eye could be eluded. A number of Montana ranchers raised horses in preference to cattle, although horses require twice as much forage. The A. C. Huidekoper outfit on the Little Missouri, the IJ outfit of the Judith Basin country, and the Flowerree Horse Ranch on the Sun River were early-day examples.

At Stevensville in the Bitterroot Valley, Marcus Daly, of Butte copper renown, raised and trained the Thoroughbred track winners that brought fame, purses, and ribbons to his stables. Three gentlemen, who later became either Montana territorial or state veterinarian surgeons, were brought here by Mr. Daly to take care of his horses. They were English-born Herbert Holloway, who crossed the Atlantic in 1878 with a shipment of horses for the Daly stock farm; Robert Bird, a Scot, who had practiced his profession in England and Australia; and Morton E. Knowles, a native of Indiana. James Maudlin, whose Willowburn Farm was on the west slope of the Ruby Mountains, raised exceptional draft horses. They were foaled by Percheron mares and sired by his famous Norman studs, Louis Phillipe and Mingo, which he imported in 1874.

Under the date April 19, 1890, the Miles City *Yellowstone Journal* carried an article headlined "A NATURAL HORSE MARKET," extolling the advantages and commercial possibilities of that location. Miles City became nationally known as a horse center. In 1900, Fort Keogh was turned into a cavalry remount station, the largest of three in the United States, where hundreds of unbroken horses were introduced to saddle and bridle and topped off by durable bronc stompers. Unsuspecting yellowlegs at distant cavalry posts must have had a few surprises when assigned some of the four-legged graduates of the Fort Keogh school of equitation.

During the roundup, work started at daylight, right after the cook had invited the crew of sleepy cowpunchers to "come and get it before I throw it out." The nighthawk brought the cavvy into the rope corral that had been strung on stakes from the wheels of the bed wagon. The horses to be ridden on circle were roped as they milled and dodged in the frail enclosure. The foreman assigned riders to cover designated drainage areas. It was their business to circle stream and coulee heads and gather cows and calves as they found them. They were routed out of brush and breaks and added to an ever-growing bunch that the riders kept moving downgrade to converge at a central point picked by the foreman.

While the riders were on circle, the cook and night wrangler moved camp. War bags and bed rolls had to be neatly rolled, tied, and deposited by their owners in the bed wagon, where they rode with the canvas fly, the cook tent, and the sleeping tent. The latter was not used in mild weather. The cook drove the chuck wagon, with the stove bouncing along behind on a two-wheeled trailer whose short tongue was supplemented by a safety chain. The nighthawk drove the bed wagon. A new camp was pitched on the chosen branding grounds at the focus of the various drainage courses being combed by the circle riders. The fly was stretched to the side or rear of the grub wagon and the cantankerous culinary artist, with flour-sack apron knotted around his waist, began preparing lunch for the ravenous riders who would descend on him at noon.

When they arrived with their cows and calves, the bunches were thrown together to form one herd. In the first general confusion, calves became separated from distressed mothers and until things settled down it was a dust-raising, bawling melee. Incidentally, wild cows found their calves much more readily than do the tamer, more stolid mothers of today, who are inclined to be somewhat indifferent if their babies go astray. Wood was dragged in at the end of a rope by riders to build the branding fire, and the irons were heated therein. The loose-herded cattle adjusted to the unaccustomed situation. Then riders worked their way into the herd very quietly, taking pains not to alarm the cattle. When a calf was identified by its mother's brand, a roper dropped a loop over its head and started for the fire, dragging the bawling, bucking midget behind. Apprehensive mamma joined the procession, sometimes on the prod. When the calf reached the fire, a wrestler flanked and dumped it so that he and another hand could hold it down fore and aft, and the hot iron was applied. An owner received credit in the tally book as to the number and sex of his calf crop. Bull calves were castrated, except for those chosen to be future range sires, these in a set proportion to an owner's heifer calves. When a calf had received full treatment, the bewildered tyke was turned loose to find its mother, and eventually all were turned back on the range to seek their accustomed haunts.

In working the herds, great care was taken not to unduly excite the cattle, so there was a minimum of movement and noise by the cowboys. Occasionally a calf was stamped with the wrong brand by mistake, in which case compensation was made by branding another calf which would offset the error. If a JO cow had her calf branded with a Bug, then a Bug calf would be branded with a JO. Both babies would be marked with a jaw brand so that when either owner found one of his cows seemingly taking care of a neighbor's calf, he would know what had happened. Reps were responsible for the branding and tallying of calves identified as belonging to the outfits they represented, and were expected to throw or start their owner's stock towards the range on which they belonged. If a wandering cow, missed in the roundup, was found later with an unbranded calf far from her owner's range, an ethical cowman would brand the calf with its owner's brand, figuring that the distant neighbor would do as much for him under similar circumstances. This was known as a "courtesy of the range." The roundup was all hard work that called for cooperation and synchronized effort if the operation was to run like a production line.

On the eastern range, diversion of sorts was sometimes furnished by Orshel Brothers of Miles City, merchants with a nose for business. They stocked a "band wagon" with hats, gloves, underwear, and other clothing, knickknacks, even forbidden whiskey. For many years, this peddling caravan was driven by one Johnny Frye to the roundup camps and ranches of eastern Montana.

Association rules governed the disposal of mavericks. It was assumed that every cow would know and claim her own, but sometimes a calf was left an orphan, or at least a waif, when its mother met with an accident and its philandering father went off with another cow. At one time a maverick was deemed the property of the stockman on whose "accustomed range" it was found. The usual Montana method of dealing with mavericks was to sell them at roundup to the highest bidder, slap on his brand, tally them to him, and turn them loose with his other cattle. The accumulated money went into the roundup fund that paid the horse wranglers and the reps who were sent to other districts.

Versions of how "maverick" became a synonym for an unbranded critter are numerous and stick fairly close to the same pattern. However, Samuel A. Maverick, the gentleman whose name was borrowed, was not a big cattleman, as many of the stories allege. Mr. Maverick reached Texas from South Carolina, after graduating from Yale, and engaged in land speculation and the practice of law in San Antonio, when Texas was under Mexican rule.

He had arrived well heeled and was adding to his capital in a substantial way when he signed the Texas Declaration of Independence. He was captured by Mexican troops in 1842 and held prisoner in Mexico City for some time.

In 1845 Maverick accepted 400 head of mixed cattle in lieu of cash due him on a $1,200 note. The cattle were on long, narrow Matagorda Island, four miles off the Texas coast. An irresponsible Negro family, who seemingly came with the cattle as part of the deal, was in charge of them. At low tide in the Gulf, the longhorns could wade to the mainland and a lot of them did. The Negroes were not very conscientious herders and few calves were branded.

During the Mexican War, Sam Maverick was knee-deep in business and political affairs. He paid slight attention to his island bovines and, due to defections by restless members of the herd, they still tallied 400 after he had owned them for eight years. In 1853, he had them moved from the island to the mainland, their Negro caretakers coming with them. They mingled with the herds of full-time stockgrowers who kept their calves branded and who were forever on the lookout for "slicks." When they found one, it was a twenty-to-one shot that it was one of Maverick's critters, which didn't deter them from slapping their own iron on the beast. And so unbranded cattle came to be known as mavericks. In 1856 Sam Maverick sold his herd, stipulating 400 head, range delivery at $6 per head. They were the only cattle he ever owned.

The roundup went on day after day until the district had been thoroughly combed. No owner wanted any of his calves overlooked. They might fall prey to the first rider who found them and who could run his own brand on with a hot cinch ring. There were also artists capable of picking a "hair brand" on a calf; they used a jackknife to remove hair in the semblance of a brand that would pass casual inspection until the calf was weaned. Then they could happen on the little fellow again and burn on their own brand with a stamping iron and a show of legitimacy. There were even some people so low as to split a calf's tongue so that it couldn't nurse. It would then abandon the milk station and lose affection for its mother, and soon thereafter become a maverick.

In the boom days, there wasn't much time gap between spring and fall roundups. During the interval there was always other work to be done. Some outfits put up hay, mostly for horses that were kept up during the winter. There were corral poles to be cut and hauled; corrals and line cabins to be built and repaired. Range broncs were gathered and broken to saddle. Winter was the time when work was really slack. Then some of the hands who had been laid off would "ride the grub line," sponging on the hospitality of the larger outfits for board and a place in the bunkhouse until they became a nuisance. Others holed-up and "bached" in a cow town. Some of the boys were kept on as "line riders." They lived by pairs in a lonesome cabin built on the owner's range limit. They rode out from there each day to keep the outfit's stock from straying off their home range. It was an isolated life that could bring on acute cases of cabin fever.

On the fall roundup, the "circle" system of gathering the stock was the same as in the spring. Late calves, dropped during the summer, were branded and tallied, but the primary object was to gather and select the beef herds of fat steers and dry cows that would be trailed to the railroad for shipment east. In the open range days, a steer wasn't judged ready for slaughter until he was four years old. Three-year-olds might be sold for feeders in the corn belt.

If it was desirable to examine a steer's brand or make other close inspection, one rider would rope the animal around the neck and another would heel it. By taking dally welts around their saddle horns and pulling in opposite directions, they could dump and "stretch" the subject. The smart cow ponies would keep the lariats tight while the examination was made. It might be necessary for a cowhand on foot to use the critter's tail as leverage to throw the steer. One man could rope and throw a steer on the open prairie by the technique known as "busting" it. The animal was hazed into a high lope across country. The rider would drop a loop over its head, take a couple of dally welts, then rein his horse to the left at a sharp angle after dropping the rope along the steer's right side. When the rope came tight across the steer's haunches, it slid his hind legs out from under him. It took a fast horse, a good rope, and a stout cinch to accomplish this stunt and it didn't always do the steer much good.

When the beef herd reached a cow town on the railroad, there had to be suitable bed and feed grounds on which to hold them until they could be loaded. If other herds had reached the shipping point just ahead of them, it might be necessary to take the late herd back on grass and "loose herd" them. The cowboys who chaperoned the shipment to its destination rode in the caboose, which was changed at every division point, forcing sleepy punchers to change bunks at ungodly hours of the night. This was the cause of much complaint, and eventually a through caboose was provided. At points the entire shipment had to be unloaded for feed and water and then reloaded, a tedious, exasperating procedure. In spite of the best care en route, there was always weight shrinkage.

After the cowhands reached the big city and delivered their charges, they were not always as naïve as they have been reported. When they had had a fling at sightseeing, they were not only ready, but eager, to be back home on the range. As for the sentimentalists who love to sing about the home on the range, it was too often a squat, dirt-roofed, log ranch house in a cottonwood grove, with a bunk house for the hands, who were not too orderly as housekeepers, a few pole corrals, and that was it.

# 11. ROMANCE OF THE RANGELANDS

With Westerns dominating TV programs, the myth of cowboy glamour is being perpetuated throughout the land. Even adult, native Montanans are falling for it. Small boys riding broomstick steeds have always done their share to emulate the cowboy but they no longer invoke a ventriloquistic "Bang! Bang! Bang!" from wooden sidearms. They have become more realistic. Nowadays, they fan and twirl a plastic-handled hog-leg loaded with endless strips of caps that make a horrific noise and stench. On the TV screen, loping knights of the plains still help or hinder the sheriff's posses, storm through the lightning-rent night to swing the big stampede into a mill, or rescue frail schoolmarms from a fate worse than death. The good guys always beat the bad guys—usually to a pulp. Fact and fancy, with the latter predominating, have been blended until a traditional pattern of suspense, surprise, violence, and romance has been created and accepted for extravagant tales of strong, silent characters who shoot from the hip and never miss. It is wonderful, but considerably overplayed.

There were no schoolteachers in the range country for many snows because there were no potential scholars in that womanless wilderness. Moreover, when the self-reliant tutors did arrive, they were capable of holding their own with a handy stick of stove wood against almost any predatory man or beast. There are still some cowboys in Montana, but they are few and far between—largely superseded by dude wranglers, rodeo contestants, guitar-playing, nasal tenors, and that man-of-all-chores, the ranch hand. The last roundup of old-time cow-waddies in Montana was instigated by Paul Campbell, hotel man of Glasgow, and Dick Nelson, rancher. It was held at the John David–Dick Nelson horse camp, thirty-five miles northwest of Glasgow, Montana, on July 1, 1951. It was a gathering of old-time riders of the range that can never be duplicated—a day for reminiscing and stowing away barbecued beef served hot from the tailgate of the chuck wagon; for the corraling of "fuzztails" that had been "spooked" out of their coulee haunts by airplane and then turned over to veteran riders who eased them across the rolling benchland and into a pole corral, proud, suspicious studs in the lead; a powwow of cowland's riding remnant.

When cowboying of the virile variety was in its prime, there were no limiting qualifications for a candidate insofar as age, conformation, place of birth, education, or previous employment were concerned. He could be the second son of a duke or a kid from the Ozarks; a college graduate or an illiterate; an adolescent or a weather-beaten old silvertip. Considering his responsibilities and the value of the investment entrusted to his care, he was a hard-working, underpaid character whose calling kept him on the fringe of the frontier. He sweltered and froze, thirsted and hungered, faced hazards, solitude, and lack of entertainment—none of them without complaining. His employment, loyalty, and morals were often elastic.

John Clay, in *My Life on the Range,* describes an episode that happened at spring roundup on the headwaters of the Powder River in Wyoming:

> The cowpunchers, headed by Jack Flagg and men of his stripe, struck for higher wages. They had said nothing when engaged or on leaving for the meeting point. Few or any owners attended or rode with the roundups. The foremen did the work and they, after some show of resistance, laid down and granted the demands of the boys. It was not the advance in wages that made so much difference. It was the way it was done. Gatlin, who on an occasion of this kind was like a piece of putty, threw up his hands at once. He lost control of his men and if you wish to be ridden over, stomped upon, get a cowboy to do it, and more especially the brand we employed in those days in the Sweetwater region. They were the real, simon-pure, devil-may-care, roystering, gambling, immoral, revolver-heeled, brazen, light-fingered lot and yet a dash of bravado among them that was attractive to a stranger. They had no respect for a man and little for a woman. Yet they were good workers.

Many of them had, individually, good instincts. In the herd they were mean and to hesitate with them meant losing. If they bluffed you, goodbye to discipline.

The ladies' impression of the typical cowhand is tempered by those feminine instincts that urge them to make allowances for bad and bashful boys. Mrs. W. W. Alderson, Tongue River pioneer ranchwife, said, "I have been dependent upon them for courtesies, protection, and kindness, and have always received them in the fullest measure." Ann Kenneth McLean, who married a cowhand, found them romantic. She described them as they appeared to a young and popular ranch girl of the 1880's.

In his picturesque togs, large sombrero, colored shirt, chaps, riding boots, silk kerchief, tie, and silver mounted spurs, he is a modification of the Spanish cavalier. His horse's movements give him grace. . . . The man of forty, as a rule, is no more bowlegged than the fourteen year old beginner. As for entertainment, say all the pretty things you can think of about his horse and soon he will expound the merits of his mount. If he comes to the house do not ask for his hat or he is lost and will not remain long. He rolls his hat, readjusts the hatband, looks at the lining, and for the first time discovers the name Stetson. His parting salute is "Well, I must be hittin' the trail—so long," or "Adios!"

Yet another viewpoint is this one, penned by Teddy Roosevelt and taken from the *Stockgrowers Journal* of March 3, 1888:

Cowboys are smaller and less muscular than the wielders of ax and pick, but they are as hardy and self-reliant as any man who ever breathed—with bronze, set faces, and keen eyes that look all the world straight in the face without flinching as they flash out from under their broad-brimmed hats. Peril and hardship and years of long toil, broken by weeks of dissipation, draw haggard lines across their eager faces, but never dim their reckless eyes, nor break their bearing of defiant self-confidence. They do not walk well, partly because their chaperajos or leather overalls hamper them when on the ground. But their appearance is striking for all that, and picturesque, too, with their jingling spurs, the big revolvers stuck in their belts, and big silk handkerchiefs knotted loosely around their necks over the open collars of their flannel shirts.

When drunk on the villainous whiskey of the frontier towns, they cut mad antics, riding their horses into saloons, firing their pistols right and left, from light heartedness, rather than from any viciousness, and indulging too often in deadly shooting affrays brought on either by the accidental contact of the moment or on account of some long standing grudge, or perhaps because of bad blood between two ranches or localities; but except while on such sprees, they are quiet, rather self-contained men, perfectly frank and simple, and on their own ground treat a stranger with the most whole-hearted hospitality, doing all in their power for him and scorning to take any reward in return.

A. C. Huidekoper, Roosevelt's neighbor, had another impression of the men he hired:

> The cowboy is as finicky about his dress as a girl. One year he has one style, the next year, another. They are a mighty fine lot of men and except when full of rum are a very dependable lot. . . . I can remember but few who were not good fellows, efficient, brave, and clean. My first impression of their cleanliness was formed by an incident at the ⊢T⌐ ranch. The cook slept near a partition so that the conversation could be heard from the adjoining room. After the cook had retired, some cowboy said, "I don't like the cook—he never takes a bath. I believe he is lousey." Another said, "You don' say so! Well, if he is lousey, he can't stay here, and if he stays we will have to hang him." The manner of hanging was discussed in loud tones quite sufficient for the cook, listening on the other side of the partition, to hear. The next morning before daybreak, the cook was gone.

So there you are—five perspectives, the manager of a big cow outfit, the motherly ranchwife, the idealistic young lady, an amateur ranchman from the East, and another easterner who became an old-timer. Consider their opportunities to observe the cowboy in all phases and their ability to reach unprejudiced decisions concerning the gentleman, then draw your own conclusions. The tersest definition of a cowboy is "a man with guts and a horse."

Certainly the average cowpuncher was neither the bashful, awkward guy on foot who became a centaur when he forked a horse, nor was he the rootin', tootin', tough, and shootin' son-of-a-gun of song and legend. He fitted somewhere in between. Moreover, as other generations have come along, the sons and grandsons of early cattlemen are as adept at working stock as were their fathers or grandfathers, although they may have a college degree and an appreciation of the classics.

When millions were being invested in the West's open range, the cowboy's pay was in the neighborhood of $30 a month and found, and a top hand might draw down as much as $40 or $45. The pay of a trail boss ran a mite higher and a range foreman got the magnificent stipend of $125. A cowboy's tools were few and highly specialized and he was an expert in their use. An individual might have some special talent or preference for a particular phase of the business—roping, bronc stomping, cutting, calf wrestling, or branding—but he was expected to make a hand at any or all of them if called upon.

Equally, or possibly more, important to a cowhand than personal ownership of a horse was his rig. That and his bedroll, which he was required to
furnish, constituted, in his own parlance, his "forty years gatherin's." For
many years you could identify a cowboy's original range by the style of his
outfit, such as the design of his "hull" or saddle—its horn, cantle, stirrups,
skirts, cinch, latigo; his spurs, taps, and chaps; his rope, hat, boots. On
the Montana range, Spanish idiom mingled with Missouri, Oregon, and Yankee vernacular; thus, a local lingo peculiar to the trade developed.

The Texas men, accustomed to running down dodging longhorns in
brush country, used a short rope and then bet all their chips on the turn, by
tying their lariat (from *la riata*) to the squat, broad horn of their double-
cinch saddle. The northerners and Californians used a long rope and when
they dropped a loop over a critter, they took "dally welts" around the small,
high horn of their single cinch, or "center fire," saddle. With this safety
measure accomplished, they could cast loose in an emergency without losing
rope and saddle, although they might lose a thumb or finger if the wraps
around the horn tightened on a stray digit.

Granville Stuart described the dress and rig of what you are led to believe was a typical cowboy; Teddy Roosevelt had himself photographed in
regalia that purports to be the habiliments of a frontier rancher—fringed
buckskin shirt, hair chaps, and all. A survey of Barthelmess and Huffman
photographs of actual working cowboys belies the foregoing samples, as do
Charlie Russell's faithful sketches and paintings. Charlie's characters wear
broad-rimmed hats with buckstraps to keep them on during violent action or
high winds. They aren't ten-gallon jobs, either—just a few quarts. The ker-
chiefs about their necks were not ornamental; they were pulled up over
nostrils and mouth when dust swirled thick. Their unbuttoned vests provided pockets for matches and "the makin's." Their pants were sometimes
foxed on the seat and down the inside of the legs to take the wear of saddle
leather. Their boots reached almost to their knees and were high-heeled—
not low-cut, gaudy, inset contraptions that hobble she-dudes and atmosphere
buckeroos of today—the kind that are worn with one pant leg carefully tucked
in, the other half in and half out, with studied carelessness. Charlie Russell's
colorful pictures have many of his characters smoothshaven or wearing a
three-day beard. The storytelling drama of his paintings does clothe the cowboys with a bit of glamour. The Barthelmess and Huffman photographs of
actual, nondescript characters with walrus mustaches take it off.

Cowboy gear has been described time and again and some of it that you
see today is a sad travesty on the original. Suffice it to say that there was a
utilitarian reason for almost every detail of rig and apparel, with a certain
amount of deference shown for the aesthetic. A shadow rider going to town
paid considerable attention to the rake and style of his Stetson as silhouetted
by the sun, the cut of angora or batwing chaps, the jingle of bit and spur

chains, his horse jewelry, the conchos and the stamping on saddle skirts and leather cuffs. A run-of-the-herd cowpoke didn't pack a six-gun to perforate crooked dealers, to destroy back-bar crystal, or to protect schoolmarms. When he wore one, it was no sartorial addition of the George Patton pearl-handled type, but a serviceable, single-action Colt .44 or .45 that made a loud noise and threw a vicious slug. It came in handy to fog a stray wolf or coyote, to put a sick or crippled animal out of misery, and to harrow the jumpy nerves of townspeople.

The getting-to-town interludes were few and far between. After a cowboy got there, his first stop was the livery stable or corral to leave his horse, then to the barbershop for bath, shave, and haircut. The settlement didn't offer much originality in the way of sin—the activities were simply designed to transfer the visitor's bankroll as rapidly as possible from his pocket to a dealer's kitty, a barkeep's till, or a lady's stocking. Inasmuch as he didn't have much money on arrival, it usually didn't take long to clean him. By the same token, it didn't give him time to raise too much hell. Perhaps he was entitled to the derisive, defiant salute with which he sometimes blazed his way out of the spider's web as he started back to the lonesome places.

When making a hand for an outfit, there were long, monotonous hours spent in the saddle, riding line, riding circle, riding herd, and just riding. There was hot, dirty work on the roundup. The shift was sunup to sundown and then some—seven days a week. The grub was a consistently uninspired menu, compounded of such staples as black coffee, sow bosom, frijoles, doughgods, fresh-killed beef, dried fruit, ashes, corral dust, with "son-of-a-bitch-in-a-sack" as a special treat. Tarpaulin-enveloped soogans unfurled to make a none-too-comfortable bed on the ground. This talk about a saddle being a pillow is a figment of some fiction writer's imagination.

Unquestionably, there were adventure, danger, tragedy, and comedy in life on the open range, but, truth to tell, while the old-time cowboy's modus operandi may have been wild and untrammeled at times, there never was much romance attached to his sweat-provoking trade. There has been less since an irrigation shovel and a posthole digger have become essential parts of his successors' accoutrements. From Madison Square Garden to Medicine Lodge, people will always thrill to TV cowboys, but a ranchhand riding a tractor behind a bullrake at haying time just isn't glamorous.

Colonel Nelson A. Miles, attached to the Fifth U.S. Infantry, and afterwards Commanding General of the United States Army, came up the Missouri and Yellowstone Rivers from Sioux City, Iowa, with his command in 1876. That fall, he built a cantonment at the mouth of the Tongue River. It was to winter troops then in the field pursuing Indians. The winter was long and cold and the cantonment was a temporary shelter designed as a combination of stockade and earth embankment. During the winter, the construction of two new Army posts was authorized in Montana Territory, one to be Fort Custer on the Bighorn River and the other Fort Keogh, which was located about two miles west of the mouth of the Tongue. The Fort Keogh plan included officers' quarters, barracks, storehouses, a hospital, and a stable. It was expected to accommodate five companies of infantry and six troops of cavalry. It was ready for occupancy in the fall of 1877.

The original military reservation was ten miles square and extended on both sides of the Tongue River. In the winter of 1877–78, Congress put the portion east of the river back into public domain. A little settlement called Milestown had been built on the Yellowstone, just east of the original reservation line. On February 16, 1877, the legislative assembly of Montana Territory passed an act stating that "a small town near the Tongue River about two miles below Ft. Keogh is hereby named, and shall hereafter be known as Miles, and same is hereby declared the county seat of Custer County."

Pioneers had a custom of appending "City" to the names they gave settlements, no matter how small or inconsequential they may have been. Perhaps it was frontier humor or maybe it was sincere optimism. When land closer to the fort became available, Miles City came into existence and for a brief period there were two towns until the die-hards of "Old Town," or Milestown, gave up and moved to the new metropolis, Miles City. The military was the sole source of civilian support at the time.

In 1877 the families of officers and soldiers, as well as the Fifth Infantry band, came in by steamboat. Social activities looked up and took on tone, at least around the post, whose population exceeded that of the "city." Supplies were freighted in from Bozeman, Fort Buford, and Bismarck by the Diamond R line, even hay being hauled from the last two points. The work stock of the freight outfit were turned out to rustle for themselves in winter and were the first cattle on the range in eastern Montana.

By 1880, Miles City, though an infant in years, had acquired mature habits. Granville Stuart stopped there overnight while looking for cattle range. In his book, *Forty Years on the Frontier,* he comments on the town's lack of suitable sleeping accommodations for itinerants. "The people that frequented Miles City in those days," he writes, "usually came to town to stay up all night and see the sights. They did not feel the necessity for a bed or much to eat. They were just thirsty."

Another visitor in 1886 observed that the town was "wide open" and that many inhabitants were preoccupied professionally or experimentally with faro, monte, roulette, and poker. Well, why not? The town's strategic location gave it many advantages. It became a trading and banking center for stockmen. It was on the Long Trail from Texas; it was on a river—two, in fact—and later on a major railroad line. Just across the Yellowstone, the grass country spread north to the Missouri. South were the vast ranges draining to the famous Tongue and Powder Rivers. It was an outfitting and supply base for early Black Hill mining operations. It promised future stability and growth not always inherent in pioneer sites. Today's modern Miles City still maintains its enviable reputation as a cow town of note from the Nueces to the Athabaska.

The West has always been tolerant of human frailties and has made allowance for unavoidable circumstances when they have interfered with good intentions. It has been related that one of Montana's well-known cow towns began with a nondescript population that didn't permit its hankering for domesticity to be hampered by the absence of parties qualified to administer ecclesiastical or civil marriage rites. When a preacher finally came to town, some two dozen belated wedding ceremonies were voluntarily performed, with appropriate festivities and no embarrassment to anyone involved.

Other queen cities of cowland reigned more or less briefly—Glendive, Wibaux, Lewistown, Ubet, Two Dot, Utica, Wolf Point, Glasgow, Malta, Havre, Dillon, and Forsyth, for example—with lesser cities in their train from Medora, North Dakota, to Cutbank, Montana. All had their day in the sun—when the cowboys came to town.

Medora, in Pyramid Park of the Little Missouri badlands and on the Northern Pacific just east of the Dakota line, was founded by the titled and handsome young Frenchman, Antoine Amedée Marie Vincent Manca de Vallombrosa, the Marquis de Mores. He found the West and wealthy Medora Von Hoffman, of New York, very fascinating. He married Medora and brought her to the fringe of the Dakota badlands, where he built a frame chateau overlooking the turgid stream—a chateau with twenty-six rooms and one closet, and it wasn't a water closet.

The Marquis de Mores became an enthusiastic investor in the West. He owned cattle and a stagecoach line out of Deadwood, the coaches having reflectors fore and aft, corresponding to an automobile's rearview mirrors. With vision ahead of his day, he built a packing plant at Medora in which to process meat right from the range. It didn't work out quite the way he planned.

The Chateau de Mores is still there, also the Marquis' statue, erected by his sons. When Queen Marie of Rumania was en route to the west coast on her much publicized visit to America in the fall of 1927, slumbering Medora awakened to make the headlines once more. The Queen's special train stopped there by prearrangement. A delegation of booted and spurred riders rent the air with cowboy yells and gunshots as their horses clattered across the little station's wooden platform. With many courtly flourishes, the Queen was welcomed by this reception committee and escorted to a sway-backed palfrey equipped with a sidesaddle. Her son and daughter were put astride docile mounts, and a procession of cowboys and cowbelles, headed by bearers of the American and Rumanian flags, wended its way to the stock-

*I'm Scareder of Him Than of Injuns, by Charles M. Russell*

Now the day of the cattlemen reached high noon. Throughout the 147,000 square miles of Montana Territory, man, horse, and cattle moved to the center of the stage.

*A Fighting Chance, by R. Farrington Elwell*

Courtesy of Dale Wilder

Wherever man rode or looked—from the Canadian line to Wyoming, from the sharp peaks of the Rockies to the alkaline coulees of the Dakota Bad Lands—were cattle, cabins, and cowboys. *Above:* a Montana beef herd on the way to market, 1900. *Below:* a quiet gathering of neighboring ranchers at the Paul Bretesche Trail Creek Ranch near Stinking Water, Hot Springs, in what is now Carbon County.

Sometimes many men and animals from many ranches gathered at places like old Utica for a roundup. Shown below is the Judith Basin roundup crew of 1885. (Charles M. Russell can be identified as the fourth man from the right.) At these gatherings such dignitaries as Louis Kaufman, Jesse Phelps, and Roundup Captain L. B. Taylor could be found eating beans and beef with cowboys Charlie Russell, Pres Larcum, Jack Whitcomb, Hank and Gene Gray, Joe King, Jack Murphy, Dan Martin, Alex Tuttle, Tom Waddell, Johnny Sellers, and Terry McDonald— the group in the bottom picture. (Russell is seated third from left, front row.)

L. A. Huffman photograph

*Line camp of a cow outfit on Crow Indian land*

A man's home has always been his castle. Most of those in the "Cattle Kingdom"—even the abodes of the knights and lords, were small, crude, and rough-hewn. They were often windowless, their log sides chinked with mud, sod-roofed. Yet they served the times well and if anyone suffered it was women and children; men were inured by day-to-day toil in sun, rain, wind, and snow. The wealthiest ranches had only more buildings and corrals. What little glitter, culture, and comfort there were existed in the cow towns and cities, miles away.

*An early southeastern Montana ranch*

*Coburn cowboys north of the Milk River, in the 1890's*

*Dining room, old Grand Central Hotel, Fort Benton*

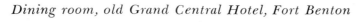

Just as the honest men of the gold camps finally turned to vigilante justice, so did the early stockmen. *Above:* pen-and-ink drawing by Montana artist Irving ("Shorty") Shope. *Below:* facsimile of a pledge signed by early Sun River cattlemen in forming the Sun River Protective Organization to eliminate horse thieves.

We the undersigned residents of Sun River valley pledge ourselves as men to strictly adhere to the following by laws and regulations governing the Sun River Protective Organization and in the event of failing to comply with their demands will pay all fines imposed on us

The object of this organization is to protect our property against horse thieves and all other law breakers that are now and will hereafter infest our section of county

This organization shall be under the command of one Captain who may appoint as many subordinates as emergencies may require, who shall hold office for six months, unless sooner removed by a two third vote of the Company, and the Captain shall preside at all meetings and have power to assemble members at any time and place at his discretion,

There shall be a Secretary elected who shall also act as Treasurer whose duty it shall be to keep a strict account of all moneys collected and expended by him

The services of all members for looking after stolen horses shall be adjusted by a two third vote of the members, and all funds collected for the purpose of horse thieves and other law breakers and for looking after stolen stock shall be assessed pro rata, in proportion to the number of horses owned by the members,

If any member of this organization gets into any trouble in the pursuit of horse thieves or other law breakers We as members pledge our all our property and our lives if need be, to his or their assistance,

Parties wishing to become members of this organization their names shall be handed in by a member at one of our meetings and shall receive a unanimous vote of the members before being admitted to the organization,

We do hereby pledge ourselves as members—our honor as men and do solemnly swear or affirm to keep inviolate all secrets and all business of this organization

We do hereby pledge ourselves to cooperate with all other organizations that are now or will hereafter organize for the same object.

Signed

Gabe Sargent
James H Adams
H M Strang
Jos F Sargent
John Winder
Rob Vaughn
W. Farrelly
Wm Mulroy
Presly H Rowe
Stephen Woodhurst
Robert S Ford
Wm Ulm
W J Hill
J P Ford
W A Sinston
W H Beall
F B Sargent
George Steell

*The Herd Quitter, by Charles M. Russell*

*Branding cattle on the Shonkin Range out of Fort Benton*

*White Sulphur Springs as a thriving cow town before the turn of the century*

*Settlers Braving the Blizzard*
*by E. S. Paxson*

Civilization was on the march. Land-hungry settlers, unmindful of the weather and the harsh realities of wresting a living from the soil, moved in. And the first cattlemen who moved into central, eastern, and northern Montana were the last to see the wild native cattle; the buffalo, like the wild Indians, disappeared almost overnight in the early 1880's. These two paintings, by Paxson and Russell, illustrate both happenings more graphically than many words.

*No Ketchum, by Charles M. Russell*

CHOTEAU HOUSE

No man can estimate the countless train loads of Montana cattle hauled to the eastern markets; but the rails became a double-edged sword, for they were soon bringing back homesteaders to parcel-up and fence the open range. *Top:* an early Northern Pacific cattle train hauling Con Kohrs' beef to market. Meanwhile, life in such towns as newly-born Choteau settled into an orderly, complacent pattern except when the cowboys—"rough, ready, their pockets full of jingle"—roared into town for a hard-earned spree. *Bottom:* the old Choteau House.

Although the cowboys and cowmen considered their work routine, they lived an epic, adventuresome life which soon blossomed into an enduring American saga. *Above:* cowboys on the range between Havre and Shelby. *Below:* "Branding Time—Waiting for the Next Calf—Big Dry, 1904," an L. A. Huffman photograph.

On all of these thousand hills there was heard the ever-pounding hoofs of tens of
thousands of foraging critters—their most unique feature, the brands they wore.
*Top:* Circle Diamond herd coming to water on the Milk River (date unknown).
*Bottom:* James Fergus beef herd trailing to the railhead near Clagett, about 1896.

Bankers, bartenders, bullet-molders, boot makers, saddlers, and sloe-eyed senoritas were all part and parcel of the open-range way of life. As Teddy Blue said later, most literature and lore of the range "told all about stampedes and swimming rivers and what a terrible time we had, but they never put in any of the fun—and fun was at least half of it!" *Above:* "Get Your Ropes," an 1899 water color by Charles M. Russell. *Below:* typical Montana advertisements of the day. The saloons and senoritas didn't need to advertise.

A new range filled rapidly. When Granville Stuart set up the DHS outfit in 1880, he was "a hundred miles from nowhere." By the next summer James Fergus was on Armell's Creek; Kohrs & Bielenberg had 3,000 head on Flatwillow; the Powers Brothers, Charley Belden, Bob Coburn, John Dovenspeck, and Henry Sieben all had sizeable herds in the vicinity. Wherever there were herds, there had to be horses. As "Rawhide" Rawlins said, "The range hoss was God-made—the best; they cost the man that branded an' claimed 'em nothing. They lived on the grass an' water the Almighty gave 'em . . . an' was needed everywhere."

*Right: Theodore ("Teddy") Roosevelt.*

*Pierre Wibaux, Mrs. George Liscomb, and Jack Serruys, fore*

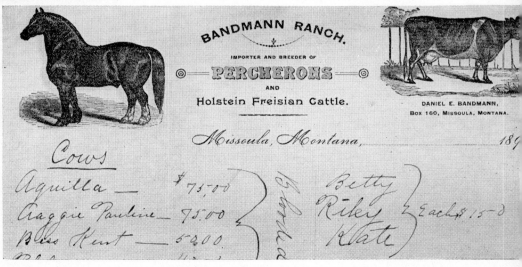

As the open range reached its historic apex a galaxy of glittering personalities appeared on the scene—Eastern socialites, foreign noblemen, theatrical personalities, soldiers of fortune—all eager to make quick fortunes in the "beef bonanza." Among many who came, few toughed it out long enough to make a mark. Among those who did were the sophisticated Marquis de Mores and Pierre Wibaux, of France; Theodore ("Teddy") Roosevelt; the Huidekopers and Biddles, of Philadelphia; Captain Howes, Major Campbell, and Oliver H. Wallop, British peers; and the colorful Daniel E. Bandmann, noted Shakespearean actor, whose letterhead appears above.

The old order continued to change. Although it was still essential for cowboys to live in the open on the range during the roundups (see *above*), some cattlemen sunk their roots deeper by building large ranch houses and elaborate homes in the cities. Pictured below is the Yellowstone River cowman's manse of Paul McCormick in the new city of Billings, with a view of its interior shown on the right.

But many were to carry the old way of life well into the twentieth century. Except for the advent of barbed wire and fencing, and the end of the giant-scale, open-range operations, most ranch life changed only superficially between 1870 and 1910. Huffman's old-time camera recorded a "Snug Little Home Among the Cottonwoods" (*above*) and "A Calf Branding" (*below*).

Photographs by L. A. Huffman, courtesy Ruth Huffman Scott

yards. A few Rumanian sheepherders had been flushed out of the hinterland to give the show added interest. At the stockyards, the local talent put on a rodeo for royalty. After Queen Marie waved a gracious farewell from the rear of her observation car, Medora went back to sleep.

Lewistown started as a trading post—Reed's Fort. It grew to be a cow town and supply point for the Judith Basin and Flatwillow country. Its early days are recalled most often in the tale of the bloody street affray on a Fourth of July, in which Rattlesnake Jake, who was really Charley Owen, and his pal Charley Fallon, erroneously called Ed Owen, were the losing principals. Glasgow, Malta, Chinook, and Havre, along the High Line of the Milk River Valley, were shipping points that offered hospitality and entertainment to visiting cowboys. The latter was a particularly seething cauldron because its clientele was made up of such violent and conflicting elements as soldiers from Fort Assinniboine, coal miners, railroad workers, and range riders. Shorty Young's temple of divertissement catered to them all and there was never a dull moment.

Former cow towns, whose streets echo to the jingle of rowels only at rodeo time, are now modern and highly respectable. They have been gentled under the refining influence of plow and farmers' co-ops. No more do they reverberate to the roll of personal artillery. Old-timers miss the masculine brass rails and the solo game in the rear. Almost every one of these towns has a Stockmen's Bar or its equivalent, but they are not the same as Shorty's Saloon, described by Johnny Ritch in his inimitable book of verse, *Horse Feathers*. The honkytonks, the harness shops, livery stables, corrals, and "Chink restaurants" have relinquished their locations to movie palaces, dime stores, filling stations, parking lots, and drive-ins. Implement dealers purvey tractors and manure spreaders as symbols of the times, and stark grain elevators stand guard by the tracks while the transcontinental streamliners whizz by.

# 12. FREE GRASS GROWS DEAR

*It is scarcely a figure of speech to say that the tide of white settlement during the last few years has risen over the West like a flood; and the cattlemen are but the spray from the crest of the wave; thrown far in advance but soon to be overtaken.*

—*Theodore Roosevelt*
Hunting Trips of a Ranchman, 1885

The odds on a roulette wheel can be figured precisely; a man had to outguess the vagaries of the elements and many other variables if he was to win in the range cow business. There were such hazards as drouth, blizzards, settlers, plows, fences, railroad expansion, avarice. It just couldn't last forever. Discouraged by the chain of adversity that had blasted high hopes, many livestock owners charged their losses off to experience after the hard winter of

1886–87. They quit. Some didn't care to start from scratch again; others might have had the inclination to continue but lacked capital or credit. Absentee shareholders of large promotional concerns were disillusioned. What they had been sold as a gilt-edged investment had turned out to be a losing speculation. The gold mine had been salted.

This is not to assert that all the big ranch spreads were badly managed. There were notable exceptions. Montana's short-grass land was a finishing pasture for big Texas companies that belonged to men who were raised raising cattle. They continued to bring yearlings and two-year-olds from the south to double-winter on northern range. The N–N (Neidinghaus Brothers Co.) lost 20,000 head in 1886–87, but that didn't deter them from driving up herd after herd during the following years. They were said to have paid taxes in 1891 on 100,000 head ranging in Custer, Valley, and Dawson Counties. In '93 they worked eleven wagons on roundup and shipped 23,000 head to market in Chicago.

As for Montana stock owners of the plains country, when there was a scramble on the part of many to sell the remnant of their herds, old-timers, who had seen hard winters before, took a quick inventory of their chips as represented by remaining cattle and bank credit. They then decided to stand pat and bet their stack while those with less fortitude were tossing their hands into discard. The stayers figured that the shortage of beef steers that was bound to ensue would bring an upturn in the market, and that it was the time to buy young stock that would fill the vacuum in a year or two.

A. J. Davis, Butte banker and former DHS partner, offered to lend Conrad Kohrs $100,000 without security to buy cattle. In the spring of 1888, Kohrs took him up and bought 9,000 head in Idaho for Montana ranges. Before the turn of the century, CK herds were roaming the Circle country of eastern Montana with the W Bar Stock of Pierre Wibaux. The shrewd ones who could, stayed with it and hedged their bets to some extent by making at least a little provision for the care of their stock during severe storms. It had been a hard lesson but it had its compensations. Methods would change—were changing. The big companies bought large blocks of railroad land. Small owners close-herded their stuff. They planted hay—redtop, timothy, alfalfa—and irrigated it. In 1880 there were 56,800 acres of Montana land in hay; by 1900 there were 712,000. And by the same token, there were 6,000 brands recorded in 1889 and 16,000 in 1900.

Pierre Wibaux's career in the cattle business is a classic example of how adversity may sometimes be licked by tenacious sagacity, assisted by Lady Luck. Twenty-four-year-old Monsieur Pierre, scion of a well-to-do French family, came to America in 1882 to find out why friends of his English fiancée were so enthusiastic about this country's range-stock industry. Wibaux's father was annoyed by this inquisitive quirk in his son, having expected him to participate in the management of the family textile mills and dyeworks. He cut Pierre off with $10,000 as his sole inheritance.

When young Wibaux arrived in America, he conserved his resources and spent some time at the Chicago stockyards, where he could absorb the livestock atmosphere and acquaint himself with cow critters from the range. There he met a fellow countryman, the elegant Marquis de Mores, who was established on the Little Missouri as a neighbor to an equally naïve but enthusiastic neo-westerner, Teddy Roosevelt.

Pierre went west with the Marquis and located in Beaver Valley in the extreme eastern part of Montana. There he met Gus Grisy, of French extraction, went into partnership with him, and in no time at all they had the G Anchor W iron stamped on several thousand cattle. Wibaux was a hard worker. Grisy was a drone. The partnership was of short duration, with Pierre soon running the W Bar outfit on his own. He had wisely chosen a range that was exceptional for grass, water, and shelter. He was willing to work with and learn from his experienced cowhands, so his outfit was better managed than the average in that area. It prospered accordingly.

The winter of 1886–87 struck with just as much severity there as in the rest of the range country, and Wibaux's losses must have been great. At this time, however, he was in France soliciting capital to expand his business. He got back to the range with a sizable stake, perhaps close to half a million dollars. Not having been there to witness the disaster, he could take a detached view of it, and so profit by it. He bought cattle at bottom prices from individuals and outfits forced, or willing, to sacrifice their remaining stock and go out of business.

The range was no longer overstocked and the cattle Wibaux bought were the hardy survivors of the herds that had occupied it. He was a keen trader and student of market fluctuations. By 1890, he had 40,000 head. That year he branded 10,000 calves. In 1899, like some others, he began getting out of the cow and calf business. He invested liberally in Texas steers, which he matured for market in the big area surrounding the town of Circle. By shrewd investment, hard work, and close study, he increased his original capital more than sixtyfold before his death in 1913. His statue now stands in the town of Wibaux, overlooking "the land he loved so well."

Kohrs and Wibaux were exceptions. It is no wonder that Association meetings were poorly attended for several years after the catastrophe. At the 1887 fall meeting in Helena, only twenty-seven members were present. Very little was accomplished, and the meeting adjourned at the end of the first session. There was a constantly diminishing membership. In 1888, at least 25 per cent of the enrolled members were technically subject to expulsion for nonpayment of dues—many of them substantial citizens. Since the Board of Stock Commissioners had been assigned the responsibility for stock inspection and the employment of detectives, there didn't seem to be much necessity for an association of stockgrowers. Incidentally, the Board was functioning so successfully that it attracted the attention of the Wyoming Association and its members secured similar legislation.

Perennial arguments with the railroads continued as a matter of course. Two new types of stock cars were presented by their competing inventors, each claiming superiority for his product. Before committing themselves to an endorsement of either type, the cowmen cagily decided on further investigation, at the same time letting it be known that in their estimation the railroads, who claimed to be partners in their business, gave them plenty of lip service but were not too liberal in extending economic assistance unless compelled to do so. President Joseph Scott expressed their attitude when he stated, "Another question presents itself to me and that is transportation. We have always had a committee appointed to fight the railroad company."

The vast expanse of grassland that extended north from the Missouri River to the Canadian line, and west from the Dakota boundary to the foothills of the Rockies, had intrigued users of the open range to the south of it. The enormous strip, cut lengthwise by the Milk River, was hunting grounds reserved for Blackfeet, Gros Ventre, and Assinniboine Indians. In 1886 cattlemen sent T. C. Power to Washington, D.C., to try to get the reserve thrown open. Congressman Joseph K. Toole also worked on the project in 1887. Their efforts were successful. In 1888, the tribes were allotted three reservations, the Blackfeet, the Fort Belknap, and the Fort Peck, of rather limited proportions inasmuch as they were deprived of about seventeen million acres by the official action. This land, on which the buffalo had ranged such a short time ago, was thrown into unreserved public domain and cow outfits promptly moved in, although the losses of the hard winter had so drastically thinned the Territory's cattle census.

The Helena meeting in the fall of 1888 was a carry-over and rehash of subjects from the spring meeting. A resolution of thanks to the Northwest Mounted Police of Canada, and to the Canadian authorities in general, was adopted, expressing appreciation for courtesies that "we have never been able to properly reciprocate . . . simply because our regular army is more ornamental than useful." The railroads were accused of starting prairie fires. The stockmen wanted improved stacks on engines or else spark-suppressing bonnets attached to present stacks. They didn't seem hopeful of getting a favorable response. One of them said, "It is a hard thing to get justice out of the railroads in this matter. We encounter opposition that is very formidable."

The Miles City correspondent of the *Montana Livestock Journal*, writing under the pseudonym Uriel, filed a dispatch to that publication, under the date March 19, 1889, that graphically portrays the condition of the cattle industry in Custer County at that time. It was also applicable to most of the

range country of Montana Territory, which was about to attain the dignity
of statehood. He wrote:

> This metropolis of eastern Montana received the news of assured statehood
> with much equanimity. Most of us have lived under state government before
> and know that to the average citizen there is but little difference whether he
> is a territorial vassal or a citizen in whom is vested all the proud attributes
> of statehood. In fact, if the misguided Bourbons had not made the keeping
> out of the territories a party measure, I don't believe there would have been
> any popular clamor for the admission of Montana for some time to come.
> Certainly not from eastern Montana as the monied interests here, as repre-
> sented by the cattlemen, do not desire any of the increased expenses that come
> with statehood or the prominence that the territory at large will naturally
> be brought into by the translation from the territorial chrysalis to the regal
> butterfly existence of statehood.
>
> Our cattlemen . . . are a singularly retiring and modest class of people
> who have been foisted into an undesirable notoriety by the sensational press
> of the East which has painted them with an artist's brush, though in lurid
> colors, in the guise of feudal barons who, having appropriated the western
> range by most questionable methods, proceeded to parcel the grazing grounds
> out among themselves to the exclusion of all other people and the extinction
> of all other rights but theirs.
>
> It is true that, comparatively speaking, a few men and a few cattle occupy
> the vast ranges of Custer County over which, though we are reputed to be
> the banner cow county of the Territory, one may travel for hundreds of
> miles and never see as many cattle as would supply one tenth of the demand
> of the Chicago market on a brisk day. The idea of there being any traits
> in common with our mild-mannered cowmen and the blood-thirsty and acquisi-
> tive barons of the medieval ages is simply preposterous. Take the courtly
> and reticent Joe Scott whose comings and goings are shrouded in inscrutable
> mystery; jolly John Holt, with broad face and capacious smile; plain, home-
> spun Colonel Bryan; or that prince of goodfellows, "Skew" Johnson; or
> H. R. Phillips, known by the sobriquet of "Little Phil" because he weighs 280
> pounds; or a score more that I could mention, and the simile fails entirely.
>
> The cattlemen occupy the ranges now because there is no one who cares
> to dispute the occupancy with them, but not because it could not be done
> successfully. The history of all range countries will undoubtedly be repeated
> here. The cattlemen, who are the true pioneers, come first in the majority
> of cases, disputing their holdings with the Indians and suffering much more
> by their predatory and hostile instincts than the outside world has any
> knowledge of. Following him comes the speculative squatter who plants him-
> self near some spring or water course merely for the purpose of being bought
> out, and "ranches" in a hand-to-mouth way until the desired end is attained.

Then comes the bona fide settler whose intent is to make a home and, although he may, in isolated instances, interfere with rights and privileges that his range neighbor had previously enjoyed without let or hindrance, he meets with no persecution. On the contrary, if he sets earnestly or intelligently to work to improve his condition, he finds in his neighbor, the range cattleman, a purchaser for much or all of his surplus crop of hay and grain besides getting many an odd day's work around the ranch or on the round-ups. Thus their relations become mutually agreeable and their interest rarely conflicting.

As the settlers continue to come in, the bottom lands are taken up, but as these are only, at rare intervals of drouth, of any value to the range owner, and as his most desirable grazing grounds, the benchland and breaks of the badlands, are of no value whatever to the settler, the "baron" yields territory without protest. In the nature of things, with the advent of railroads and the settlement of the country, he must inevitably be forced out here as he has been elsewhere, and as he will be everywhere, until range growing ceases to be practicable.

That this is not theory merely, I can prove by citing the operations of several large owners in Custer County who have, for two or three years past, been preparing themselves for this change by the purchase of land, the erection of substantial and commodious buildings, the taking out of water for irrigation purposes, and the shrinkage of their range herds down to a thousand or two thousand well-bred cows, to be close herded, served with the bull at the proper time, and fed and protected during the few weeks of severe winter when they cannot care for themselves. The idea is to merge the business into gigantic stock farms, taking all advantage of the wonderful adaptability of this country to stockgrowing by using the range at least ten months in the year and, at most, feeding but two, while competitors in the eastern states are subjected to feeding expenses, either of pasturing or yard feeding, all the year round.

The men who are adopting this idea are what is known as "she stock-men," who believe in the advantage of this northern country for breeding purposes. Another class, the "steer men," look upon our ranges as desirable only for the maturing of market beef, their routine being the continuous shipping in of Texas "ones," "twos," and "threes" in the spring for maturing on our rich feed and shipping to market in the fall of all double-wintered stock, and sometimes even single-wintered, if the outlook for winter feed is not favorable.

At present the "steer men" number the greatest constituency as the hard winter of 1886–87 virtually wiped out the she-stock and bulls of the country, while a fair percentage of steers pulled through. She stockmen maintain, however, that if calves come at the right time, and this they propose to regulate, and there are means at hand for feeding and sheltering for the comparatively brief period that such care is necessary, the losses can be held down to a lower percentage than obtains in farm herds in the East. As a matter of fact, three weeks of continuous storm caused the enormous losses of three years ago, though feeding would have been necessary for a longer period as there was but scant feed on the ground that year.

Of course the outfit that runs over 2,000 head can't make any preparation for winter feeding and care. The outlay would be enormous and the attempt would be impractical in the extreme. Such outfits necessarily represent the steer idea, and are not as valuable to a community as the "she stockmen" whose system I have detailed. These latter are the permanent settlers who, every year, add tangible, taxable wealth to the country, that cannot, like the property of the "steer men," be removed whenever personal interest suggests it. But while the breeding branch of the cattle business in this locality is temporarily a secondary one, I am satisfied that it will shortly and permanently take the lead.

While we have in our countless valleys broad stretches of bottom lands, than which there is no richer or more fertile land on the face of the earth, we claim nothing as an agricultural country for the reason that we know we have a much greater and more productive resource in stockgrowing and, with the enlargement of this industry, enough agriculture or "granger-ranching," as we call it, will follow to make us self-supporting, and that is all we care for. Let us furnish the beef to the nation and we care not who furnishes the flour. We want no bonanza farms or single crop farmers who, year in and year out, never have a dollar that someone else has not a prior claim upon. We do not encourage this class of emigration and the prospector who asks if this is a farming country is flatly told, "No!'

The man who will come here and start with a few cows, depending on the soil for an existence only, and giving his attention to his stock, will in a few years find himself on the road to wealth and subject to none of the vicissitudes and misfortunes that perennially beset the path of the granger. Such a settler adds annually to his wealth by almost geometrical progression and in a few years becomes a valuable citizen more permanently rooted to the soil than the mortgaged wheat farmer of Dakota, because he has a future that rests not on the successes or reverses of the "cattle barons" nor yet on the allegorical but highly unsatisfactory "tickling the earth with a hoe that she may smile with a harvest" but in the appropriating and utilizing to the fullest extent the superior resources of the country as applied to stockgrowing and relieving providence of that portion of the work that has heretofore been put upon its shoulders. We propose to build our fortunes on Montana beef, born and bred right here, and in a few years there will be no more going to Texas, Arizona, or New Mexico for beef stock, even among the "steer men," if there be any left at that time.

Uriel was right. There were two ways to play it, one to make a fast buck while there was still open range; the other to build for permanency, as had been done in the western valleys of the Territory. However, Uriel's time schedule was wrong. The change did not come as quickly as he anticipated. When his prophetic essay appeared, the steer men were monopolizing most of the range. Less capital was needed for "plant" and the turnover was faster than with "she stockmen."

A story printed in the May 11, 1889, issue of the *Weekly Yellowstone Journal and Livestock Reporter* of Miles City, taken from the *Cheyenne Leader,* indicated the trend. It read:

> The shipment of 200,000 head of Texas cattle over the Cheyenne & Northern will commence next Monday and will be completed about August 1. This great herd is the combined purchase of Montana men and the cattle will be unloaded at Wendover (Wyo.) and driven north. These cattle will occupy about 500 trains which will be run on passenger time from start to finish. Arrangements are being made for three trains daily over the Cheyenne & Northern from this point although an unlimited number can be handled if necessary. Three additional train crews will be employed and extra engines will be brought from points on the western portion of the system.

"Steer men" could look forward to many years of open-range operation.

The gayety customarily credited to the nineties did not extend to Montana for the first half of that uneasy decade. The killing winter had hastened the inevitable. The natural grassland could support just so many head of cattle even when there was a bumper crop (theoretically, one critter to about twenty-five acres), and the crowding of more and more stock onto the uncontrolled range would have brought dire consequences anyway, regardless of adverse weather. A hindsight analysis lays much of the blame on the speculative fever that had forced weak, unacclimated cattle onto overcrowded drouth-depleted range, with the hard winter as a potential, but really secondary, factor. The tragic loss of cattle was not a blessing to anyone by any means, but it did eliminate ill-founded promotion that had no chance of success even had weather conditions remained favorable—promotion that was a hindrance to legitimate, well-managed enterprises.

The majority of the survivors reluctantly reached the conclusion that the flush days were gone and that the safe way to play it now was to follow Uriel's sage advice: reduce the size of herds, own some base land supplemented by convenient open range, and put up hay. Notable exceptions to this doctrine were the opportunists like Kohrs and Wibaux, but the prodigal concepts of the old range-days were no longer good promotional material. This very fact prevented restocking to the point of overstocking by speculators, and canny "steer men" profited thereby for a number of years to come. Nevertheless, the trend was towards more and smaller outfits owned and personally operated by individuals. The granger-rancher was taking over where farming and stockgrowing could be combined. The day of the cowhand who despised a plow was drawing to a close. Students of the industry were strongly advocating home feeding and finishing, their theory being that it was sheer waste to ship cattle east to feed lots and for processing, and then to ship the finished product back to where it originated for local distribution and consumption. This was exactly what the Marquis de Mores thought when he built at Medora a packing plant that failed.

The change in operations was not confined to Montana. The winter of 1885–86 had also played havoc with stock on southern ranges. During the summer that preceded it, over 200,000 head of cattle had been forced off leased land in Indian Territory by Presidential proclamation. Those cattle that couldn't be marketed had to be moved to range that was already well stocked. The results were deplorable. The combination of overstocking and a severe winter played havoc. Setting a precedent for what was to happen in Montana, a lot of southern cowmen got out of the business. The glamour and their confidence were gone. In the fall of 1886, the Chicago livestock market touched a record low.

The spring meeting of the Montana Stockgrowers Association, held April 15, 1890, produced no new themes among the orators. Dr. C. J. Alloway extolled the superexcellence of the Twin City stockyards, only to have General Mark D. Flower, of South Saint Paul, give an even more glittering description of the comforts and courtesies that awaited train-weary cattle at his spread. Bristling spokesmen clashed for the glory of their respective railroads, but the fireworks of the session were furnished by S. S. Huntley. With consummate and preconceived cunning, he awaited a general exodus of members before lighting the fuse. With a bare, and packed, quorum present, Mr. Huntley moved that the Association by-laws be changed so that Helena would alternate with Miles City as host to the annual meeting, this plan to start the next year with a spring meeting in the capital city. Miles City members were particularly disconcerted because three prominent eastern Montana men were supporting this treasonous idea. It took a two-thirds vote to carry the motion. The balloting gave Helena fifteen and Miles City ten, thereby saving the latter from defeat. It seemed futile to continue holding fall meetings in Helena so Con Kohrs moved to abolish them. This passed without a dissenting vote.

The *Yellowstone Journal* of Miles City summed up Custer County sentiment under the heading, "HELENA DOWNED":

Argument that Helena is the more central location [of the cattle industry] lost force in view of the fact that five counties in Eastern Montana have 60%

of the cattle and one half of the horses in the entire state. Our position as the center of the stockgrowing industry, though fully assured today, will be strengthened year by year and even at the next meeting will be so indisputable that not even Helena will think of attacking it.

Only fifty members answered roll call in 1891. There were fully as many satellites present. The secretary reported that seventy names had been dropped for nonpayment of dues, nearly all of whom had quit the livestock business. Offsetting this to some extent were Dakotans who had either not joined or who were delinquent. At last they had begun to appreciate what they had been missing in the way of inspection benefits. They wanted to join, or to get back in. At the 1891 session, Russell B. Harrison, who had served as association secretary for seven years and whose western career had somewhat disturbed his eminent father, tendered his resignation and was succeeded by W. G. Preuitt.

The Crow Reservation had always had a great attraction for cattlemen. Its beautiful, well watered valleys and grassy hills were close to rail transportation. White men coveted this land and there was a never-ceasing demand that it be opened to them. Whites who had married Indian women to procure grazing rights on the reserve were stymied when Congress decided that squawmen had no tribal privileges. In 1882 an act was passed that permitted the Crows to sell limited grazing rights, but three years later the U.S. Attorney General held that the Indians could not give valid leases without special authorization of Congress. In 1891 another act provided for leasing both allotted and unallotted Indian lands. In the spring of that year leases went to the highest bidders and, moreover, the Crow Reservation was reduced in size by almost two million acres.

The leases were given for a three-year period, renewed in 1894 for one year, and in 1895 for five years. The system proved satisfactory to almost everyone concerned in spite of a few minor complications. Those who had no leases complained about it, and those who did get the opportunity to run their stock on Indian land took the attitude that it exempted them from paying the county tax levy for stock inspectors and detectives. Some of them made voluntary contributions, but bowed their necks and stopped when Custer County asserted its right to collect.

In 1892 convention attendance was pitiful. Only twenty-six members checked in. The old vexing problem of rustlers came up and the Association bravely pledged its "honor and support to stock raisers to suppress this character of crime." The entire economy of the nation was in an unstable condition, which gave the public a bad case of jitters. The inordinate, speculative mood of the eighties had run its course and the reaction that was setting in was national in its scope. Decline of the nation's gold reserve was not reassuring, even among those to whom the science of economics was a mystery. It all culminated in the Panic of 1893, when banks failed, railroads went into receivership, and something like 15,000 commercial failures were reported. Prices plummeted; people were broke. What chance had the average cow-man who was trying to recover from a recent licking? There was no credit, no market. It was the year of Coxey's Army. No wonder Association meetings were uninspiring, attendance small, and the programs routine for the first six years of this woeful closing decade of the century.

By 1894 there was a glimmer of encouragement. At least the promised Association assistance rendered to members in the matter of rustler-suppression had brought gratifying results. Many a cattle thief was now plaiting hair bridles in his leisure time at the state penitentiary in Deer Lodge. The annual convention attendance showed a slight increase though still leaving much to be desired. For the first time, a politician was on the program. Senator Tom Carter, the Republican candidate from Missoula who had beaten W. A. Clark, of Butte, in their rather unsavory senatorial contest, contributed half an hour of verbal pyrotechnics. In spite of membership losses, the Association was beginning to command more than passing attention from those in and out of office. Another innovation was having a speaker from the yearling State College at Bozeman; in this case, Professor Emory, who referred to the financial depression of 1893 as the blackest period in the history of Montana. With wisdom beyond the times, he advised the convention that no settler should pick a location where there was no chance for irrigation.

Predators, particularly wolves and coyotes, were in the limelight again. There were the lengthy arguments and never-ending differences of opinion as to bounties, their size, who should pay them, and how the money should be provided. Two professional wolvers, who were sitting on the sidelines, explained that best results could be obtained by using the profit incentive and placing the bounty high enough to induce men to really work at it. They claimed that hiring men by the month killed few predators. There was another side to that. High bounties did set trappers to working in earnest, but as soon as they had thinned the predator population sufficiently to reduce their income, they were prone to switch to other work until nature brought the predator census back up to par.

The state had been issuing certificates in lieu of cash payments when the balance in the bounty fund went dry. These were being accumulated by bankers at from two to four bits on the dollar, and if the state legislature did, by some miracle, vote to replenish the fund, the money provided would go to redeem the certificates and the financial situation would not be improved except in banking circles. The prevalent notion was to let the bankers hold the sack, for it was strongly suspected that most of the certificates had been issued for pelts brought across the Dakota and Canadian lines.

As a compromise, members of the Montana Stockgrowers Association were committed collectively and individually to employ a poisoner in each roundup district from June through November. His salary was to be pro-rated among the stockmen in each district. A committee of three in each district would select the man and oversee the details of operation. It was purely an experiment and didn't work too well.

# 13. NOT-SO-GAY NINETIES

Jim Hill's St. Paul, Minneapolis & Manitoba Railway came west up the Milk River Valley to reach Havre in 1887. It joined the Montana Central, connecting link between Havre, Great Falls, Helena, and Butte, and in 1889 they were combined with other holdings as the Great Northern Railroad, destined to reach the west coast in 1893. The Milk River country became known as the "High Line." Local roundup associations had formed in that part of the state when the herds were given access to the benchland that spread from the Missouri River to the Canadian border. It was a long, roundabout journey from that section to attend Montana Stockgrowers Association meetings at Miles City. In 1895 M. E. Milner, spark plug of the Shonkin Stock Association, became the moving spirit in the promotion of a merger to be known as the Northern Montana Roundup Association. Forty cattlemen signed at the initial meeting in Chinook. Tom O'Hanlon was elected president and Milner secretary, a position he held when the curtain was rung down on the range-cattle industry of that area.

The Shonkin Stock Association, one of the first and most aggressive "locals" in the open-range country, had been organized in 1881, primarily to "take care of Indians," as Bob Ford often said. Eventually it expanded its interests and activities and in 1887 drove and shipped cooperatively. The Highwood Mountains were the hub of its range. The grass country swept north from the Shonkin Sag, abandoned channel of the prehistoric Missouri, to the present big bend of the river below Fort Benton, and south along the Highwoods to Belt and Arrow Creeks—country that is still undisturbed by arterial highway and rail traffic.

The Northern Montana Roundup Association gained prominence in a hurry. The second annual meeting, held in Chinook in April, 1896, had all the earmarks of a Montana Stockgrowers Association conference. At least seventy-five members were present and almost twice that many visitors, including, of course, the ubiquitous rail, commission, stockyards, and packing plant contingents. The "Northerners" had even reached the stage of affluence and aggressiveness where they could retain a prosecuting attorney.

An executive committee was elected, consisting of top hands J. T. Harrison, John Survant, Colin Hunter, L. E. Kaufman, C. W. Price, Tom Clary, Sam Miller, Con Kohrs, John Lepley, Henry Sieben, Will Coburn, M. E. Milner, W. K. Flowerree, A. W. Kingsbury, and Tom O'Hanlon. As things turned out, there was little change in the personnel of that committee during the existence of the Association. They did the work and the membership at large approved their actions and policies. They battled the railroad as a matter of course, but their major activity was the suppression of rustling. They were once defined as "a large, well-equipped and excellently organized detective bureau." It boded ill for any rustler who attracted their attention.

Interest was gradually reviving in MSGA affairs, benefits, and objectives. President Joe Scott opened the eleventh annual convention, held April 16, 1895, with the hopeful assertion that the dawn of prosperity was breaking. To demonstrate that Association interests were not confined to petty, local matters, he touched on the discrimination of Germany and France against good American beef, both nations having barred importation of our meat products.

Secretary Preuitt, in a brief résumé of Association accomplishments over the ten years of its existence, cited the recovery of 80,000 estrays valued at nearly $3,000,000, the inspection of 2,000,000 cattle, and everything was amicable until Mr. Ben Remney, of Great Falls, took the floor on the second day. He offered a resolution to amend the by-laws and change the place of annual meeting. Friends of Miles City had suspected that some such skulduggery might be afoot, but didn't think the plotters would sink so low as to broach the subject at the noon hour when many Miles City members had gone to lunch. The matter was quickly referred to a committee of three—Con Kohrs, S. S. Huntley, and S. F. B. Biddle—who in a matter of minutes recommended adoption, with Mr. Biddle dissenting. Mr. Huntley supported the majority report of the committee by arguing that a change of pasture for the convention would create interest in western Montana, stimulate increased membership, and bring about an infusion of new blood. Miles City backers started delaying tactics and countered by asserting that if the change were made, new members might be enlisted in the west but any hoped-for gain would be offset by eastern members dropping out. In the meantime, their confreres were scurrying up and down the street and in and out of swinging doors in quest of reinforcements. When the vote was taken, they had mustered sixteen in favor of tabling the resolution, as against ten in its favor. Again the day was saved for Miles City.

There was a brief flareup in the 1896 meeting of the MSGA, when some of the members intimated that the selection of officers had been an arbitrary and undemocratic procedure. It was customary for the president to appoint a nominating committee. The slate submitted by this committee was automatically accepted by the members present, no further nominations being made from the floor. As a matter of fact, popular and efficient as President Joe Scott had been, the monotonous regularity of his re-election had created a feeling that was not helpful to increasing the membership. There had been some variation in the more or less honorary offices of first and second vice presidents. Captain William Harmon expressed the feelings of many others when he arose to say that many eligible "small" owners who should, would, and could be valuable members had not joined MSGA because they believed that a select few dominated, and that they would have no voice in the Association's procedure and policies. There was much truth in what the captain said and, although it didn't change things then and there, his opinion made an impression.

At the 1897 meeting, the railroad complaint of the year dealt with the two-dollar terminal charge on shipments to the Union Stockyards in Chicago. It was called exorbitant, unjust, discriminating, unfair, extortionate. Then, having expressed themselves in this mild manner, the members went further and formally protested the charge. Nor did the Association hesitate about advising Congress concerning its responsibilities. The stockgrowers wanted an amendment tacked onto the pending tariff bill that would protect the price of hides. The prevailing low price due to cheap imports was depriving Montana cattlemen of important revenue.

Professor Emory, of the State College, gave one of his short, practical talks on future possibilities, again emphasizing experimental home feeding and suggesting that a more stable price for cattle might be maintained if shipments could be spread out instead of flooding the markets for two or three months each year with the entire output of the range.

The nominating committee surprised everyone by presenting a list of nominees that failed to include the familiar names of former officers. S. F. B. Biddle, Philadelphia socialite and misogamist turned cowman, supplanted President Scott, one-time miner in Alder and Last Chance Gulches, John Harris and H. R. Phillips were elected first and second vice presidents, respectively. The thirteenth annual meeting also had the distinction of being the best attended in the history of the Association, yet it still left room for improvement in both attendance and enrollment.

Since 1883, attempts had been made to organize stockgrowers on a national basis. When the Montana legislative assembly of that year sent a memorial to Congress expressing concern and requesting federal control over areas in which contagious pleuropneumonia existed among cattle, they were reflecting the thinking of all cowmen. The disease was then prevalent in some eastern states. Moreover, the United States had no proper inspection of American cattle shipped to England, although pleuropneumonia was feared over there quite as much as on this side of the Atlantic. After protests from England threatened to put a quietus on our very lucrative export of cattle to that country, Congress became disturbed and created a so-called Treasury Cattle Commission to investigate the situation and make recommendations.

The commission called a meeting of stockmen in Chicago that fall of 1883, to give individuals a chance to express themselves. One hundred and seventy-five attended, the range country of the Northwest being well represented. The stockmen agreed that the states and territories had no setup for detecting, restricting, or treating the disease and that control by quarantine seemed to be a proper federal function and the only practical solution. A small committee was selected to present this view to Congress. As an end result, the Bureau of Animal Industry was finally created—a typical example of how the passage of an apparently simple and beneficial piece of legislation can be complicated by sectional prejudice, political finagling, and opposing interests. Incidentally, it also touched off a chain reaction that led from the inspection of cattle for disease, to inspection of meat, and at length to the inspection of foods and drugs.

With 175 cowmen in close conference for several days, it was only natural that such favorite and vital subjects as shipping, marketing, and the disposition of public domain should come in for much discussion. It was just a step from that to talk of the benefits that might accrue from national organization of the industry. This led to formation of the National Cattle Growers Association of America.

Texans refused to participate in, and fought the recommendations of the first Chicago meeting and the legislative proposals that came out of it. They were extremely sensitive about tick fever. Their cattle were themselves immune to the fever, but they carried the ticks to other ranges. The public had long since dubbed the disease "Texas fever," which implied that its source was with Texas cattle and not with Texas ticks. The first winter on northern ranges destroyed the ticks but, nevertheless, owners of northern cattle held longhorns suspect when there was any chance of an intermingling of herds.

When the Texans took up the cudgels against the inspection plans proposed at the Chicago meeting, lest such inspection affect their drives, the Chicago stockyards' dealers, and packers who didn't want to offend valuable customers, chipped in with them. They reckoned without the aggressive, young Wyoming Stockgrowers Association. Fourteen Wyoming cattlemen had been at the Chicago session, and Wyoming now got into the free-for-all by threatening to boycott the Chicago yards and ship elsewhere. The Chicago interests pulled in their horns.

When the delegates to the initial 1883 Chicago gathering decided to meet the following year to perfect their organization, the stockmen from the southwest, who had been very sparsely represented, decided not to be outdone. They called a national convention to be held in St. Louis three days after the scheduled 1884 Chicago meeting. This, of course, presented complications for the peaceful founding of a truly representative national association. However, something like 1,200 attended the St. Louis gathering. Montana was very much in the minority, with only 40 delegates.

It soon developed that the chief object of the meeting's sponsors was to pressure Congress into donating a strip of land from the Red River to Canada, which would constitute a "National Cattle Trail" six miles wide, to benefit no one but Texans and their close neighbors. Montana and Wyoming protested vigorously, but were snowed under by an avalanche of oratory. At that time, Montanans were not much alarmed over the possibility of tick fever being brought to northern ranges by cattle driven from the south, but they did object to further crowding of their ranges. Since their protests were brusquely overridden, they decamped the second day of the meeting. The National Livestock Association organized at this meeting was unharmonious and short-lived.

The Long Drive from Texas to Montana was finally superseded by rail shipment to Ogallala, Nebraska, from Texas points, with the cattle then being driven the balance of the way to northern ranges. This put a definite stop to the move for a National Cattle Trail. Such transportation gave no chance for change of climate to kill the ticks and resulted in the issuance of quarantine proclamations by the governors of Wyoming and Montana against all Texas cattle coming by rail, until they could be inspected. Rail shipments also threatened wide distribution of the tick fever due to contamination of the stock cars.

Another St. Louis meeting was held, but this one accomplished nothing. The National Association of Cattle and Horse Growers did join forces with the National Cattle Growers Association of America, the merger being called the Consolidated Cattle Growers Association. To quote John Clay, who became secretary:

> They held a meeting in 1886 in Chicago and at Kansas City in 1887. Both of these meetings were slimly attended, but with a strong Executive Committee much work was done. Several deputations went to Washington and the result was the creation of the Bureau of Animal Industry which continues as our main support in the control of disease. . . . We made an effort to keep the Association alive but the winter of 1886–87 had cooked the cattleman's goose. We were too poor, too dejected, to do more than look after our own business, and as far as I recollect, we never held another meeting. But we left one monument, the Bureau of Animal Industry, to our credit.

Lack of unity, which prevented important accomplishment by these early associations, accounted for the brevity of their existence and hindered further attempts to organize the beef cattle industry on a national scale. However, in November, 1897, the Denver Chamber of Commerce, cooperating with the Colorado Cattle Growers Association, sent out a call for a convention to revive the last, moribund national association or to supersede it with an association of similar scope, and to "discuss and devise measures for the protection of the livestock industry." It was also planned to influence Congress to grant relief and other benefits wherever and whenever needed in the livestock industry. The invitation was all-inclusive. It went to federal and state officials, all livestock associations, individual breeders and owners, commission men, packers, stockyard and railroad men. Over 1,000 came, from twenty-eight states, and the meeting convened in Denver, January 25, 1898. Membership was extended to anyone who had the slightest claim to a direct or indirect interest in livestock; the result was stormy weather. Expecting sheepmen, cattlemen, packers, exchange men, and railroaders to hit it off in complete peace and amity was asking too much.

Payment of dues was slow, member associations became disgruntled about this and that, there was dissension between factions, and the dynamic executive secretary, Charles F. Martin, died. Reorganization was attempted in 1904, confining membership to producers and feeders of livestock. Finally, in January, 1905, after two days of scuffling and recriminations, the cattlemen pulled stakes and founded the American Stockgrowers Association, headed by Murdo MacKenzie, manager of the Matador Land and Cattle Company. Later in the year, a truce was declared, differences were adjusted, and the two associations merged as the American National Livestock Association, membership limited to growers and finishers of livestock and their state and local associations.

The fourteenth annual meeting (1898) of the Montana Stockgrowers Association reported a slight drop in enrollment. Secretary Preuitt advanced a three-barreled theory about this recurring problem. He laid it to (1) excessive fees (the initiation fee was only $5 at the time and annual dues another $5, (2) lack of interest and effort by members in soliciting applications from their neighbors, (3) the Board of Stock Commissioners had the responsibility of inspection for which all stockgrowers were taxed, and from which all received benefits, so many were contented to remain outside the association.

The secretary deplored this shortsighted attitude, which did not take into account the advantages of cooperation in securing passage of new laws and setting up machinery for their enforcement. He was quite right, for after all, there would have been no Board of Stock Commissioners had it not been for the cooperative effort of cattlemen to procure such legislation. The $5 initiation fee was subsequently dropped in deference to Preuitt's plea, but it is doubtful if that reasonable sum was ever an actual deterrent to membership.

When the United States declared war on Spain over the Cuban affair, a generation with no experience in war was red-hot to participate. President William McKinley called for 125,000 volunteers in April, 1898, and the patriotic youth of the nation sprang to arms in true Minute Man tradition— but the arms weren't there. The War Department was a trifle short of them and other equipment for the sudden increase in army enlistments.

Three regiments of cavalry were authorized. They were to be made up of westerners, who were credited with superior ability to fork a horse or sling a gun. They were designated the First, Second, and Third Regiments of the U.S. Volunteer Cavalry. Dr. Leonard Wood was organizer and colonel of the First Regiment; Judge Robert A. Torrey, of Cheyenne, headed the Second Regiment; South Dakota's attorney general, Melvin Grigsby, commanded the Third Regiment, known as Grigsby's Rough Riders. The First Squadron of the Third Regiment consisted of Troops A, C, D, and K, and was known as the Black Hills Squadron. The Second, or Inter-Dakota, Squadron was made up of Troops B, E, G, and H. The Third, or Montana, Squadron included Troop F from Missoula, Frank J. Higgins, Captain; Troop L from Butte, D. Gay Stivers, Captain; Troop M from Billings, John C. Bond, Captain; and Troop I from Miles City, commanded by Captain Joseph T. Brown, later president of the Montana Stockgrowers Association. They were known collectively as the "Cowboy Cavalry."

The Montana Squadron was mustered in May and eventually reached Camp Thomas, Chickamauga Park, Georgia. They expected to be assigned to the Puerto Rican campaign. For some time after their arrival, there was a dearth of horses, saddles, and bridles—quite a handicap to a cavalry outfit— but there was no shortage of rain. After Commodore Winfield Scott Schley wheeled his battle wagons into action against Cervera's fleeing fleet at Santiago Harbor on July 3, the war collapsed. The Montana boys, who were still marching through Georgia, were mustered out on September 8. Home on the range looked pretty good to them.

The river valleys of central and eastern Montana were solidly settled by the turn of the century. Settlement had started years before in a small way when buffalo hunters became squatters, when domestically inclined cowboys got married and started small spreads of their own, when nesters began cutting native hay along the bottom land, and when larger outfits had established home ranches close to wood and water by homesteading or purchasing and then acquiring additional pasture and meadow. Homesteading in the western valleys of Montana had started in 1864, the Territory's No. 1 filing being on land in the Prickly Pear Valley, just north of Helena.

The *Yellowstone Journal* of Miles City commented as follows in its February 11, 1897, issue:

> Farming by irrigation is very different from the old style [eastern type]. Twenty acres is as much as one man can take care of in truck farming; forty acres is a good sized general farm; and one hundred and sixty acres is the limit. With all under successful cultivation, results are surprising. Forty acres here, under irrigation, will produce more than 160 acres in Minnesota, Iowa, and the Dakotas.

The editor was, of course, referring to a one-man operation of the truck-garden type, but granger-cowmen were using controlled water on their land, too. The current belief among practical students of the livestock industry was that open-range practice was well on its way to extinction. It would have been a deaf cowman of the old school who had not heard the repeated predictions and warnings. They didn't have to be told that the small rancher was in the ascendancy. He had more than a foot in the stirrup—he was firmly seated in the saddle. His irrigated forage crops of redtop, timothy, clover, and bluegrass replaced native grass. In the western valleys, ranchers had diverted mountain streams to flood hay meadows long before extensive irrigation was practiced east of the mountains. Montana's first alfalfa field was planted in the Madison Valley about 1880.

Professor Shaw, of the Minnesota State Experimental Station, and Mr. Rantoul, a representative of the Northern Pacific Railroad, were speakers at both the 1898 and 1899 Association meetings. Each emphasized the changing conditions. Shaw said that, while he was not opposed to range interests, he was preaching to Minnesota farmers to feed their grain to their own stock and not to follow the practice of selling young stock to range men who sent it back to be fattened when matured. He stated that if Minnesotans followed his advice, in a short time Montanans would no longer be able to buy their young stuff and would have to change their system. He further counseled that the natural advantages of Montana not only made it easy for a rancher to raise and feed his own calves but they would mature more rapidly than eastern stock.

Rantoul also advised Montana stockmen to pay more attention to breeding. He warned that, unless they bred their own stock, they would one day find themselves without herds. He declared that the small stockman was the winning factor in the cattle business of Montana. From the tone of these talks it is easy to deduce the trend of the times in eastern Montana stock-growing.

Indians were still an annoyance, though hardly a menace. Colonel George W. H. Stouch, government agent for the northern Cheyennes, while admitting that his charges had killed some range cattle, told Association members at the 1898 meeting that the reports of their misdeeds were greatly exaggerated. He ascribed the depredations of the Indians to their "hunting instincts and the confused condition of their reservation rights." He said:

> The Indian is shown the enclosures belonging to white settlers having prior rights and is told that he must not trespass upon them, but that all of the rest of the land belongs to him. He reasons from this that if the things that are on the white man's land are the property of the white man, the things that are on *his* land belong to him or else should not be there, and the logic is not bad.

When the Cheyenne Reservation was created by Presidential order in the winter of 1884, the order stated that

> any tract or tracts included within the . . . described boundaries, which have been located, resided upon, and improved by some bona fide settlers prior to the last day of October, 1884, to the amount to which such settlers might be entitled under the laws regulating the disposition of the public lands of the United States, or to which valid rights may have attached under said laws, are hereby excluded from the reservation hereby made.

This left the white settlers within the prescribed boundaries of the reserve, surrounded in most instances by Indian land, which accounts for the "enclosures" referred to by Colonel Stouch.

According to the colonel, if one of the settlers' steers strayed onto Indian land, a Cheyenne would be under the impression that he could pounce on it with impunity. The colonel's conclusions would indicate that one cause of the settlers misunderstanding Indian motives was their deficiency in proper analysis of Indian thought processes, which are sometimes startling in their simplicity, and at other times very complex.

When 1900 rolled around, President John M. Holt's opening comment at the April MSGA convention was that the country was prosperous. The Spanish-American War had not disturbed cowland seriously. Former Association member Theodore Roosevelt was still leading a "strenuous life"—one which had included the charge up San Juan Hill. The Klondike gold rush was a matter of indifference to stockgrowers, and when Gentleman Jim Corbett took the pugilistic sceptre away from "Jawn" L. Sullivan, it made nary a ripple on the range.

There was a large attendance at the meeting. The total enrolled members now numbered 362 and 75 per cent of them were classified as "small owners." That fact probably accounted for the resistance that developed when the subject of leasing public lands was brought up for discussion, a controversy that was to go on and on. Judge Strevell, of Miles City, expressed violent opposition to government-leasing on the theory that big outfits would control the range to the detriment, if not elimination, of small owners. His argument carried the day and the Association went on record to that effect.

In 1898 the Montana Stockgrowers Association had been cordially invited to join the current national association and the matter had been referred to the executive committee, which had deferred action. Not having received a favorable reply, a representative of the national organization appeared at the 1900 convention and eloquently presented the advantages of such an affiliation. He was persuasive and this time the executive committee reported favorably, with instructions that the secretary make application for membership.

# 14. GROWING COMPLEXITIES

There was much social and political unrest throughout the nation during the nineties, and this carried over to the first decade of the new century. Population increase and the diminished supply of desirable free land were major factors in creating it. A tremendous influx of aliens, bringing their different racial temperaments and traditions, diluted the heritage of American colonial principles in many sections of the country. Michigan, Wisconsin, and Minnesota became havens for the Scandinavians, who took to logging until the woods were full of them—cities, too—with a broad overflow on farm land extending into the Dakotas.

With steamboat traffic on the Missouri River replaced by transcontinental railways, any migratory increment added to the Montana population came from that northern row of states, via "Yim" Hill's Great Northern. A certain amount of family movement crossed Montana from east to west with Washington as its goal, for Montana valleys along the Northern Pacific were solidly occupied and the dryland expanses on either side of the Great Northern held no attraction as yet for prospective settlers. In 1900, 73 per cent of Montana's total acreage was unappropriated, unreserved public land; 12 per cent was reserved; only 15 per cent was in private ownership or covered by homestead entries.

Politically, western Montana, as a producer of silver, was deeply concerned with the coinage question that divided the nation between "gold bugs" and the "free silver" advocates. Big business, fostered by improved transportation and larger metropolitan areas, reached proportions that attracted national attention, including envious resentment from certain elements of the seething melting pot. It became a target for the muckrakers, who filled magazine pages with reports tending to inflame public opinion against the trusts that had taken the place of pools when the latter were outlawed. In the spring of 1902, the New York *World,* campaigning against the "Beef Trust," cited the outrageous cost of meat, under the headline, "PRICES THAT STAGGER HUMANITY." The prices quoted were: sirloin steak, 24¢ a pound, lamb chops, pork chops, ham, 18¢ a pound. On July 20, 1959, a bargain was offered in round steak at a Butte supermarket. It was 89¢ a pound.

For some time there had been persistent dissatisfaction among cowmen with the wide spread between the price of beef on the hoof and the ultimate price to the consumer. E. W. Martin, South Dakota's Congressional representative, had been prodding the Secretary of Commerce to investigate possible collusion among cattle buyers who seemed to be in control of the market. The Montana Stockgrowers Association decided to encourage the Honorable Mr. Martin by voicing its approval, whereupon Senator Tom Carter, who had been asked to speak at the 1902 MSGA convention in Miles City, took the opportunity to enter the lists and break a lance against the Beef Trust.

The senator opined that it was quite evident that someone was making an enormous profit at the expense of the grower and the consumer. He called attention to the action of the U.S. District Court at Chicago in enjoining the packers from combining in restraint of trade and said that there were still flagrant violations of the order. The senator's speech whipped up proper indignation. It was bad enough to have wolves and rustlers harassing stockmen on the range but now the human wolves, the erstwhile pals, whose jovial, free-spending reps attended every Association meeting, were at their throats. It was almost more than an honest cowman could bear. So the executive committee was authorized to cooperate with the United States Department of Justice in an effort to ascertain any violations or conspiracy in manipulating the livestock market.

At the same session, President Theodore Roosevelt was made a life member as a gesture of friendship to an old neighbor and former member. Teddy, who had been so dexterously pigeonholed in the Vice-Presidency by Boss Platt of New York, emerged from that obscure position as a popular crusader when the assassination of President McKinley placed him in the White House. He plunged into the arena of public affairs like a bronc peeler coming out of a rodeo chute with spurs scratching fore and aft. Dedicated to his "strenuous life," his activities ranged from battle with the industrial mighty, to conservation of natural resources, to spelling reform.

One of the first movements of particular import to the West that won his support dealt with large irrigation projects, designed to store water and distribute it on arid land. The potentialities of putting wasting water to far-flung, beneficial use had a fascination that enlisted the all-out enthusiasm of some people. Young, energetic, and eloquent George H. Maxwell was one of them. He left his law practice in California to dedicate his organizing and administrative abilities to a realistic campaign of public enlightenment on the subject. He became president of the National Irrigation Association and in that capacity was invited to address the 1902 MSGA meeting. His impressive talk urged Association recognition of the benefits to accrue from more elaborate and comprehensive irrigation projects, be they privately or governmentally financed. George Maxwell's Irrigation Association, which had been formed in 1897, gave persistent support to the cause that finally crystallized in the creation of the United States Reclamation Service, on June 18, 1902, but even more credit should go to Major James Wesley Powell.

Major Powell was a man of many parts—geographer, geologist, ethnologist, and Civil War veteran. He had headed a number of governmental exploring expeditions and was as familiar with the West as were any of the early, nomadic fur trappers. He was blessed with imagination and vision of a practical type and was equipped with the scientific training to recognize and analyze the economic limitations and latent possibilities of the West. In the spring of 1878, the Secretary of the Interior had transmitted to Congress a report prepared by the major, entitled "Lands of the Arid Regions of the United States." The report contained several recommendations distinguished by their originality. They eventually had far-reaching effects. Others, had they been heeded, would have altered the history of western cowland, probably for the better.

The major proposed a classification of public lands under the headings of mineral, timber, coal, irrigable, and grazing. He advocated a change from the accepted rectangular system of public land survey to one that would recognize the importance of water in the arid West, and conform to water frontage so that the most good might accrue therefrom to the greatest number on an equitable basis. He suggested that Congress make provision for two distinct classes of landowners—irrigation farmers and stockgrowers. Irrigable land was to be divided into districts which could be filed on by not less than nine individuals, to the extent of eighty acres each. Stockmen were to be permitted to file in groups of nine or more on public domain classed as grazing land, each to receive title to 2,560 acres and to have access to water.

Major Powell was a prophet and also a doer. Unselfishly and meticulously, he prepared the way so that other men might build and profit. His wisdom and sagacity are even more apparent in retrospect. He recognized certain facts and principles that were unheard of at that time, but which have been so thoroughly demonstrated since that they are now accepted as having always been self-evident. The major knew more about the grasses of the western range than the stockmen did themselves. He knew what overgrazing and injury to the sod would do to them and worked against it, as he did against careless irrigation. He knew that small allotments of arid land would not suffice any farmer and that "the great areas over which stock must roam to obtain subsistence usually will prevent the practicability of fencing the lands."

The Powell report aroused so much Congressional interest that it resulted in the United States Geological Survey, of which the major was made director. This agency measured stream flow, kept records, and procured complete and exact data pertinent to plans for future developments. This took time. Records of erratic western streams had to extend over many years to be of value. The testimony of old-timers was no doubt sincere, but it was frequently unreliable. The work finally produced sentiment, which grew ever stronger, in favor of direct action for reclamation of the West's arid lands by the federal government.

The Reclamation Act of June 18, 1902, created a federal service to build, maintain, and supervise irrigation projects too large for cooperative financing but which, in the course of ten years, were expected to be self-liquidating, with complete ownership and management being transferred to the water users. Four of the nine initial projects approved for construction in the public land states of the West were in Montana. They were the Upper and Lower Yellowstone, the Sun River, and the Milk River projects, all in the heart of cow country. The Flathead Indian Reservation project was added by arrangement with the Indian Service.

This great, official, social experiment was given national publicity. A beneficent government was going to assist a portion of its people to a fuller life close to the soil. It soon became evident that the effort was to have many ramifications.

With enthusiasm born of inexperience, far too alluring pictures were drawn to attract settlers. Such phrases as "altruistic effort" and "spirit of practical brotherhood" were used to describe the experiment. As a result, many impractical dreamers envisioned themselves and their families living a prosperous life of ease and contentment in a vine-covered cot, with not much to do but watch things grow. It didn't work like that. It did bring an influx of settlers and drew national attention to western public lands and to a method of farming that was far from new to Californians of Spanish descent and to the Mormons of Utah.

Paralleling in time and partially responsible for the aroused public interest in the nation's natural resources, as exemplified by reclamation of arid land, was the attention given to forests. In 1891, Congress empowered President Benjamin Harrison to establish forest reserves from public domain. Acting on that authority, the President immediately designated a reserve in Wyoming covering over 1,250,000 acres. Other reserves were created by President Harrison and also by President Cleveland. The administration of the tracts was given to the General Land Office in the Department of the Interior.

In 1895 a National Forestry Committee was appointed. Serving on the committee was Gifford Pinchot, a zealot in the cause of professional forestry. Much sentiment was aroused in the East for adequate administration and protection of forest reserves by people trained in that vocation. Particular emphasis was placed on one part of the committee's investigation:

> A study of the forest reserves in their relations to the general development and welfare of the country shows that the segregations of these great bodies of reserved lands cannot be withdrawn from all occupation and use, and that they must be made to perform their part in the economy of the nation.

Complementing this committee opinion, the Sundry Civil Appropriation Act of June 4, 1907, limited the type of land permissible in the reserves, as follows:

> No public forest reservation shall be established except to improve and protect the forests within the reservations, or for the purpose of securing favorable conditions of water flow and to furnish a continuous supply of timber for the use and necessities of the citizens of the United States; but it is not the purpose or intent of these provisions, or of the Act providing for such reservations, to authorize the inclusion therein of lands more valuable for the mineral therein or for agricultural purposes than for forests.

And yet, just a short time before, President Cleveland had created by proclamation thirteen reserves of almost 21,500,000 acres, in which were included excellent homestead sites. East and West tangled over it. Easterners who had become so acutely conservation-conscious through propaganda knew nothing about the supply and sources of water in the West and equally as little about western land suitable and available for homesteading. Finally, homesteaders were given a limited time to file on the Cleveland-made reserves.

In 1905 President Theodore Roosevelt, prompted by Gifford Pinchot, succeeded in transferring jurisdiction of the then existing sixty reserves, totaling around 56,000,000 acres, to the Department of Agriculture and in direct charge of a Forest Service, Mr. Pinchot heading the latter organization. In 1907 the original term "forest reserve" was altered to "national forest," lest the former term imply a withdrawal from economic use.

Creation of the national forests met with popular approval. No reasonable person could find fault with a program of preservation of timber resources from exploitation or destruction by fire. Their orderly harvesting, propagation, and the protection of their watersheds to curb excessive erosion at lower levels was simply good sense. However, there were those who believed that any additional reserves should be made by Congressional authority rather than by Presidential proclamation. Agriculture Information Bulletin No. 83, Forest Service, Department of Agriculture, entitled *High Lights in the History of Forest Conservation,* reports the following, which occurred in 1907:

> A Western element in Congress opposed to the national forest enterprise, succeeded in attaching to the agriculture appropriation bill a rider prohibiting any further additions by Presidential proclamation to the forest reserves in Oregon, Washington, Idaho, Montana, Colorado, and Wyoming. President Theodore Roosevelt signed the bill carrying the rider to be effective March 4th, but before doing so, he signed thirty-three proclamations on March 1st and 2nd, by which new reserves were created and areas were added to already established reserves so that a total of 14,645,631 acres were added to the forest reserve system. California, Arizona, and New Mexico were added to the list of restricted states a few years later. Addition to the national forests or creation of new ones in these states can [now] be only by action of Congress.

Of course, the evasion of the intent of Congress took connivance on the part of the Forest Service. Gifford Pinchot and other makers and supporters of the President's forest reserve policies were elated by the strategy used to circumvent the pending law. Those on the other side of the fence quite naturally viewed the Presidential action as a piece of slick political chicanery.

No official provision had been made for multiple commercial use of the national forests but, starting in 1906, stockmen were issued permits for sheep and cattle to graze on forest summer range for a fee. A system of rules and regulations was set up. The fees were based on animal-unit months instead of per acre as had been the custom on leased land under private ownership. There were instances where stockman and forest official didn't see eye to eye, but on the whole things ran along amicably for a long time before there was a serious rift.

The packers were not having a happy time. Aside from their troubles for alleged irregularities, such as rebates and concessions of various kinds to favored customers, they were beset with other difficulties. They had received adverse publicity off and on, ever since the "embalmed beef" scandals of the Spanish-American War. In 1906 ardent socialist Upton Sinclair authored a book entitled *The Jungle*. It was fiction, based on his personal observations while working at the stockyards in order to gather material. Primarily, the author's intention was to stir up the public in the cause of anti-capitalism by exposing some of the sordid social evils of the day. His hero was a Central European immigrant who was outrageously exploited by all with whom he came in contact. For a time the book was a best seller, but its impact on its readers was disappointing to Upton Sinclair. Instead of the expected indignation over the treatment of immigrant labor around the stockyards, it stimulated renewed interest in the processing and purity of meat products coming from the packers.

While such matters of national import affecting the cattle industry were of interest to Montana stockgrowers, affairs of state caliber were also claiming their attention. All in all, 1901 was not a bad year for them, although it must have been a trifle rugged in parts of Texas. Mrs. Anna E. Taylor made a trip over Niagara Falls in a barrel to raise funds for the mortgage on her Texas ranch. The Denver *Republican* offered the suggestion that Mrs. Taylor seemed to be taking a lot of credit that belonged to the barrel. The Texas oil boom had started that year near Beaumont, but Texas is a fairly large state—not as large as Alaska, of course—and perhaps the Taylor ranch was too far from the oil discoveries to profit by the boom.

The Lone Star State had no dearth of cattle. The limitless stream that flowed north had not been dammed or entirely diverted by 1902. Neither had the admonitions and warnings of Minnesota's Professor Shaw brought about a cessation of shipments back and forth between eastern feeder belts and the Montana range. Under the date March 16, 1902, the *Yellowstone Journal* carried a story from Fort Worth, Texas, headlined "BIG DEAL IN CATTLE." It read:

> Frederico Terrazas, son of the former Governor of the State of Chihuahua, Mexico, is here closing one of the largest single firm deals ever made in this country. The sale includes 25,000 head of cattle which will go to Colorado, Montana, Wyoming and the Dakotas. . . . To transport this large number of cattle will require 550 cars making forty trains. The approximate freight bill on the stock to various destinations will be $96,000.

On April 22, 1902, the *Journal* printed a story copied from the *Rocky Mountain Husbandman* that said there was still a strong movement of young stock towards Montana to range and winter and turn off a year or two years from the following fall. It further stated that thousands of Texans were to be unloaded; that yearlings from Minnesota, Iowa, and Nebraska were to come into Montana because cattlemen were expecting good prices to hold for five years at least, and so were investing in young stock that would grow into money. The extra herds of Texans were being imported because the buyers expected to feed them in competition with the Corn Belt. The *Husbandman* prophesied that at the then current rate of imports the herd owners would be forced to rely on meadows, hay, and fenced pasture to carry them through the winters. It further predicted that there would have to be an increase of forage crops and the development of meadows, considered impractical a few years earlier.

In 1903 it was again demonstrated that the vagaries of Montana weather could do unexpected things to the hopes of cattle ranchers. Drouth and grass-hoppers combined to clean a 75-by-100-mile strip of range in southeastern Montana—the equivalent of 312 townships. Strangely enough, there was good feed west on the Crow Indian Reservation and also east of the Powder River. Outfits on the lower Tongue, the lower Powder, on Pumpkin and Mizpah Creeks, were forced to move their herds. Their cattle became scattered from the Yellowstone deep into the Dakotas, along the Belle Fourche River, and as far south as the Platte. In 1904 50,000 head of thoroughly mixed brands had to be rounded up and returned from a 200-square-mile area.

The LO, Flying E, Bug, D, Three Circles, Cross, Six Half Circle, 4J, WM, SA, TJ, and Circle Bar outfits were among the participants on this last really big roundup. One hundred and fifty men rode circle and camped with nine wagons. A few of them have not forgotten the big rain that over-took them near SA Lake. It rained for ten days until the land was a swamp and the draws were raging torrents. The Circle B chuck wagon was on one side of a small coulee, the bed wagon on the other. On the third day of the deluge, the men had to swim their horses to cross back and forth. It took two years to gather all the strayed cattle.

In 1904 the huge area east of the Musselshell, lying between the Yellow-stone and the Missouri, was being combed at roundup time by big outfits. The XIT and CK wagons covered the section east of the Redwater. The middle segment was range for the Hat X, CK, H Cross, 79, and Bow and Arrow irons. The west portion was taken care of by the N Bar, Lazy J, LU Bar, and Cross K riders. The N Bar had passed from the Niobrara Cattle Company to Tommy Cruse, of Helena. It was hard to believe that this big chunk of dry land would ever be anything but cow country.

Action of Montana's 1907 legislative assembly affecting stockgrowers re-ceived a mixture of praise and condemnation at the annual meeting of the Montana Stockgrowers Association which followed on its heels. New legisla-tion provided for the appointment by the Governor of one owner of cattle or horses from each county as a member of the Board of Stock Commis-sioners, to hold office for two years. The newly constituted board was to divide the state into as many districts as they deemed necessary for assignment of inspectors and administrative purposes. The secretary of the board was to be the recorder of marks and brands, with a fee of $2 fixed for each recording. The law stipulated that the State Treasurer should hold the proceeds of estray sales in a separate fund for one year and if not claimed and paid to owners in that time, they were to be placed to the credit of the State Stock Inspector and Detective Fund. All estray money in the hands of the State Board of Stock Commissioners, or the Montana Stockgrowers Association, "or anyone else, received from sale of estray horses and cattle" was to be transferred to the State Treasurer and placed to the credit of the Inspector and Detective Fund within thirty days after passage and approval of the bill.

Furthermore, the State Examiner was to scan the books of the Board of Stock Commissioners and of the Montana Stockgrowers Association to see if the estray money had been properly used and accounted for in the past. He was then to submit a report to the governor. All future money derived from the sale of estrays was to be accounted for by the secretary of the Board of Stock Commissioners, who was required to keep a record of brands and marks and full data on sales, turning over the proceeds, when possible, to the owners. Unclaimed funds remaining with the secretary after May 1 of each year were to be advertised in four newspapers (in Helena, Billings, Miles City, and Fort Benton), and after "such publication and proceeds from sale of such animals shall have remained with the Secretary for two years," they were to be paid to the State Treasurer and credited to the State Inspectors and Detectives Fund.

There was merit to this legislation that was palpably designed to safeguard estray owners and unclaimed funds accruing from the sale of estrays. Referring to this law, the Miles City *Independent,* commented rather unjustly:

> Hereafter neither the Stockgrowers Association nor its Secretary will have anything whatever to do with the receipt and disbursement of funds derived from the sale of cattle belonging to unknown owners, or estrays, this duty devolving, under the new law, on the State Board of Stock Commissioners through its Secretary. The Stock Association becomes in effect merely a social organization.

Of greater importance was the legislature's creation of the Livestock Sanitary Board, its membership to consist of the president of the Board of Stock Commissioners, the president of the Board of Sheep Commissioners, and the president of the State Board of Health. The new board was "empowered to govern quarantines, establish and maintain livestock sanitary regulations, direct and regulate slaughter of all diseased animals, provide for meat inspection, and provide for the payment of indemnity when required." The state veterinarian surgeon, appointed by the governor, was to act as secretary and executive officer of the new board without extra compensation.

What caused consternation among stockmen was the action of the legislature in repealing the special tax on livestock for inspection and detective purposes. The attorney general had rendered an opinion that the tax was unconstitutional although it had been levied on stock interests alone for many years and was used solely for their protection. The repeal deprived the Stock Board of funds for inspection and for procuring evidence against rustlers, the primary service for which the board had been created, as the unclaimed estray money that was to go into the state treasurer's Inspectors and Detectives Fund would be insufficient to maintain such service. By cutting the inspection force to the quick, the board hoped to make their small bank balance carry them through until another legislature convened.

The necessity for, and the status of, stock inspectors and detectives never has been known to the general public. Prior to the employment of inspectors and detectives in an official state capacity, stockmen themselves voluntarily served in those roles and also, betimes, as prosecutors, judges, jury, and executioners. Floppin' Bill Cantrell was Montana's first "private eye" connected with the stock business and of course, insofar as the law was concerned, his status was unofficial.

Montana's stock detectives have been particularly well endowed with a talent for avoiding publicity and for remaining inconspicuous. It may be commendably modest, but it left the record of their accomplishments very short of published detail. When their employment was put on an official basis, it became possible to hire men of ability and experience and to give them authority to gather evidence and make arrests that resulted in convictions. These special officers had to possess patience, fortitude, courage, and brains. They had to outthink, outguess, and outshoot the outlaws against whom they were pitted. Their record is long and honorable.

The role of brand inspector carries no glamour but has been indispensable in the cattle industry from the time stock started going to market by rail. Copies of the first brand book issued by the Montana Stockgrowers Association were placed in the hands of every inspector, detective, sheriff, Canadian Mountie, railroad official, and commission house. The books were powerful agents in the suppression of cattle rustling. They also were potent arguments to induce non-Association cattlemen to join. With the creation of the state office of Recorder of Marks and Brands, the registering of brands was not confined to MSGA members only. Though an expert inspector's memory for brands was encyclopedic, no one man could begin to memorize the thousands of brands that had come into use; 16,000 Montana brands in 1900, 20,000 in 1910. Equipped with official records, the inspectors at the central markets could identify the ownership of thousands upon thousands of estrays that got mixed in with shipments. Their integrity was unassailable.

In the open range days, a beef roundup inevitably included cattle from outfits that had no rep with the crew. If these critters were far from their home range—some of them did wander astonishing distances—and were in shipping condition, it would have been a disservice to their owners to have left them behind, eventually to die of old age. Moreover, they would eat grass that would support some marketable steer who knew enough to stay on his accustomed range. So they were deliberately included in the beef shipment as a "courtesy of the range," with the assurance that an alert brand inspector would spot them and the owner would receive payment. Such cattle were sold on the same basis as those with which they were shipped, and the sales money remitted directly to the owner of the estray when instructions were on file for such disposition of the funds.

In case the owner could not be determined, the sales price was sent to the secretary of the Association, before it became a state responsibility, with a report of marks and brands for each estray. The Association staff searched the records and made inquiries in a thorough effort to locate the owner; as soon as ownership was established beyond a doubt, the money was remitted to him. By this system, close to $625,000 had been recovered for owners during the year 1898 alone.

In more recent years, and even today, if the various brands of a train-load of cattle are not well mixed at the time of loading, they are very likely to become mingled at the stops where they are unloaded for feed and water. When they arrive at the terminal market, it is the task of the Montana brand inspectors to check them, one by one, against the descriptions listed by the shipper, a duplicate having been sent to the Livestock Commission office in Helena. Brands must be verified and ownership accounted for before the owner's authorized commission men can sort and grade his cattle in lots for sale.

A prime objective of the Livestock Commission is to provide every safeguard against error in determining correct ownership of all Montana stock received at a market. For years, Montana has led in the efficiency of its brand inspection system at the major markets to which Montana cattle have been shipped. Chicago has been a favorite shipping point. Western representatives have been maintained there since the 1880's. Effective January 1, 1959, the resident inspector was withdrawn to assume other duties in Montana, thereby closing another chapter in the story of Montana livestock. At one time (1937), five Montana inspectors were kept busy in Chicago. Today, home markets have cut into the Chicago traffic so heavily that the Livestock Commission finds the cost of maintaining a year-round inspection service there prohibitive. Hereafter, cattle shipped to Chicago by rail will have to be inspected before shipment. In October and November only, an experienced man will be on the job at the Union Stockyards "to see that cattle consigned to the special feeder sales are properly identified by lots."

Association affairs were not without interest and benefit to the members between 1901 and 1910. At one meeting they framed and adopted a resolution designed to make Congress recognize the cow business by creating the office of Second Assistant Secretary of Agriculture, "who shall be a gentleman fully advised as to the livestock industry of the nation, whose duties shall be solely to attend to the welfare of this industry." Copies were transmitted to the state's Congressional representatives. Association members were never supplicants. They issued orders whenever they decided to take a hand in national maneuvers. The idea must have bogged down in the morass of Congressional procedure, or perhaps they could not find the specified paragon to take the job. At any rate, no Second Assistant Secretary of Agriculture who is a gentleman solely devoted to the cow business has yet appeared upon the bureaucratic horizon.

Unsatisfactory bounty laws and fraudulent claims thereunder still plagued all members, and another abortive attempt to move the annual meeting place to Helena kept Miles City supporters enraged. Judge Strevell, whose loyalty to the cow capital dated from his terms of office as secretary-treasurer of the Eastern Montana Stockgrowers Association, hotly contested the proposed change, saying that Helena was primarily a mining town whose residents were not interested in stock raising. Con Kohrs countered by alleging that sheepmen were fast taking over eastern range and that Miles City was no longer the center of the cattle industry. He called attention to Jefferson, Madison, and Beaverhead Counties as having large cattle holdings and extensive range that entitled them to consideration. Miles City proponents *didn't* think so by a sufficient vote to gain their point.

The harmony of the 1907 Association meeting was disrupted to some extent by the secretarial aspirations of H. R. Wells. Mr. Wells had arrived in Montana a few years earlier as manager of the Hat X spread. He lined up the Association members from the eastern end of the state in an unprecedented campaign for the office of secretary-treasurer and received a vote of 79 to 58 against the incumbent, W. G. Preuitt. The secretary's business office was moved to Miles City and remained there until Mr. Wells again appeared on the hustings and was elected to the more lucrative job of sheriff of Custer County, whereupon W. G. Preuitt was restored to his former position with the Association.

There were 579 members in good standing at the 1908 meeting. Signs of the changing times were underscored in George W. Brewster's response to the welcoming speech when he reiterated what was becoming an old story—the old-time roundup was fading out as the larger outfits went out of business and benchlands were settled by ranchers who combined stock raising with farming.

To fill the financial gap left in the Board of Stock Commissioners' budget by discontinuance of the state's special tax levy, a resolution was passed that provided for a three-cent assessment per head on cattle and horses belonging to Association members, this fund to pay stockyard inspectors and range detectives, the latter to work in the interest of members only. Following the Texas pattern, each member was obligated to file with the Association secretary a list of his marks and brands, with a list of all cattle and horses for which he was claiming protection, the number to be no less than that returned to the authorities for taxation. The penalty for noncompliance was loss of membership.

Whether or not the assessment had a dampening effect on membership, the paid-up members listed for the Silver Anniversary meeting of April 1, 1910, showed 369, a dismal drop of 210 in two years. The bulk of the roster was made up of eastern Montanans. The twenty-fifth anniversary meeting was an appropriate time to review Association history, and this was done with nostalgic references to the "good old days" (which were never quite as good as they seem in retrospection), to the old Macqueen House that burned in 1898, never to be rebuilt, to the famous and continuing roast pig of Miles City Club lunches, to Northern Pacific Railway side tracks lined with chartered Pullmans. The character of the membership and meeting agenda had changed. Controversy with railroad solicitors and commission men over rates and service and the fixing of roundup dates and boundaries were no longer as important as interstate commerce laws and rates and the effect of a State Railway Commission.

# 15. THE FREE GRASS IS FENCED

About 1900, H. W. Campbell, of western Kansas, tried an agricultural experiment. It had long been evident in his part of the country that average annual precipitation (about 15 inches) was too scant for profitable farming as it was practiced east of the 100th meridian. Maybe the combined rainfall of two years would be sufficient to produce a respectable yield. Runoff, plant life, and evaporation used up each year's supply of water. In flat Kansas, runoff control was no problem, so if you could eliminate vegetation on a piece of land and protect the accumulating moisture from the sun and wind, you might be able to conserve it.

Mr. Campbell planted some acreage to crop and let an equal amount of adjoining ground lie fallow. By plowing the idle land deep and assiduously harrowing it at proper times, he permitted no plant growth and conserved below surface all moisture that fell. The following year, he reversed the status of the two tracts. It worked. Of course, only half of his land was in production each season, but half a crop was far better than none. The method became known as "dryland farming" and was immediately seized upon by optimists as an infallible formula for successful cultivation of arid land.

At that time, you couldn't give land away in the so-called Benchland District, north of central Montana's Musselshell River. In 1904 a gentleman with gambling instincts turned over the sod, seeded to wheat, and harvested forty bushels to the acre. Farmers flocked into the Musselshell, Flatwillow, and Grass Range areas. The two foregoing agricultural accomplishments put a crimp in the current plans of the Public Lands Commission for classification of public lands. A brand-new speculative land boom started. Many land agencies in the Twin Cities concentrated on prairie tracts in the Canadian province of Saskatchewan, but the western states were not overlooked in the search for any remaining "free land" that by a stretch of the imagination might qualify as arable. It took just a few seasons to demonstrate that a 160–acre homestead in a region of limited rainfall was not enough to support a family when only half of it was in crop. Over 80 per cent of the original entries were relinquished.

In 1907 a proposal to grant greater acreage for dryland homesteads was introduced in Congress. It did not get the support of cattlemen, who were skeptical of the efficacy of the newfangled farming process and did not want to see virgin sod plowed under in an ineffectual attempt to turn grassland into wheatland. Oddly enough, the bill was defeated because of the general, but mistaken, belief that the measure would be advantageous to stockmen, who were still regarded as the villains of the wide open spaces. This was but a temporary delay. A besieged Congress yielded to the unreasoning clamor for more free land and, on February 19, 1909, passed the Enlarged Homestead Act, applicable to the thirteen public-land states of the West.

The act permitted claims of 320 acres on surveyed public domain if the land were nonirrigable, unreserved, unappropriated, and contained no merchantable timber. Nonirrigable land was interpreted to be land in areas where the average rainfall was insufficient to grow crops with customary methods of cultivation and for which a water supply for irrigation was not available at reasonable cost. Something like 26,000,000 acres were so designated; Montana had lots of such land. All told, more than 18,000,000 acres were filed on in the fiscal year 1909–10—an all-time record.

The land fever took another angle. National forest boundaries included considerable land that was unforested but deemed necessary, or at least helpful, for proper administration. Some of it looked very good to prospective followers of the plow, who believed that anything designated as "forest" land should be timbered. Their protests became so clamorous that the national forest land was reclassified and almost 1,000,000 acres eliminated. This happened in 1910; two years later, Congress, in spite of conservationist opposition, required that all potentially arable land within national forest preserves be returned to the jurisdiction of the Department of the Interior as tracts open to homesteading. For once, cowmen and ultraconservationists found common cause. Reclassification and elimination of grassland from the national forests cut down grazing quotas and took away summer range on which small cattle owners were dependent.

Inspired by the Enlarged Homestead Act and by dryland farming propaganda, a surge of miscellaneous land-seekers rolled into Montana in 1910, especially along the High Line. They filled the arid benchland from the Milk River south to the Missouri River breaks, and north to the Canadian border. Promoter James Jerome ("Jim") Hill, head of the Great Northern Railway and known as the "Empire Builder," employed analyzers of soil and climate whom his publicists advertised as experts. The promoters painted a very alluring picture for land-hungry urbanites of free land waiting under a big sky. They came from the crowded cities by trainloads, but they were decidedly not the type of clear-eyed, self-sufficient pioneers who had come land-seeking through the Cumberland Gap.

"Locators" boarded coaches down the line and signed up passengers for service. Most of the prospects were not well-heeled. They didn't need to be. The land was free, wasn't it? They rode in day coaches that had been equipped with cook stoves for housekeeping of sorts en route. For a cash consideration, the locator or his agent would drive the land-seekers out across the billowing landscape and show them sections of unclaimed land. When they found 320 acres to their liking, they were shown the corners and given a legal description for filing. It didn't take long for the grassland to be covered by entries at the local Land Office. In 1910, 21,982 original homestead entries were recorded in Montana, and that was just a starter. Entries averaged 16,000 a year for the next seven years. During that time, wheat acreage jumped from 258,000 to almost 3,500,000 acres. In 1876, W. A. Clark had bragged in Philadelphia about Montana's 40,000 acres of wheat and oats combined.

The newcomers fenced the range and plowed under the hardy native grass. They built shacks and had to tie them down with guy wires to keep them from going with the wind. They drilled for water and sometimes got it—alkaline. This was to be the "progress" so dear to Chambers of Commerce. Density of population was, in some magic way, to spell prosperity and happiness for everyone. It would attract commerce and industry; smoke would belch from furnaces; crowds would congest city streets. Competition would remain about the same, just so many doctors, lawyers, bankers, and barbers per thousand, but more of them in the aggregate; streams would receive more sewage and refuse; there would be more orange peel, and discarded cleaning tissue would make great white ways out of highways. But where would the stockgrower take his herds?

Squatters came and holed up on unsurveyed land in shanties, soddies, and even caves dug in cutbanks. They petitioned the United States Land Office to set section corners so that they, too, might file. They sifted into the Big Dry country, a hundred miles from a railroad. They tried to raise grain on the Missouri Flats of the upper Madison River at an altitude where it was impossible to mature a crop. By 1912, some of the hopeful were beginning to think that dryland farming was not what it had been cracked up to be. Dryland farming did best when it rained occasionally. The customary wail for help went up—for more acres per homestead when they couldn't handle 320; for a curtailment of residence time required; for other concessions. Despite the painful experience of others, newcomers continued to file.

To complicate the situation for Congress, there was a hue and cry on the part of western state administrations for federal land to be turned over to them. They wanted to acquire the remaining grazing land to supply state revenue should agitation for the leasing of public land ever attain its goal. There was bitter jurisdictional jealousy between the Department of the Interior and the Department of Agriculture as represented by the Forest Service. Each wanted exclusive control of public domain, regardless of its classification. Montana stockgrowers who had opposed leasing of public domain, on the theory that it would benefit big owners only, were changing their minds. Anything now to preserve the grass, that protective covering of the high prairie that held the soil in place and that had learned to thrive on a minimum of moisture.

The short, perennial buffalo grass and blue grama built a very dense sod. Before they were disturbed, they accounted for about 90 per cent of the forage on much of the great plains country. When seasons of severe drouth came—with a haphazard pattern of irregularity, as drylanders were to learn—stems were seared by hot winds and roots parched in the desiccated soil, but the grass never gave up. When its thirst had been slaked by the delayed rains, it came back with astonishing vigor and luxuriance, to provide a storehouse of nutrition for the animals that grazed on its broad expanses. Where the grass blanket is missing, torrential rains lash the exposed soil and disintegrating bedrock and erosion carves fantastic forms in regions known as badlands. Major Powell knew this and warned against disturbing the shield of forage that protected so much of the northern plains—a natural resource for annual harvesting. His wise counsel was filed and forgotten.

Grass supported the buffalo, and buffalo had supported a race of people for centuries. That same enduring grass also supported thousands upon thousands of range cattle, and stockmen fought hard to conserve it. To accuse them of willful abuse of their greatest asset is stupid. Grass was their everything. Without it, there would be no livestock industry. True, the open range of Montana was overgrazed in the boom days but that was not

*Assigning riders for the roundup circle*

Apart from the cowboy-artist Charlie Russell, a photographer named L. A. Huffman also foresaw and was saddened by "the end of the frontier." With exquisite feeling he captured its last moments on glass plate and film between 1878 and 1900. Huffman's eastern Montana range photographs are now considered gems among all Western documentaries, as attested by the fine examples reproduced on these pages. The pictures following show *how little* the scene has actually changed between then and now—much less than is commonly believed.

*Roundup outfit breaking camp*

*Andy Speelman, saddling the wild horse*

*Going to the roundup*

*A typical trio*

*Putting on a hackamore*

*The nighthawk in his nest*

In 1910, almost 400 miles north and west of Huffman's beloved range, Charlie Russell (third from the right), the Con Price family, and neighbors gathered at the Lazy KY ranch house in the Sweetgrass Hills.

In the typical cow town of Dupuyer in the winter of 1899—in snow deeper than normal, but not phenomenal—cowmen managed to ride in to the Klondike Saloon to exchange news and greetings and to warm their innards.

In 1898 in extreme eastern Montana's Dawson County, just a whoop and a holler from the Dakota Bad Lands, cowboys munch a chuck-wagon meal near their tent-camp (*below*), the canvas shelters being the most notable change in twenty years. In 1910, eleven years later, Bob Kennon, salty cowboy friend of Charlie Russell, took this photograph (*bottom*) of a Judith Basin roundup crew in central Montana. Little had changed since the roundup of 1885 at Utica, already pictured.

In 1916 the huge Biering-Cunningham herd (*top*) ranged out of the Madison Valley in ranch country pioneered in the 1860's by such stalwarts as Ennis, Jeffers, and Story. *Bottom:* winter sometimes comes early in the Rockies. In 1943 Don Hunter moved his stock from the higher meadows down into the Big Blackfoot Valley for winter feeding. The manner of trailing has changed little in eighty years.

Come spring—many moons ago, last year, or decades from now—the scene above will repeat itself as cattle again move from the winter lowlands to summer range—a never-changing pattern in Montana's cattle economy. And in the winter, too, they'll sometimes have to be moved, as the Belden photograph below indicates.

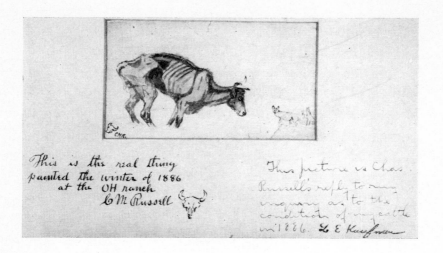

*This is the real thing painted the winter of 1886 at the OH ranch C M Russell*

*This picture is Chas. Russell's reply to my inquiry as to the condition of my cattle in 1886. L E Kaufman*

The full cycle runs its devastating course. The Terrible Winter of 1886–87, in which Charlie Russell dramatically portrayed the last of 5,000 OH cattle to perish (*above*), started as a dry summer. In the 1930's the most fearsome drouth the Great Plains ever experienced left this Montana critter (*below*) dead of starvation and thousands of stockmen facing bankruptcy.

due to the first occupants, who deplored the situation but had no authority to bar public range to the newcomers who swarmed in.

Cattlemen have not always agreed among themselves as to the proper disposition of public domain, but on one thing they have always been in harmony: that the ultimate beef product of a grass-covered section of dryland is more valuable than the crop of weeds and thistle that ultimately finds toe hold after the plowed soil of that section is gone. Grassland is a natural resource of tremendous importance, but a government that prided itself on conservation of water, timber, and the reclamation of land by irrigation gave grass scant consideration until it was almost too late.

Drylanders were not the only irritant that galled Montana cowmen. The winter of 1916–17 was one of the hardest in thirty years. The heavy winter kill might be chargeable to their own poor judgment; it had happened thirty years before. The loss was confined largely to scrub easterners that had arrived in the fall; these cattle were unused to range feed, their coats were thin, and many of the cows calved during the worst weather. But this winter loss came on top of the heavy stock shipping of the summer of 1916, when more than 100,000 cattle were shipped out of state. In 1917, 333,000 more were shipped out. The alarming feature of this exodus was not immediately apparent. It had been partially brought about by a short grain crop among the granger-stockmen, but it was also stimulated by high prices caused by the war in Europe. The large number of cows, calves, and young cattle included in the shipments boded ill for the future.

Although the big operator might be shipping his surplus only, all signs led to the belief that the small owner was cutting into his foundation stock, which it would be hard for him to replace later. The granger-stockmen who had depleted their herds would not have credit to buy more. They would have to mortgage their holdings and could not get back on a sound basis until they had successfully raised at least two or more grain crops. The man who kept his base stock in spite of alluring, fancy prices stood to reap big profits from his expendable calves, and would be far better off in the end. The war abroad accounted for many abnormal things that were happening in America.

The war, however, could not be blamed for the inevitable. The law of averages overtook the drylanders. There was a drouth in the summer of 1918, and a worse one in 1919. It reduced to mere trickles the state's largest rivers. Ranchers forked trout out of the shrinking, overcrowded pools that remained in the bed of the upper Jefferson River and smoked them, rather than let them starve slowly. Tragedy stalked the range. Individuals lost everything. Most drylanders, the "honyockers" of local parlance, didn't have much but hope to start with. A Montana ranch has been called a piece of dry ground with a water right attached. The drylanders didn't even have that. When they quit, they had nothing to take with them. They just spit on the fire and whistled for the dog. There were tough times in Montana and a lot of disillusioned people.

The long, intense dryness increased premature selling of young cattle and breeding stock. Over 600,000 cattle left the state, some to southern pastures, and most of them didn't return. Livestock Commission inspectors hunted for available pasture and the railroads cut rates on incoming feed and outgoing stock. Cattlemen were filled with gloom. Many of them sold out. Just before the catastrophe, big blocks of railroad land in central Montana were being optioned by wholesale realtors who were passing them on to syndicates, both local and out of state, as speculative ventures, the blocks to be broken up and resold to individuals. Devastating reports of the drouth were reported in the East and put such a damper on the ardor of prospective buyers that the promotions came to a halt.

It took courage to weather those trying years. In the minds of the majority, only a few activities recorded in the annals of the Montana Stockgrowers Association were of sufficient import to the members to justify the Association's continuance. A core of loyal, tenacious believers in the basic worth of the industry kept the organization going. Wallis Huidekoper, son of pioneer stockman A. C. Huidekoper, gave life to the office of vice president. His interest and activities in the MSGA were immeasurable. His excellent ideas and leadership deserved something better than the pall of apathy which enveloped so many of the members. His personality, unfailing energy, and sound counsel were a power in eventually getting the Association back to a status of influence and of beneficial aid.

Wallis Huidekoper was elected first vice president at the 1914 convention and held that office for four terms. At that meeting, Secretary Dan Raymond, successor to W. G. Preuitt and his son, E. K. Preuitt (who had filled out the year 1909 after his father's death), recommended a change of meeting place every other year, but it was not until the 1917 assembly that a slim attendance sanctioned the biennial switch to host cities other than Miles City. Great Falls and Billings were contenders for the 1918 honor. It went to Great Falls, the Electric City.

It was not lack of fighting spirit or home-town loyalty that caused Miles City backers to concede every other meeting to some other city. It was wisdom recognizing expediency. That the innovation was beneficial was proven by the jump in membership enrollment from 264 in 1917 to over 1,000 when the April 8, 1919, convention opened. Had there been further delay in accepting the change that picked up membership and interest, the Association might have died on the vine. New zip had been pumped into the hardening arteries of the organization at Great Falls, where the stockgrowers were welcomed by Shirley Ford, banker son of Robert S. Ford of pioneer days. Mr. Ford produced figures to show that while the production of cereal grains had increased tenfold in Montana from 1902 to 1916, the livestock census had remained static. In truth, there had been a decrease. Not that this meant a gradual and ultimate extinction of the stock business in the state, but it did illustrate the tremendous change in economic conditions and concepts, some chargeable to World War I. Ford warned that it was a change that must be met by stockgrowers with new methods if they were to survive. The Great Falls convention ended with an eloquent and much applauded speech by Malcolm Clark, Blackfeet Indian and stockman, who pledged the support of his tribe in the cause of democracy and for the welfare of the Association. Quite a difference from the days not long gone when Lee M. Ford's father was organizing stockmen in that very area to "attend to" Indians who "needed looking after."

Wallis Huidekoper was elected to the presidency at the Miles City meeting in 1919, and Billings was chosen for the 1920 get-together. The wisdom of a change of venue was again demonstrated there. The attendance was good and the tone of the sessions had altered under Huidekoper's influence. There were better-prepared talks on key subjects, given by a cross section of experts. However, any optimism for the immediate future of the livestock business was blasted during the balance of the year and again in 1921. Reaction had set in after the war. Money was tight, credit was restricted, men were being forced to liquidate their assets on a prostrated market. Back East, veterans were selling apples on the street corners. Everywhere people were out of work and curtailing expenditures. Imports of livestock from Canada and frozen beef from South America, Australia, and New Zealand, were not helping the western cattle situation.

With matters at such low ebb and getting worse, the professors of economics, the self-appraised experts in and out of Washington, D.C., the vocal, and the scribes all over the country were offering panaceas, analyzing and admonishing, but Montana cowmen suffered in silence as they sat it out. Not that they didn't talk things over among themselves. The Association continued to hold annual meetings and a program pattern of informative addresses made them worth attending, although membership was down again with some 40 per cent in arrears, a condition that was deplorable but not unusual.

Prefacing the spring meeting of 1922, held in Butte, grasshoppers had taken over during the previous summer, the winter had been a bad one, everyone was hard up, there was a shortage of cattle in the state, and prices were lower than the cost of production. This formidable situation led Association President Jack Burke to state, as an opener to a brief but masterly summary of existing conditions, "1921 will, I believe, stand in the stock history of Montana as the hardest year it has ever seen." He added a faint note of hope, ". . . but I believe we have not only reached the bottom rung but are once more climbing the ladder to better times."

He cited his belief that there was economic waste in a marketing system that sent Montana feeders to a distant point where shippers had to take what was offered them upon arrival, only to see men from the Corn Belt purchase them, the commission houses collecting fees from both Montana seller and grain-belt buyer. In many cases, the stock retraced a portion of their rail travel to reach the feed yards, a process that added cost and also disturbed the cattle. Jack's theory, and it had many supporters, was that "if the feeder and the producer could in some way organize and deal direct, it would save both of them a great deal of expense." Jack Burke was just a little ahead of his time.

In reference to the recent precarious state of stockmen's finances, President Burke said that "the banks had gone their limit and only through the cooperation of the government was a great disaster averted. The bankers of the state deserve the thanks of this association for the splendid manner in which they stood behind us during these trying times." He called attention to the unsatisfactory bounty laws and expressed himself in favor of all-out cooperation with that well-equipped and experienced agency, the U.S. Biological Survey. He decried the inequities in taxation of grazing land, attributing it, and the inflated values placed on all land in the state, to the craze for making little counties out of big ones, each new entity in the county field requiring revenue to pay its political officeholders.

On the subject of freight rates, Burke commented that

> possibly we of Montana . . . must go farther to reach a terminal market than any other area of the country that produces stock in the quantity that our state does. We are most unfortunately situated in this regard and therefore must constantly be on the alert lest freight rates or other impositions tend to stifle our industry.

He estimated that since June, 1918, the yearly advance in freight rates on cattle going to eastern markets was almost three quarters of a million dollars, and stated:

> You can see . . . the huge weight that those rates are around the necks of the Montana stockmen who are just now straining . . . to recoup their losses of the disastrous year of 1919 that left every stockman in the state, big or little, in mighty hard straits. Even without these high freight rates, the Montana stockman has sufficiently heavy burdens, in his efforts to rehabilitate the ranges and again get going in the stock business, to discourage any . . . group of men.

In commenting on the Association and on the members themselves, Jack Burke characteristically pulled no punches. He said:

The past year has been so hard on stockmen that very little has been done to push membership but I believe that stockmen cannot afford to be without an association in hard times more than in good. . . . I am not here to lecture you, but I can assure you that your officers have a pretty hard time creating any interest among stockmen. Some stockmen have the idea that you are pushing it for your own personal benefit and I get letters asking me, "What has the Association ever done for me?" This Association was formed by the amalgamation of the eastern and western stockgrowers' associations. The old-time stockmen knew the value of numbers, and that they would have greater strength and weight acting as one than as several small associations acting independently. The old saying "United we stand, divided we fall" remains true.

These remarks of the president are a good index to the prevailing atmosphere of the times. It was frustrating to Jack Burke, but fortunate for the Association, that his terms of office came during those discouraging depression years. With a lesser man in the lead, the Association might have disintegrated. As it was, Burke's sound judgment and dynamic personality bolstered lagging spirits and made the organization more valuable than ever to its members.

When the legislature of 1917 combined the Board of Stock Commissioners and the Board of Sheep Commissioners to form the Montana Livestock Board, Jack Burke was appointed president of the new body by the governor. Burke, Dr. William F. Cogswell, the president of the State Board of Health, and Dr. W. J. Butler, the state veterinarian surgeon, constituted the Livestock Sanitary Board, which was given new powers and duties. A diagnostic laboratory was authorized in Helena.

By 1922, through the close cooperation of an exceptionally talented and experienced staff, supported by the best livestock laws of any state, Montana had attained an enviable reputation for progressiveness and business administration in the nation's cattle industry. Dan Raymond had served as secretary of the Livestock Commission until his retirement in 1921, when he moved to the Madison Valley to manage cattle interests of his own. He was succeeded by Edwin A. Phillips. Dr. W. J. Butler was chief executive officer of the Livestock Sanitary Board; Dr. Emil Starz was in charge of the chemical laboratory; Dr. Hadleigh Marsh capably directed the bacteriology and pathology work. This exceptional team, with the backing of leading men of the industry who were serving on the board, made remarkable progress in the suppression and elimination of disease on ranch and range. The new board was not only of vast benefit to cattlemen, but its inspection and control of food products in the state performed a great public service. Not only was attention concentrated on livestock disease, its cure and prevention, but research was constantly in progress concerning such matters as diet and breeding.

The Act of 1921 provided that

> it shall be the duty of the Livestock Sanitary Board to supervise the sanitary conditions of livestock in Montana; to circumscribe, extirpate, control and prevent infectious and contagious diseases in livestock; to foster, promote, and protect the livestock industry in every way possible; to establish and maintain a laboratory; to define the standards for all dairy and meat food products; to issue dairy, creamery, and slaughter house licenses; to inspect all dairies, cheese factories, butter factories, condensed milk factories, ice cream factories, milk plants, receiving stations, slaughter houses, and meat depots, and to promulgate and enforce necessary regulations governing these duties.

Many parts of the Montana Livestock Sanitary Board law, and the regulations established by the board itself, became patterns for federal legislation and the laws and regulations of other states. All of this, of course, had been brought about by the stockmen themselves through the Montana Stockgrowers Association and was a pretty squelching answer to the gentlemen who wrote Jack Burke, asking, "What has the Association ever done for me?" No legislature would have bothered about cattlemen's difficulties and woes had the cattlemen not presented a united front and taken the initiative in the introduction and advocacy of bills for their own protection.

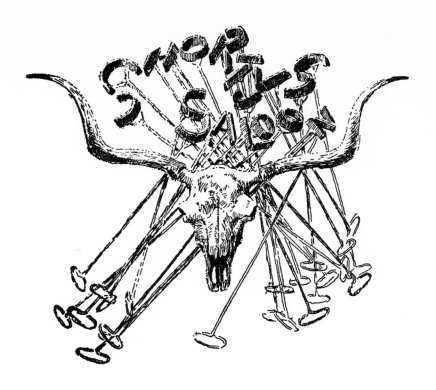

# 16. GUN SMOKE

Presidential candidate Warren G. Harding's campaign slogan in 1920 was "Back to Normalcy." It echoed the nation's desire to recover from the abnormalities imposed by World War I. In spite of victory for the Allies, the world had taken a beating. The return to civilian life of a generation that had been regimented in its formative years, the sudden industrial change that found factory capacity far in excess of consumer capacity and requiring conversion, a national debt that had been increased twentyfold in seven years, strikes, inflation, unemployment—all had disrupted social and economic standards in America to a point where a muddled public was in despair.

During the difficult, postwar period of readjustment, the War Finance Corporation, created in March, 1919, had functioned for about a year. Its activities were then suspended, only to be revived in the fall of 1921 because of credit emergencies engendered by a collapse of commodity markets. Its Agriculture Credits Section came to the rescue at a time when there was general demoralization in all branches of agriculture. Things were in a sorry plight. Among stockgrowers, breeding herds were being sacrificed at an appalling rate. To quote banker Trevor O. Hammond, of Helena: "There was forced liquidation and hasty selling, impaired buying power, and this in turn brought about a reduced demand for the products of industry. Bank deposits were being withdrawn and reserves depleted, and our whole banking structure was seriously threatened. Into this situation the War Finance Corporation brought the machinery which enabled the banks to extend credit to farmers and livestock men in general, with the result that prices immediately stiffened and a crisis was averted."

Out of the conditions of the day, there also came the privately owned and operated Montana Livestock Finance Corporation. It grew out of the need for an institution that could come to the relief of large livestock operators who were not eligible for loans through the government agencies. The larger banks of the state supplied 60 per cent of the required capital, but it will come as a surprise to the cattlemen of today to learn that the Corporation, from which there was little or no expectation of profit, really owes its existence to the generosity and loyalty to Montana industry of John D. Ryan, chairman of the board, and C. F. Kelley, president of the Anaconda Copper Mining Company, and John A. Spoor, president of the Union Stockyards of Chicago.

"Back to normalcy" was a laudable objective but it had not yet been achieved when the Montana Stockgrowers Association meeting of 1923 convened at Miles City on April 7. On the contrary, almost everyone present was despondent over what many called the deplorable condition of the industry. Everyone was hard up and to hell with it. They were ready to let the Livestock Commission have all the responsibility while the MSGA convention became a forum for casual exchange of views, a chance to meet old friends and get acquainted with new ones, and an opportunity either to support the Commission's achievements and policies or to kick about them. The market was still lower than the cost of production and the West was short of cattle, although the South and central states seemed to have plenty.

Nevertheless, Jack Burke, who was then completing his second year as president, didn't let the pessimists sing the blues for long. A splendid convention program took their minds off their troubles. At the opening of the meeting, Burke again sounded the right keynote by saying, "We all have a heavy grind ahead of us and it will be only by hard work and perseverance that the stock industry will ever get back on its feet."

Quite naturally, the return to Miles City prompted a bit of nostalgia and historical review by the speakers. A verbal tilt between Montana's attorney general, Wellington D. Rankin, and Samuel O. Dunn, of Chicago, representing the railroads, was hardly in that classification, although the bone of contention between them was an old one. Between them, they presented a pretty thorough analysis of the subject under rediscussion. The gist of Mr. Rankin's oration was that "the rates should be reduced." The nub of Mr. Dunn's speech was, "I could cite you many cases of railways which at this very time are actually tearing up their lines and going out of business, or seeking permission to do so, because they cannot make enough money to live."

Some of the cattlemen's other chronic worries had lessened, among them "Indian trouble." At the 1923 meeting, F. C. Campbell, superintendent of the Blackfeet Indian Reservation, in a talk entitled "Indian Reservations as They Concern the Livestock Situation in Montana," presented quite a different picture than that which had existed when red and white men were disputing the range. Emulating the stockgrowers, the Blackfeet Indians now had their own livestock association, divided into chapters under the guidance of such worthy chiefs as Bird Rattler, Feather Ear Rings, Black Weasel, and Aims Backwards. They solicited lessees for their surplus grazing land and, in extending an invitation for the stockmen to visit the tribe, Mr. Campbell said, "Our Indian people will welcome you and will be glad to show you the wonderful resources of their reservation." The Indians had not been as hospitable when uninvited whites were coveting their much larger grazing areas without the formality of a lease.

Predators, too, while not extinct, were not the individual or Association responsibility that they had once been. The U.S. Biological Survey had taken over with gratifying results. E. S. Piper, of Denver, speaking as a representative of the Survey, said:

> In view of the destruction by predatory animals in the states of the West, amounting to from twenty to thirty million dollars annually in livestock, correspondingly heavy loss in game, spread . . . of rabies among wild animals over a great part of the West, increasing appeals for assistance, and along with this a very evident lack of means to cope with the situation, the matter of predatory animal control takes on aspects of a special business—a business that not only warrants but demands every advantage of organization, of methods, and of persistence that can be brought to bear.
>
> Effectiveness of organized methods is best illustrated in the case of the big, gray wolf. Efforts have concentrated against this animal from the first. Just so far as means will permit, we have responded to appeals of stockmen and have kept hunters after these animals. I could take up the rest of the morning telling you stories of the killing of wolves and eradication of wolf packs. Among the wolves brought to an end are many of the worst animals that had become notorious through continuous depredations over periods of ten or twelve years, even with substantial prices on their heads. In some cases it has taken weeks, in others months, and in a few instances a year or more, to capture some particular wolf. Almost without exception, such work

has been carried out successfully and to the satisfaction and relief of stockmen.

Effective work has been done on gray wolves here in Montana. Certain large ranges have been entirely cleared of them. . . . General knowledge of the situation would place the number of wolves now at large in Montana at something more than two hundred and fifty. They are making their reappearance on certain ranges where organized work had all but eradicated them in 1918. . . . Little is accomplished by killing a few wolves out of a band, leaving enough to breed to full numbers again the next spring. Success in wolf work means everlastingly staying with it until the animals are eradicated. Records clearly prove that this task is best left to a reliable hunter, backed by the experience and methods of the Service, who can be definitely assigned to the job.

It began to look as though predators were about to join uncontrolled disease and wild Indians as worries of the past. But lest cowmen grow smug and carefree, new difficulties kept confronting them.

Again the resolutions committee of the Association ran the gamut from commendation to condemnation. Resolution No. 16 was unique. It made no bones about including every Montanan, beef eater or vegetarian, in its scope. It read:

> *Whereas* the livestock industry of the United States has bestowed more confidence and happiness upon a larger proportion of the inhabitants than any other industry known to civilization . . . an industry that converts the grass and moss and sagebrush and other vegetation, that would be otherwise worthless, into a palatable article of food and a staple article of clothing, and which not only materially increases the taxable valuation of the state but adds much to the grand sum total of human happiness and comfort. . . . Notwithstanding its importance to a commonwealth and the welfare of its people, it is buffeted and blown about by the winds of prejudice, politics, and speculation until its destruction seems certain.
>
> *Therefore it is Resolved,* That it is the opinion of this Association that the remedy lies in greater cooperation. That it is the duty of every man and woman in the State of Montana who is either directly or indirectly interested in the growing of livestock to become a member of the Livestock Association of Montana and also go further and become a member of the National Livestock Association, thereby lending his influence financially, socially, and politically to the upbuilding and maintenance of the industry.

With the adoption of this uninhibited declaration, the 1923 convention adjourned, to meet in Dillon the following year. President Jack Burke had been fatally injured in a car accident and C. M. Simpson occupied the chair. He introduced a new sentiment when he said:

Stockgrowers should use their influence in favor of fair treatment of the railways. My attitude towards the packers, stockyard companies, and the Livestock Exchange is the same as towards the railroads. They are the medium through which we market our livestock and I think we should refrain from constantly throwing a monkey wrench into the machinery of these organizations.

This fair and straightforward announcement was in contrast to the antagonistic, chip-on-the-shoulder attitude that had marked past dealings with the outfits to which Mr. Simpson referred. It was a refreshing change that indicated a better understanding of the other fellow's problems, and which might be attributed to the placing of their representatives on annual programs.

Things were still not too good in 1924. Bank failures had hurt during the past four years, yet everyone was feeling a bit encouraged. From the stockgrowers' angle, the cause of the tough years for them was summed up as overproduction due to the war; the competition of dairy stock, caused by the postwar demand for cheapness from a hard-hit public; the inferior quality of grass-fattened cattle, due to drouth and the resultant poor feed; the competition of cheap pork; imports from Canada; the excessive cost of production. But all that was now water over the dam. The first mention of baby beef or finished yearling was made at this meeting. Willard G. White, from Armour and Company at South St. Paul, said, "The future of the beef industry and the stimulation of beef consumption depend not on quantity production but on quality animals."

The year 1924 marked a radical change in method, from the maturing of four-year-old steers to the raising of feeders for the corn country—calves running from 300 to 400 pounds. As this phase took over, Montana stockgrowers encountered another hazard. They became dependent on feeder-belt conditions—weather and crop failure—as well as their own. Government controls were to come later as added complications but, in the meantime, the fortunes of Montana producers matched the resilience of the country's other industries and bounced back. By 1925, there was a predominant demand for baby beef in the markets. Everything looked brighter.

That August, President Herbert Hoover wrote Montana's former governor, Joseph Dixon, then Assistant Secretary of the Interior, about his plan to transfer surface rights of unreserved public domain "to state governments for public school purposes." Among the reasons given was this:

We must seek every opportunity to retard the expansion of federal bureaucracy and to place our communities in control of their own destinies. . . . The federal government is incapable of adequate administration of matters which require so large a matter of local understanding. . . . Therefore, for the best interest of the people as a whole and the people of the Western States and the small farmers and stockmen by whom they are primarily used, they should be managed and the policies of their use determined by the state government.

The winter of 1925–26 was a mild one. Spring found the range in excellent shape, the stock in better-than-average condition. The nation was riding the crest of the wave and everyone was speculating in stock—the kind that is bought and sold in Wall Street. Millionaires were being made by the minute—on paper.

Of more lasting importance to the West, several ranchers met that spring at Miles City with the Custer County extension agent, Paul Lewis, and E. W. Hall, agricultural agent of the Milwaukee Railway, to hash over the well-worn subject of played-out range. South of Miles City, between Mizpah Creek, tributary of the Powder River, and Pumpkin Creek, branch of the Tongue, there was a tract of over 100,000 acres of grazed-off, plowed-up, wind-blown land that had once been blanketed with good native grass, but was now taken over by sagebrush and prairie dog towns. The title to it was a balled-up mess of public domain, private, state, and railroad ownership.

Mr. Hall had not been indoctrinated with the belief that certain things just couldn't be done, such as fencing public domain with special permission from Congress to do so. He conceived the idea of the cattlemen owning land in or on the fringe of the Mizpah–Pumpkin Creek area forming an association, obtaining long-term leases on the seemingly worthless deeded acreage for fees sufficient to cover taxes; and inducing Congress to withdraw the public domain sections from right-of-homestead entry and permit the fencing of the block for private use. It seemed to be a large order, without much chance of having it filled.

Hall, Lewis, a rancher named Nick Monte, and A. A. Simpson, supervisor of the Custer National Forest, decided to tackle the job and their enthusiasm was contagious. Powwows were held and a plan worked out. A local association would be formed and given the responsibility for details of operation, while general policies would be in the hands of the Department of the Interior. Ranchers in or adjacent to the tract, who had sufficient land of their own and proper facilities along stream bottoms to carry stock for four months in winter, would be eligible for participation. Fifteen of them signed up.

Pumpkin Creek is a far cry from the Potomac, and how to convince skeptical Congressmen of the importance of this small, revolutionary plan for tampering with sacred public domain was the next hurdle. Montana's congressman, Scott Leavitt, was approached and he approved the scheme. He had been in the Forest Service at one time. The land classified as 25 per cent belonging to the Government; 41 per cent railroad land; 6 per cent owned by the State of Montana; and 28 per cent in private ownership. The railroads and private owners agreed to grant ten-year leases for just enough rental to cover taxes. The State Land Board turned control of its property over to the district association after an ineffectual attempt had been made to trade state sections for federal sections located elsewhere—something which was accomplished in 1929. The Department of the Interior agreed to lease the federally-owned land for $20 a section per annum, and rebate the first three payments if the money was used for range improvements.

Congressman Leavitt introduced a bill which passed the House of Representatives. There were objections raised, of course, but these were largely farfetched. For example, ranchers from other areas claimed discrimination and World War veterans didn't like the principle of withdrawing *any* land from homestead entry for the benefit of a few ranchers. Senator T. J. Walsh supported the bill after satisfying himself, through personal investigation, that it was meritorious. On March 29, 1928, it passed the Senate and so the first legally organized, cooperative grazing district in America was created.

A survey of local experts determined the carrying capacity of the district. They made a conservative estimate of not less than 3,000 cattle or more than 5,000, bearing in mind that the grass must be given a chance to come back. The project was fenced, a range rider hired, prairie dogs poisoned, reservoirs built, stock allotments and grazing fees fixed. At first the fees were set at $1.50 per head for eight months' grazing; this was later reduced to $1.25. The barren, sorry-looking range came to life with a carpet of grass. The Association discussed, and agreed upon, the number, type, and quality of bulls to be turned out and then purchased them cooperatively, each individual being assessed in proportion to the number of cows he grazed in the district. Project Mizpah-Pumpkin Creek was a success.

When prosperous stockmen met in Butte in the spring of 1929, the outlook was the best for years. Not only the governor of the state, but the governor of the Federal Reserve Bank in Minneapolis, railroad presidents, editors, and other VIPs were glad to accept invitations to address the cowhands. Hard times were forgotten. Association membership, which had dropped to 557 during 1924, was edging back up to par. A long-delayed action was taken; it was decided to hire a full-time secretary.

Association presidents, who were in closest touch with the accomplishments and possibilities of a close-knit, smooth-functioning machine were well aware of the advantages of such a move. Some problems had been licked or had become obsolete, but even more vexing ones were always taking their place. Nothing less than eternal vigilance was required to forestall and fend off threats and adverse actions that could, and did, originate at the most unexpected times and places. In a state the size of Montana, many stockgrowers of long acquaintance do not see one another for months at a time. Each is engaged in his own affairs, which necessitate daily thought and personal supervision. Vital as some matters of group interest may be, busy ranchers haven't the time to stand a day-in, day-out watch over mutual affairs. Nor has a part-time secretary. Volunteer minute men, pledged to spring into action upon sound of an alarm, can never render the same, steadfast service to a cause that can be expected from a trained and constantly on-the-alert force of paid professionals.

Both Jack Burke and Wallis Huidekoper were dynamic leaders who had long recognized the need for a full-time Association secretary. Burke expressed his sentiments at Miles City in the spring of 1923, when he said:

> We have funds enough at the present time to start a secretary out but how long he can last, I cannot say. A secretary who can serve this Association with any degree of efficiency has to be a man to whom you will have to pay some money. You can't hire him like a cowpuncher or a sheepherder. He won't work for that amount of money. He has to be an expert along many lines.

No decision was made at that meeting, but the idea was constantly in the minds of the Association officers and executive committee members. Secretaries Harrison, Preuitt, Wells, and Raymond had served well under different circumstances and conditions than the ones that prevailed in 1929. In their time, a membership of a few hundred had constituted a representative cross section of the range-cattle industry. Now times had changed. There were over 60,000 brands on record. The secretaryship of the Montana Stockgrowers Association was no job for a green hand. It required the talents of a financier, a coordinator, an expediter, a director of public relations, a legal adviser, a certified public accountant, an advertising manager, a cheerleader, a man of letters, a diplomat, and, after that, it was fairly desirable that he know a little something about cows. Such paragons are not easily found.

Edwin A. Phillips was a natural choice. Credit must be given to the wisdom of his sponsors for the further growth and strength of the Association. Mr. Phillips had grown up with Association affairs. He had worked for the Board of Stock Commissioners and for its successor, the Livestock Commission, under W. G. Preuitt and Dan Raymond, taking Raymond's place as secretary upon his resignation. He had served as acting secretary for the Association since 1921. His past experience, his familiarity with the history and personnel of the cattle business and its allied industries, and his genial personality were potent recommendations. Even for such a highly qualified person the work was no sinecure. Phillips accepted the position of full-time secretary in 1929, and was immediately confronted with a double-barreled task—to increase membership in order to finance his office and to produce a progressive program that would attract new members. The two items were interdependent.

Letter writing and personal visits were not enough to alter established routine. While there was not absolute apathy among the rank and file of membership, neither was there great enthusiasm. A medium of mass communication was needed. Ed Phillips achieved this by starting an official monthly publication, appropriately dubbed *The Montana Stockgrower*. To gauge the reaction of the membership, he first launched a modest four-page bulletin, published September 1, 1929. It met with immediate favor and he thereupon dove into the salty and ofttimes stormy sea of editorial responsibility with all the professional swimming style of an Olympic champion.

What counted, however, was results—membership results, for one thing —and Phillips got them. The four pages expanded to eight, to twelve, to twenty-four, and even to a giant ninety-two-page issue on May 15, 1947. The first eighteen issues carried no paid advertising. There were only approximately 250 members [1] receiving the bulletin and advertisers like impressive circulation figures. In the March, 1931, issue, four commission houses took a total of one and three-quarter pages and this broke the ice. From then on the paper was self-supporting. In the big edition of 1947, published just prior to the annual convention, there were over seventy-three full pages of paid advertising, covering the field from banks, boots, and bulls to serum, stallions, and stockyards.

In September, 1929, at the Salt Lake City conference of western governors, President Hoover reaffirmed his belief that "western states are today more competent to manage their affairs than is the federal government." In support of Mr. Hoover's opinion, the membership of a Committee on Conservation and the Administration of Public Domain was announced in October, its purpose to study the question implicit in its name. Under President Hoover's plan, the federal government would turn over to individual states the control of all surface rights to public domain within their boundaries, except national parks and forests. At that time there were over 6,500,000 acres of public domain in Montana, exclusive of national parks, forests, reservations, and other withdrawals. The total federally-held land amounted to 45,310,000 acres, or about half of the state's area.

The committee worked diligently to secure a cross section of public sentiment. It found opinions diverse and conflicting, even among stockmen. The committee was certainly no catalyst to speed up harmonious reaction. The U.S. Forest Service went to great lengths to discredit transfer of pub-

[1] In 1955, Swift & Company celebrated its centennial and gave plaques to eleven people in the United States who had made valuable and consistent contributions to the livestock industry. E. A. Phillips was selected as one of these. Under his secretaryship, the membership of the Montana Stockgrowers Association increased from 250 to more than 4,000.

lic domain to the states, even though forests were exempted. Actually, they wanted to increase forest areas by millions of acres. The President's plan for transfer was backed by the Department of the Interior, which exercised jurisdiction over public domain. It was recommended by the Committee. It was endorsed by stockmen's associations. It was supported by the legislative assembly of Montana. Yet, after a bill was introduced in Congress to effect such transfer, the whole ill-starred effort finally joined the other ghosts of defunct legislative measures.

# 17. BOOM AND BUST

The skyrocketing boom that took the nation to dizzy heights of unstable affluence fizzled out and plunged to rock bottom at the close of 1929. It brought unemployment, followed by poverty. It cut the props of prosperity out from under every market. The vast oversupply of food commodities caused a break in prices as dealers hastened to reduce inventories. There was nothing temporary about it. It kept up for year after year until it became an abyss instead of a depression. At the start of the 1930's, confidence in cattle-trade circles was at low ebb. With a past history of mercurial ups and downs, cattlemen's hopes waned again. Drouth ruined the range and when it seemed as though cattle prices could go no lower, they would drop another notch.

The rapidity with which the outlook and fortunes of stockmen can change is astounding. The record of the thirties is one of toil and trouble, mixed with spurts of contrasting prosperity. In 1931, half of Montana's counties were seeking or accepting Red Cross help. For awhile the price of beef was high on retail counters although the price received by producers dropped to a discouraging low. Cattlemen were looking for cost-cutting measures as shock absorbers for declining prices. The housewives blamed the high retail price of beef on the stockgrower and turned to cheaper substitutes. Again the cattleman became the "greedy cattle baron" in the public mind, and he didn't like it.

When he complained, retailers suavely explained the price inequality by asserting that their overhead had remained at the same level despite the nose dive on Wall Street. They claimed that there was always a lag between a live-product price fluctuation and the retail price, a lag that took time to adjust, but they were vague as to how much time was needed. Furthermore, they said, their basis of profit was gauged as an exact percentage of gross sales and if they reduced prices they would disturb the balance. This gobbledegook was difficult for hard-hit stockgrowers to follow. They had small chance to defend themselves with the housewife by refuting the specious reasoning of the retailers, who talked to the lady on the telephone or across the counter every day. The high retail price did not benefit the producer at all. On the contrary, it brought him only condemnation, and housewives used beef substitutes in even greater quantities. So when the Montana rancher began to have too many cattle on his hands and no way to get rid of them without loss, it was said to be "not a question of overproduction but one of declining consumption."

All of this had one stimulating effect on the thinking of a great many cattlemen. They knew that the nation was accustomed to a liberal meat diet under normal circumstances and that it could, and would, eat all the meat that the country could produce. There had been no appreciable exports of live cattle or of beef for twenty years except during World War I. Home demand had equaled home supply for, by the same token, tariffs had reduced imports of live cattle, dressed, and canned beef to negligible quantities. Now they began to suspect that they should take an active interest in what happened to the price of beef all the way from grass range to kitchen range, and to realize that stockgrowing was no longer the simple process indicated in the lines from "The Chisholm Trail": "We rounded 'em up and we put 'em on the cars / And that was the last of the old Two Bars."

It was beginning to dawn on the thoughtful that the cow industry was now full of intricacies of diet for both humans and the critters themselves. The consumer's unexplainable switching from a gourmand's demand for huge, full-flavored porterhouse steaks to a gourmet's preference for delicate, bland *filet mignon* had created a market-requirement change from heavy carcasses to baby beef almost faster than the stockgrower could keep up with it. Members of the industry wondered if there wasn't some way to attain a form of market stability that would do away with extreme price fluctuations. If a price range could be established within sensible limits that would yield a reasonable profit, yet not discourage consumption, it would take some of the grief and uncertainty out of stock raising.

Stockmen who had given the subject any thought at all were reaching the conclusion that the job of finding and maintaining an ideal, knife-edge balance in the price range was a stunt for professional equilibrists trained in research, in the interpretation of trends, their causes and effects, and in the art of good public relations. There were such complications to consider as the competition of lamb, poultry, and even fish; the eating habits of our increasing and fickle population; the effect of faddist cults and magazine articles on diet. But all of this would have to come later in less parlous times. Right now, with the depression closing in tighter and tighter, the average cattleman's sole objective was to keep out of the poorhouse by cutting expenses and hoping that people would eat more beef, of any age or grade.

When the shoe began to pinch in 1931, Association dues were cut 40 per cent and every appeal was made to the membership to keep the organization intact and functioning. In the absence of President George Clemow, who was desperately ill, Vice President Julian Terrett presided at the Great Falls meeting, which convened May 25, 1932. He dismissed ill-omened 1931:

> To recount the events of the last year calls up no pleasant memories. Depression, with its resulting shrink in assets; drouth, which made necessary the liquidation of many herds at prices that were little short of ruinous to their owners; and the serious expense involved in buying feed to winter a remnant with which to continue business, are not pleasing facts to dwell upon. Stockmen can only remember 1931 as a year of disaster. We can thank Providence that it is past.

How reminiscent of Jack Burke's talk at the 1922 meeting!

But the end was not yet. In 1932 and 1933 it rained a little—not really enough, but some. Except for that brief interim, drouth kept a strangle hold on the parched land for the rest of the decade. Stockmen were to continue grasping at every opportunity to procure cash and credit to pull them through. Paradoxically, in the midst of a national crisis when people didn't have enough to eat, surpluses of food products were building up, among them Montana beef on the hoof.

In the fall of 1932 the Helena branch of the Spokane Regional Agriculture Credit Corporation was opened, with H. H. Piggot as manager. Within a month, 1,669 applications for loans had been made by Montana stockmen, aggregating $7,371,157.22, and seventy field inspectors were at work examining and reporting on collateral. There is a tribute to Montana stockmen in the statistics for the period 1932–1936. Thirty-three million dollars was loaned to them with an eventual loss of less than one-third of one per cent whereas in other states the government took a terrific licking.

Times were so hard that Secretary Phillips took a job with the "Regional" in 1933 and voluntarily reduced his Association salary by the amount he was paid by the corporation. The distress of unemployment prevailed everywhere. The New Deal administration was frantically experimenting in the field of economics. Alphabetical administrations were piled on top of bemused bureaus, but subnormal consumer buying remained unchecked. On the meager family menus, cheap beef continued to be rejected for cheaper substitutes. From 1928 to 1933, the average ranch value of beef cattle dropped 61 per cent. What with the attempted control of the law of supply and demand by the Agricultural Adjustment Administration, the beef cattle industry was being adjusted into a jam. Corn in sealed cribs flattened the market for feeder stock and forced cattlemen to liquidate their herds.

In the fall of 1933 Harry L. Hopkins, Federal Emergency Relief Administrator, with the concurrence of Secretary of Agriculture Henry A. Wallace and the AAA, announced a plan for feeding the destitute unemployed and, at the same time, reducing the surpluses that were keeping the prices of farm products at low levels. As things were going with the cattle business in Montana, the state would have entered the winter with a surplus of over 360,000 head. Competition in the beef market from culls of dairy herds was making the situation impossible for Montana breeders. State Veterinarian Surgeon Butler said:

> The statement that the prosperity and successful continuation of a basic industry, that of stockgrowing, is at stake is not an exaggeration. The fact that millions of human beings in these United States are without sufficient food to continue in normal health, and that basic industries of food production are facing ruin by reason of a surplus, is an appalling fact and certainly one that does not reflect credit upon civilization.

The Hopkins program included the purchase and distribution of substantial quantities of range cattle of cutter and canner grade. A minimum of $10,000,000, if not double that sum, was to be used for buying, processing, and free distribution of beef from 200,000 to 400,000 cattle. Secretary F. E. Mollin, of the American National Livestock Association, did much to foster this plan of double-barreled assistance to those in dire need—the stockgrowers and the hungry public. The Montana Stockgrowers Association supported the plan and wired Washington, suggesting that it might be consistent for the government to buy Montana beef for Montana needy instead of shipping in pork from other states.

Hard-working Secretary Mollin was swamped with depression developments aside from routine matters of tariff and traffic. There were questions involving Canadian and Mexican imports; proposed regulation of

trucking which might freeze the high-level rail rates; the proposed regulation of how and where livestock must be marketed; the battle with the
dairy people who wanted complete prohibition of the sale of oleomargarine.
Four per cent of the live weight of cattle slaughtered under government
supervision was edible fat, and of the hundreds of millions of pounds annually produced, a large percentage was going to the soap manufacturers
at lower prices than if used in a food product. Also, leather substitutes were
on the market and the American National Livestock Association demanded
that they be labeled as such; the Army contemplated the purchase of great
quantities of foreign beef for use in the Philippines; there were troubles
with the U.S. Forest Service. Sharpshooters sniped at the cow industry from
every side and it took aggressive counterattacking to stand them off.

In 1934 the overwhelming drouth in Montana took a hand in adding
irritant to cowland's festering woes. At the end of the year, the AAA allotted sufficient funds for government purchase of 125,000 head of cattle in the
state. By June, 1935, the federal government, as an emergency measure,
had bought over 8,000,000 head in the general national program. It was
monkeying with the buzz saw of economics, but the purchase, plus the heavy
commercial slaughter occasioned by the drouth, reduced the national cattle
inventory to a point where the bugaboo of overproduction would not haunt
producers for some years to come. The government bought at an average
of $13.40 per head. In view of range conditions, the sale at such depressed
prices was more an act of mercy to the cattle than one of financial benefit
to the stockgrower.

The highlight of an otherwise bad year for cattlemen (1934) was the
Taylor Grazing Act, passed and approved by the federal government that
summer. The first break in federal resistance to leasing public domain to
stockmen came with the Mizpah–Pumpkin Creek Grazing District. It had
taken such a departure from precedent to activate the pilot grazing district
of the West, and the Taylor Grazing Act unquestionably received impetus
from the successful experiment.

The act was named for its sponsor, Edward T. Taylor, Congressional
representative from Colorado, and was patterned after a similar bill introduced in 1932 by Congressman Don Colton of Utah. Of the Colton bill,
Chief Forester Stuart had said that it encompassed "reasonable provisions
for the conservation of the industry dependent upon that resource [grass]."
The Taylor Act's purpose, as set forth in its title, was "to stop injury to the
public grazing lands by preventing overgrazing and soil deterioration, to
provide for their orderly use, improvement and development, to stabilize
the livestock industry dependent upon public range, and for other purposes."

Major John Wesley Powell's advice came too early; this action came
almost too late. But considering former general conceptions of western stockgrowers as avid, lawless cattle kings, it was astounding to have a federal act

concede that the "livestock industry, dependent upon public range," needed and deserved help. The Secretary of the Interior was given authority to set up grazing districts on unappropriated public domain; he was also given authority to enter into agreements with local grazing associations anywhere in the United States, and to withdraw from homestead entry land that he deemed chiefly valuable for grazing and raising forage crops when they were needed for grazing districts. The provisions of the act were calculated to give satisfaction and equitable treatment to all settlers, residents, and livestock owners in the vicinity of a district.

In the fall of 1934 the remaining public domain lands were withdrawn or reserved for disposition, pending their classification. This withdrawal served to preclude further stock-raising homesteads of the 640-acre type, first authorized for Nebraska and afterwards extended to other western states. It is still possible, however, to file on lands under the Enlarged Homestead Act, providing that, before the homestead is allowed, the land has been classified as suitable for the production of crops on a sustained-yield basis in sufficient amount to support a farm family. The amount of such land left in the West is negligible.

Shortly after approval of the Taylor Grazing Act, Assistant Secretary of the Interior Oscar L. Chapman, Denver attorney, met with two hundred Montana cattle and sheep men in Billings for a general discussion of the Act, its implications and its applications to their range difficulties. The conference was one of several held at the instigation of Secretary Harold Ickes, to get the advice and suggestions of local supervisory boards made up of cattle and sheep men directly interested in the leases and permits that were to be issued. A committee of the American National Livestock Association met in Denver to formulate other ideas pertinent to the Grazing Act.

Under the existing conditions, it took much courage for Miles City to undertake the role of host to the Golden Jubilee meeting of the Montana Stockgrowers Association. The city played its part with verve and vigor. The Golden Jubilee issue of the Miles City *Daily Star,* Thursday, May 24, 1934, paid tribute to the occasion in eight special sections. Editor Joseph D. Scanlan didn't overlook an angle. Starting with page one of the general news section, which featured a four-column cartoon by western artist Jim Masterson, it grudgingly accorded some space to national topics but ignored the depression. Louisiana peace officers had just thoroughly perforated out-law Clyde Barrow and his cigar-smoking lady friend, Bonnie Parker; rioting strikers in Toledo and Minneapolis had made it necessary to call out the National Guard in both cities; attorney Clarence Darrow and militant Hugh Johnson were exchanging verbal clouts over the "Blue Chicken" (NRA); Governor Joe Dixon had just died; politically-nimble Burton K. Wheeler was campaigning for his third term with the all-inclusive slogan "For Roosevelt, bi-metallism, for recovery, but with necessary reform"; the Hansen

Packing Company of Butte had filed a $6 million suit in federal court against Swift and Company, alleging "unlawful and ruinous competition."

Of such mundane matters was the general news. Having attended to it in the line of duty, editors, reporters, and readers were preoccupied with things of local moment. From there on to page 184, cowmen, cowbelles, and cowland took over. On the streets, store fronts were transformed into log structures. Saddle horses stood at hitching rails. Ox-teams, chuck wagons, stage coaches, and fringed surreys replaced banned automobiles. Whiskers and whiskey flowed freely. The Stockyards Post of the American Legion sent their kiltie band of pipers to accompany the Chicago Union Stockyards delegation, whose heads were bloody but unbowed from the disastrous fire that had swept the stockyards a few days earlier, destroying the Drovers' National Bank, the Exchange building, the Stockyard Inn, the Saddle and Sirloin Club's gallery of three hundred life-size oils, and the International Livestock building.

The Sioux City Stockyards Company and members of the Exchange brought the famous Abu-Bekr Shrine Temple mounted patrol by special train—thirty-two perfectly matched white Arabians and their riders. There were burros, bands, barbecues, drum corps, choruses, cavalry, Indians, cowhands, honkytonks, and parades. Never had beer been delivered with a greater flourish than when the Anheuser–Busch eight-horse hitch rolled out the barrels. Never had the traditional roast pig of the Miles City Club been more succulent. There was business, too. Perhaps not business as usual, but of a serious bent, nevertheless.

After President Wallis Huidekoper brought the initial session to order by swinging the butt end of a braided quirt in lieu of a gavel, he set the tempo of the times for Montana stockmen by saying:

Nineteen thirty-three was a year of hardship and tribulation. Prices were lower than for a quarter of a century. . . . Until we get the general mass of working men at steady, remunerative employment, we are not going to have a much higher cattle market. We must reduce our output where possible, keep our costs at rock bottom, better our herds in quality, and sit tight, for brighter days will surely come to us once again.

# 18. DROUTH, DEPRESSION, DISEASE

President Huidekoper's prediction of better times was premature. In 1935 25 per cent of Montana's population were on relief. The country continued in the throes of political experimentation. C. J. Abbott, of Hyannis, Nebraska, addressed the MSGA convention of 1935, held at Great Falls. He was a member of the Committee of Five of the American National Livestock Association, appointed to keep an eye on the "avalanche of emergency legislation" in Washington, D.C. He told the stockmen that

perhaps the most significant of the so-called "New Deal" controls is its control of agriculture. In this industry, the Agricultural Adjustment Administration is in the process of socializing by peaceful revolution the six million farm units. We of the cattle industry are told that the cattle cycle and the drouth are the ancient nemesis of the cattlemen and that periodically we must expect one or the other to strike us—either the weary, hopeless cycle of overproduction, normally recurring every fourteen years, resulting in the end in forced liquidation at bankrupt prices, or the shortage of feed that causes high feed prices, distorts the feed-beef ratio, and denies a profit. This is the argument advanced by the Administration, urging cattlemen to join this peaceful, socialistic revolution, which may be termed collectivism.

Being individualists of a pronounced type, western stockgrowers have not taken kindly to the theory of federal subsidies, especially after the examples of its folly that grew out of the economic chaos that spawned the NRA and the AAA.

At this time, an added cause of worry for leaders of state and national Association affairs was the threat of an agreement, under consideration in Washington, between the President and the Argentine Ambassador. Its ratification by the Senate would permit the importation of fresh beef from parts of the Argentine adjudged free from contagious animal disease, although at the time there were outbreaks of foot-and-mouth disease on the pampas. American cattle growers, knowing the ravages of that disease and the difficulty of controlling it, to say nothing of eradicating it, urged their associations to protest vigorously. There was a Roosevelt in the White House, but not the one who sometimes bent a sympathetic ear to the trouble of his range pals of the booming eighties.

Association members were also warned to take cognizance of a trade agreement that was under consideration in Canada. As long as the United States was capable of furnishing an adequate supply of beef to its citizens, there seemed to be no necessity for importations from our northern neighbor that might lead Mexico and other countries to demand like consideration.

That summer (1935), the Big Wind hit the High Line, searing hot out of the west. It drove topsoil to enrich farms and darken skies somewhere back east. In northeastern Montana, fences, buildings, and tombstones were buried by the drifting subsoil. In the fall, cattle prices were at attractive levels, providing a stockman had any marketable cattle left. Some of them did and were in the best position they had held for years. Cattle loan agencies reported full payment of a large volume of paper that had looked like a total loss the year before. Association dues began coming in from delinquent members. Recovery seemed on its way. Perhaps that is why Secretary Phillips found it necessary to issue repeated warnings to members not to make sales to unscrupulous direct buyers who invaded the ranches, telling glib stories of falling prices and other false data that sometimes persuaded a rancher to make a deal, to his great regret. Occasionally, drafts on commission houses had been returned unhonored.

The respite was brief. At the opening of the 1936 Association convention in Billings, President Joe Metlen said, "Business conditions are decidedly better the country over. There are ample supplies of cattle and the outlook is that there are ample supplies of feed. . . ." Metlen was whistling in the dark. The woeful plight of industry, general unemployment, and the weather continued to punish the country at large, the weather concentrating on the West. Thirty-nine of Montana's fifty-six counties were declared drouth areas. Ranchers were getting little solace out of broadcasted fireside talks. In the fall a hearing was held in Helena by the Interstate Commerce Commission on an application filed by the Montana Railroad Commission for lowering rates on cottonseed cake and other concentrated livestock foods for those stricken areas.

The Western and Southern Trunk Line Companies made a voluntary reduction of 33⅓ per cent on the through rate from southern states to points in Montana within the designated drouth area. Governor W. Elmer Holt, nephew of J. M. Holt of early association days, appointed a rail rate committee for each of the drouth counties. Without exception, one or more members of the three-man committees were Association members. So critical was the drouth that the use of Russian thistle was contemplated as an emergency feed.

Various bureaus, departments, administrations, and even individuals in the Department of Agriculture were still taking a hack at western land in one way or another. No item was too small to receive the attention of alleged experts, advisory boards, inspectors, and the time and effort devoted to writing and printing bulletins were only exceeded by that required to supplement and revise them.

On page 7 of the October 10, 1936, issue of *The Montana Stockgrower,* an eager cowman could learn something about the range program under the Soil Conservation and Domestic Allotment Act as approved by Secretary of Agriculture Henry A. Wallace, as set forth in bulletins just received by the editor. For example: "Pursuant to the authority vested in the Secretary of Agriculture under Section 8 of the Soil Conservation and Domestic Allotment Act, *Western Region Bulletin No. 2—Montana—1, revised, and now supplemented,*" the avid agrarian and keeper of livestock was told that a "payment of 60¢ would be made for each acre furrowed on the contour, furrows to be not less than 8 inches in width and 4 inches in depth, dammed at intervals of not more than 100 feet and constructed on slopes in excess of 2% with intervals between the furrows not more than 25 feet." A conscientious plowman would have equipped himself with a micrometer and a pair of calipers.

If the bulletin reader did not care for sod-busting of such a meticulous type, he could collect a payment of 30¢ per rod for the construction of "three or more wire fences" (which, presumably, meant three or more *wires,* not fences) "with posts not more than 20 feet apart, with corner posts well braced and wires tightly stretched." There were other equally attractive deals, most of them new, and of course there were conditions governing payments. None could be made unless the county committee had given its written approval, based upon examination of the ranching unit by the range examiner to make sure "that such practice will tend to effectuate the purpose of the Act." By that time the rancher might have lost interest and started reading further. If so, he would learn that,

> Pursuant to the authority vested in the Secretary of Agriculture under Section 8 of the Soil Conservation and Domestic Allotment Act, the following instructions are issued to supplement the provisions of Part VII of *Western Region Bulletin No. 1 Revised,* and the provisions of *Western Region Bulletin No. 2 (as supplemented with respect to range land for each state in the Western Region),* in connection with the effectuation of the purposes of Section 7 (a) of said Act of 1936.

If this left him glassy-eyed because he had mislaid Part VII of *Bulletin No. 1* and had perhaps effectuated the building of a fire in the kitchen range with Section 7(a) out of the supplement to the supplement to *Bulletin No. 2,* all was not lost. By persistently reading further he would learn the following:

> Within 15 days after the date of the mailing of a completed copy of Form WR-16 to the operator, the latter may appeal in writing to the County Committee for reconsideration of its recommendations with respect to grazing capacity and approved range building practices, stating in full the reasons for such appeal; if no revision is approved by the County Committee or if the revision approved by the Committee is unsatisfactory to the operator, an appeal may be made to the State Committee in accordance with the provisions of *Supplement (c), Western Region Bulletin No. 3.*

Then all he needed to do, "after assignments of grazing capacity had been determined in accordance with the foregoing," was to prepare the Listing Sheet Assignments of Grazing Capacity (Form WE-17) in quadruplicate, the original and two copies being forwarded, after approval of the County Committee, to the State Committee. It was as easy as that. He could keep the fourth copy as a souvenir, or use it in the little house out back.

The tangle of red tape did not deter 3,500 to 4,000 Montana stockmen from making application for participation in the 1936 Range Improvement Program. Reservoir construction to trap surface runoff and the development of springs and seeps as insurance against water shortage were its major projects. In the meantime, Nick W. Monte, now administrator of the Montana State Grazing Commission, and Secretary Phillips, of the Montana Stockgrowers Association, made a trip to Washington, where they worked with the Department of the Interior and got an approved cooperative agreement for Montana from the Administrator of the Taylor Grazing Act.

Under the stimulus furnished by western stockmen, the Taylor Grazing Act had begun functioning; in 1936 there were thirty-four going districts in ten Western states, utilizing 80,000,000 acres of public domain. Fifteen thousand grazing leases had been issued, 94 per cent of them to cattlemen with fewer than five hundred head of cattle—a convincing refutal of oft-repeated allegations that the districts would benefit large operators only.

Julian Terrett, twice president of the Montana Stockgrowers Association, resigned that office in 1936 to accept an appointment as first assistant to Ferrington R. Carpenter, Director of Grazing, who administered the Taylor Act. F. R. Carpenter was a practical man familiar with grazing problems of the range and he was ably seconded by Terrett, whose experience in the practice of law and grassroot education in the range-cattle business made him eminently qualified for his new post. Both men were naïve in one respect, however. They thought their government operation would require just a few competent employees and a modest budget. When the bill was being prepared, Secretary Ickes estimated that the lands involved could be administered for $150,000 a year. Actually, the cost increased year after year until it rose to over $1,000,000 per annum.

In 1935 some proposed amendments to the Taylor Grazing Act included increasing the public domain included in the grazing districts from 80,000,000 to 142,000,000 acres, there being applications for grazing districts in that amount on file; specifying that assistant grazing directors be residents of the states in which their jurisdiction was located; giving preference to men with actual range experience; providing for the transfer to various Western states of all isolated tracts of public domain not sold, leased, or included in grazing districts or marked for exchange in the next two years. President Roosevelt and the Department of the Interior objected to these amendments, and they were killed by Presidential veto. Director Carpenter fathered the idea of district advisory boards, and incorporated that principle in the regulations of the Grazing Service. The Taylor Grazing Act was later amended to make advisory boards mandatory, thereby eliminating the chance that a Secretary of the Interior might dispense with them.

During the time required for land classification and the preliminary studies needed to get the Grazing Act in the groove, temporary grazing permits without fee were issued for use of public lands. An administrative organization, known as the Grazing Service, was formed to carry out the details of grazing permits, eligibility of district members, preference rights, fees, range capacity, length of grazing season, and to formulate rules and regulations, subject, of course, to the approval of the Secretary of the Interior. Security of tenure was of vital importance to prospective permittees. Every effort was made to foresee all possible contingencies and to forestall misunderstandings and conflict between unallied interests.

The 1935 state legislature, recognizing the value of the grazing district principle, created a Montana Grazing Commission, but left it without funds. The commission's primary functions were (1) to assure uniformity of practice among grazing districts incorporated under the laws of Montana, (2) to assume jurisdiction over disputes arising between members or districts, (3) to make it easier to arrive at full agreement with the Director of Grazing under the Taylor Act. Such problems as the most economic use of grazing areas, uniform rules of issuing permits, amount of fees, and a dozen other matters were sure to come up in each district, and the state commission was to act as their mentor and arbiter. In short, the law gave it authority "to do any and all things necessary to accomplish a sound administration of grazing areas in Montana." It was a sweeping assignment, the actual working of which was to be imposed on a State Grazing Administrator, to be appointed by the governor.

As for the districts, three or more stockgrowers were given the privilege of incorporating a cooperative grazing district for a period of not to exceed forty years, "for the utilization, conservation, restoration, and improvement of forage resources on their lands and land to be acquired by purchase or lease." It was to be a nonprofit venture. The corporation could lease county land taken for taxes, U.S. land, state and private property. Grazing rights were to be apportioned to each member, and in the issuance of grazing permits preference was to be accorded those within or near a district.

Nick Monte, a prime assistant in the promotion of the Mizpah–Pumpkin Creek District, was one of the commissioners. He drew up a model constitution and by-laws for the proposed districts. As there was no money to put the legislation into gear, the State Water Conservation Board finally agreed to finance the penniless Commission, providing that Mr. Monte would take on the administration of the districts. He reluctantly agreed to do so for six months, and wound up serving for two years. Among his other accomplishments of that period, he succeeded in reducing, through mergers, the number of districts that were organized, from ninety-five to less than twenty. He also collaborated with Mel Williams, a young attorney with the Soil Conservation Service, in rewriting a state grazing district law that had been submitted and passed at the 1937 legislative session, only to be vetoed by Governor Roy Ayers. The revised bill, with minor amendments, was passed and became law in 1939. Nick Monte joined the Federal Grazing

Service in the fall of 1937, to spend many years in important administrative positions in Montana, Oregon, Nevada, and California before retiring to his present home near Miles City.

Having successfully staved off an attack made by the Montana Educational Association and the Commissioner of State Lands on the reduction of state land-lease fees two years before, the Montana Stockgrowers Association now had to combat the attorney general in 1937 on the question of renewing the reduction for another three years. The attorney general challenged the extension as unconstitutional, and suit was brought by the State Land Board to enjoin the State Land Office from issuing the extensions. The Supreme Court upheld the validity of the reduction and the extension.

As a precaution against shenanigans, Association members were warned not to let the Land Office persuade them to accept a new five-year lease in lieu of the three-year extension. Such leases carried a joker, applied with a rubber stamp and worded as follows: "The right is hereby reserved by the state to cancel and terminate this lease at the end of any rental year in case the state desires to exchange the land with the United States or lease it to a state cooperative grazing association."

The Battle of the Argentine Menace continued in 1937. Stockmen still valiantly opposed the Presidential and State Department overtures to the South Americans. They held that any diplomatic gains might be made at the cost of a national disaster to the livestock industry. Not only were cattle highly susceptible to foot-and-mouth disease, but the danger extended to every cloven-footed animal. State Veterinarian Surgeon W. J. Butler had this to say:

> We do know that foot-and-mouth disease is prevalent in the Argentine and other countries of South America. . . . these countries do not attempt to control this disease in the same manner that it has been controlled in the United States. If that disease became rooted in Montana and other Western states, the economic production of livestock in these states would be a thing of the past. I do not know a single sanitary officer in the United States or Canada who does not view with alarm and apprehension the letting down of the sanitary bars now in existence governing the shipment of livestock and livestock products from any country where foot-and-mouth disease exists. We appeal in no uncertain terms to our Senators and Congressmen to fight to the last ditch the proposed treaty, or any proposed resolution or law that will lessen the disease control restrictions which now govern the importation of livestock or meat and meat products into the United States.

Militant F. E. Mollin, secretary of the American National Livestock Association, informed all and sundry as follows:

American livestock producers have served notice that they are not willing to subject their herds and flocks to the menace of foot-and-mouth disease in order to fulfill Secretary Hull's and the President's ill-conceived ambitions for the betterment of our relations with Argentina. It is all right to be a "good neighbor" but the livestock industry doesn't approve of carrying it to such a ridiculous degree.

Aside from this major threat, 1937 troubles at home appeared to be confined to trivial matters. The bounty on coyote hides inspired a skin game very profitable to Cree Indians residing on the Rocky Boy Reservation near Havre. The pelt of a coyote pup brought just as much bounty as that of a full-grown bitch or dog coyote. This gave the Indians an idea. Instead of cleaning out a den when they found one, they permitted litters to mature in order to keep the coyote business on a going basis. By stretching a bull gopher hide and messing it up with crankcase oil, they could produce a reasonable facsimile of a coyote pup pelt. Fastidious county authorities gave the bedraggled hides only a cursory inspection when submitted for bounty payment. Collections by the Indians were reaching fancy proportions. The abnormal drain on the bounty funds in Liberty and Hill Counties interested the State Board of Examiners from a biological as well as a financial point of view. Such coyote fecundity didn't make sense. The consequent investigation exposed the lucrative experiment in coyote conservation. The Indians lost interest.

President Tom Ross, of Chinook, enumerated other minor difficulties at the April, 1937, MSGA meeting in Bozeman. He intimated that the membership might look forward to the customary natural hazards of the stockgrowing business, plus a few more. He cited recent enactments of the legislature, the need for orderly marketing, advertising, and more efficient distribution of beef and beef products. Drouth and insect damage were problems, too. Drouth continued throughout the summer, with a serious depletion of water supplies. Eastern Montana was practically out of the cattle business and the ground was alive and shimmering with grasshoppers and Mormon crickets. At the close of the year, the editor of *The Montana Stockgrower* was still writing about "Monday market gluts" and that will-o'-the-wisp "orderly marketing," which market diagnostician Jim Poole declared to be "the need of the hour."

Montana cowmen had long been accustomed to such difficulties and when 1938 rolled around, they joined right heartily in the Eat More Beef campaign initiated by the Institute of American Meat Packers and the National Livestock and Meat Board. The Board, a nonprofit organization serving the nation's livestock and meat industry, was formed in 1923 by representatives of all branches of the industry. Its purpose was "to initiate and encourage education and research with regard to livestock and meat products and to disseminate correct information about meat and its relations to health and to do all things necessary to promote the interests of the live-stock and meat industry."

Whether it was the effect of the eat-more-beef campaign or the law of supply and demand, the cattle business was booming in July, with the Corn Belt demanding more feeder stock. Employment increase was coupled with huge government spending, and once more Sir Loin was in public favor. It was a shame to disturb the brief serenity that pervaded cowland, but Association officials had no compunction about doing just that.

Back in 1934, Congress had passed a Reciprocal Trade Act, intended to encourage the exchange of surplus commodities between countries, each seeking an outlet for its surpluses and taking in exchange the things it did not produce or of which it was a deficit producer. We, for example, might find ourselves with a surplus of can openers, while the Chinese were flooded with an overabundance of chopsticks. We could swap without either country imposing a tariff on the other's product. In short, no outside com-petition would be involved. At least it was on this basis that the Act was sold to the American public, but after four years there was no longer any pretense in Washington that the Act was so limited. It was now admitted that its primary purpose was a flat reduction of tariffs on imports in the interest of diplomacy and preservation of world peace. Now there was dan-ger of Congress surrendering its tariff-making powers to the Executive branch. Agricultural imports had taken millions of American acres out of production and thousands of farm workers out of employment. Imports of cattle and beef products were affecting prices at the ranches.

Federal land administration authorities at last reached the conclusion that certain grazing land in Montana had been seriously injured by home-steading under the Enlarged Homestead Act, and that it must be returned to productive status even though such production be low. To get the sub-marginal areas back to public ownership, a program of government pur-chase was inaugurated, linked with a resettlement project that would aid the impoverished excess population on the land in question to relocate where they might have a chance to make a living and get off relief. The over-all program was initiated in 1934 under the Land Policy Section of the Agricultural Adjustment Administration, passed on to the Resettlement Ad-ministration, then shunted off to the Farm Security Administration. In 1938 it wound up in the U.S. Department of Agriculture's Bureau of Agricul-tural Economics.

By April 1, 1938, a little more than 1,500,000 acres had been purchased in three projects—the Milk River–Northern Montana Land Utilization Project that included Blaine, Phillips, and Valley Counties; the Musselshell–Central Montana Land Utilization Project that took in Yellowstone, Musselshell, Petroleum, and Fergus Counties; the Lower Yellowstone Land Utilization Project that embraced Prairie, Custer, and Fallon Counties. Reseeded and cared for, this land has been brought back to grass production, at an average cost of $2.33 an acre. Today it is known as LU (Land Utilization) land. With a small amount of help from the Rehabilitation Division, 793 families who sold were relocated; 211 families were relocated with public aid on resettlement projects. Only 168 families were left on federally purchased lands, some operating under temporary cropping and grazing agreements. It was a great day for the indigent and the administrators.

The latter informed skeptical cattlemen that their grazing district plans called for the recognition of local autonomy that would preserve local management with the minimum of interference, and that the grazing lands were being reserved for use of "local, land-owning, taxpaying, community-building citizens," with fees arranged on a sliding scale. They didn't say how this Utopia was to be maintained in the future, nor did they offer assurance that privately-owned land and the state, county, and corporately-held tracts included in the grazing districts might not again go into cash crop production with the return of a few moist years. It was suggested that the Association might induce the legislature to allow the state and counties to make long tenure leases without a sales clause. Be that as it may, there were still funds left in the kitty to purchase approximately 1,500,000 more acres within the boundaries of the three Montana projects. The dryland experiment had cost the nation's taxpayers plenty.

The year 1939 opened with a flourish for cattlemen. The popular opinion among them was that the outlook for their business was never better. There was an increasing demand for meats, probably brought about by an improvement in business and in the unemployment situation. When people are prosperous they eat better, and beef is better eating. Export demand for American beef was at a low ebb but the home market was leaving no slack. Other agricultural products were at a low-price level but not so with beef. The government cattle-buying program of 1934 had depleted herds and replacement was slow. Feed back in the Corn Belt was now plentiful and must be converted into marketable meat, poultry, and dairy products. Of course, Montana stockgrowers realized that once their drouth areas were restocked and the Corn Belt demand for converters of cheap feed to meat was satisfied, there would be more competition. They would have to accept lower price levels and like them.

The 1939 state legislature created the Montana Grass Conservation Committee to supersede the Montana Grazing Commission. It consisted of five members, appointed for staggered terms of four years by the governor and approved by the Senate, one each from the Montana Stockgrowers Association, the Montana Woolgrowers Association, the County Commissioners Association, a cooperative state grazing district, and a representative of the general public familiar with the livestock industry. The Commission was to appoint a secretary who would be the executive officer. It was given authority to supervise and regulate the organization and operation of all state districts incorporated under the Act or grazing associations incorporated under former laws. Three or more livestock operators owning or controlling commensurate property within the proposed area could incorporate a state grazing district if approved by the Commission as being beneficial and desirable for more than 50 per cent of the owners and controllers. Grazing rights were, in general, attached to dependent commensurate property, i.e., privately-owned land, not range, that requires the use of range in connection with it to maintain its proper use and that furnishes, as customary practice, the proper feed necessary to maintain stock when not grazing in the district during winter months.

The districts were empowered to buy supplies and to acquire grazing lands by lease, purchase, cooperative agreement, or otherwise, from any source. They could make range improvements, determine grazing fees, and regulate the number and kind of stock to be permitted on the range. Membership was limited to those engaged in the livestock business who owned or leased forage-producing lands within or near the district. They were obligated to lease any state land within the boundaries of the district when it was offered for lease by the State Board of Land Commissioners. All grazing associations incorporated under the 1933 and 1935 laws had to conform to the new statute and amend their articles of incorporation, if necessary to do so. The Montana Stockgrowers Association was beginning to get somewhere with cooperative leasing of public land.

The parent grazing district of the West was recognized as sacrosanct by this phrase: "No territory within the Mizpah–Pumpkin Creek Grazing District shall be included within a state district unless such Mizpah–Pumpkin Creek Grazing District shall approve and recommend an application to such state grazing district for inclusion of such territory."

There was still great world unrest and all economics were out of kilter, but when the thirties ended, it was agreed that the Montana beef industry was in good shape. Herds had gradually been rebuilt and with greatly improved quality. Prices during the shipping season had been profitable and there had been a plentiful supply of feed to carry cattle through the winter. Fortune was to continue smiling through the first year of the 1940's. Grass was good, there was plenty of water in the streams, the hay crop was abundant. Ranchers were giving more care and thought to their operations. The Association was well off financially and its membership was increasing to a record high. The weather, prices, and increase in grazing areas had given the industry three years of deserved prosperity.

All of this in spite of President Jack Arnold's affirmation: "Whatever may be your personal opinion as to the desirability or effect of government control, or interference with business, the fact remains that it exists in a tremendous degree, and the present trend seems to be to increase rather than decrease it. The cattle business is no exception to the general rule."

# 19. BULLETS BRING BENEFITS

The year 1941 started out like its predecessor. Cattle were still high and the herds had wintered in excellent shape. As the summer advanced, the weather and range conditions continued favorable. In an address before the Western Division Conference of the United States Chamber of Commerce, held May 12 at Spokane, Association President Jack Arnold spoke about an objective of long standing with Montana's cowmen:

Stability must be the criterion of successful operation as far as the livestock industry is concerned. The only way to secure stability . . . is to be able to exist under a system whereby the lands that are available for grazing use, whether forest lands, other federally-controlled or -owned lands such as administered by the Taylor Grazing Service, the General Land Office, or those administered by the Indian Service, also state- and county-owned lands, can be used with some degree of continuity in a manner which will complement the privately owned and improved lands which have been built up, cultivated, and developed in connection with and dependent upon these federal and state grazing areas.

Montana's stockgrowers were achieving stability to some degree, but they were still plagued by the refusal of the Federal Government to consider disposing of its uncommitted lands to private owners or the standardization of its lease requirements and other regulations under a single authority. Multiple controls by agencies with differing standards confused the leasing of public land, and the condition was promoted by the jealousy of those agencies.

The nation was thinking in terms of national defense. Government purchases of materials and supplies were producing a synthetic prosperity, for which the taxpayer would suffer later. The interventionists and isolationists were at each other's throats. England was suffering, Hitler was terrorizing millions, German U-boats were taking a ghastly toll of foreign shipping. In the U.S.A., the fall cattle market was excellent. Then came Pearl Harbor.

With war came the customary abnormalities and maladjustments. There was the usual shortage of labor and equipment. Priorities, subsidies, rollbacks, and rationing made headlines. The patter of the day dwelt on WACs, WAVEs, War Bond drives, sugar ration coupons, meatless days, 4-Fs, dive bombers, Lend-Lease.

The stockgrowers did not have much justification for complaint. The beef cattle census had consistently increased for five years. By January 1, 1944, there were an estimated 82,000,000 head in the United States, an increase of 8,000,000 in ten years. To be sure, there was a shortage of young, active ranch hands. Some were lured away by the high pay of war jobs, some were drafted—although draft boards were lenient about key ranch workers because boys in uniform must have meat. The slaughtering of meat animals and the consequent huge meat tonnage in 1942 had never been equalled. Growing conditions for young beef could not have been better. Debts were paid, ranch plants and stock were improved. Association membership exceeded the 2,000 mark.

In the second year of our actual participation in World War II, a peculiar situation developed. While there was ample beef on the ranches, there was a persistent rumor of beef shortage, with the blame placed on the producers. The Office of Price Administration (O.P.A.) seemed of that opinion, too, and threatened to place ceiling prices on live animals. To anyone familiar with livestock, this was an impractical, if not impossible, thing to do if any semblance of fairness was to be maintained. Association President G. M. Mungas commented:

There are very few men so skilled that they can look through the hide of a living cow and accurately tell the dressing percent and the quality of beef that the cow will yield. . . . Often times there will be three grades of beef in a single shipment, all fed for the same length of time. Stock would have to be graded, and that would require an army of competent graders to cover the hundreds of ranches, farms, and market places where cattle are sold.

President Mungas was right, of course. Cattle vary in weight, finish, grade, and hence in value, as much as any other products that are not machine-made. To lump them all under one ceiling price was manifestly unfair. This became a bone of contention that lasted until 1945, when the Office of Price Administration instituted a live-cattle ceiling, disregarding all opinions and advice from responsible representatives of the beef industry.

It was not lack of a price ceiling that was giving the country the impression that there was a shortage of beef. There were two reasons which were not apparent to the public. Government control of feed had curtailed the operations of feeders in the Corn Belt to an extent that forced some of them to quit. A price-squeeze had been placed on their business until there was the paradox of plenty of range beef in the country, yet a shortage of beef on the retail counters. What the public did not know was that stockgrowers were not prepared to furnish the packers with finished stock, or even grass-fed animals of killing age, in the quantity that the market needed.

They had changed their operations to a cow-calf business, prompted by the popular demand for baby beef years before. The feeders had become the connecting link between the rancher and the packer. With the feeders stymied by arbitrary government control of feed crops, there was no chance for the ranchers to fill the resulting void by shipping direct to the packer unless they disposed of cows and heifers that should be retained for breeding, and they could not finish steer calves on the ranch overnight.

The other reason for the alleged meat shortage was the fact that restriction of packers' quotas and meat rationing had led to expansion of the black market. Secretary Mollin of the A.N.L.S.A. said:

It seems quite possible that the drastic control imposed by the O.P.A. in the shape of packer quotas and too sharp reduction in allotment to the civilians under the rationing plan, has actually encouraged black market operations. When packers in some of the smaller cities have exhausted their quotas, when they have plenty of cattle available to kill, and when consumers in their territory have the coupons to buy meat, there isn't any sense in stopping that kind of operation. To stop it does not mean that the consumers are going to eat jack rabbit. It means they are going into the black markets to buy meat and to defeat the very purpose of the packer quota.

Rustling had never ceased in the history of Montana's cattle business. Hanging, shooting, fining, and imprisoning some culprits didn't seem to deter others. Mavericking and mass abduction went with the open range, only to be succeeded by trucks, winches, and quick getaways over paved highways. The Association enlisted the active aid of the State Highway Patrol, and the Association offer of $1,000 in reward for evidence leading to the apprehension and conviction of offenders had at least given the satisfaction of placing an appreciable number of cattle thieves behind the bars. But high prices for beef, black markets created by the war, and the cooperation of lawless butchers and meat dealers had given the illegal occupation stimulus. Under cover of darkness, a critter could be shot, winched into a closed truck, and freighted to a secluded spot for dressing, in an amazingly short time. It seems certain that rustling can never be eliminated but it can be slowed down. It is just one of those adverse variables with which the business of stockgrowing is afflicted.

In the fall of 1943 Chris J. Abbott, of Nebraska, addressed a Livestock Association conference in Kansas City and referred to the price ceiling controversy. He said:

The meat industry of the United States is the largest industry in the world. Millions of people are engaged in producing, marketing, processing . . . and distributing meat animals. Notwithstanding the complexity of an industry whose produce is so highly perishable; where thousands of traders, both wholesale and retail, trade daily; where competition is so intense that there is always livestock for sale and where livestock can be instantly converted into cash; a marketing system so sensitive that prices balance demand against supply almost to the single animal . . . a marketing system that is the envy of every other country in the world—notwithstanding the existence of this perfect machine so delicately balanced, O.P.A. simply hauled off and tossed a monkey wrench into its vital mechanism. Only a bureaucrat could be willful enough or stupid enough to fix retail price ceilings on meat during Lent when there was as much as ten cents a pound difference between the cities of Boston and Philadelphia. This is exactly what was done, and ever since then markets have not followed the pattern with which all producers are familiar—that of supply and demand—but instead have depended upon the regulation, news, and propaganda from Washington.

While this hassle was going on, stockgrowers' attention was distracted by another complex and vital question—the methods of determining income tax returns. To make a study on behalf of the industry, the National Live Stock Tax Committee was formed in the fall of 1943 in Kansas City, representing producers from twenty-seven Western and Southern states and sponsored by the American National Livestock Association and the National Woolgrowers Association. They sought clarification of the Bureau of Internal Revenue's proposals for taxing ranches. The cost method meant determination of the cost of producing an animal, that value to be used for tax purposes. The market-value method would place a tax value on each animal at a particular time. The tax committee and most cattlemen favored an inventory basis, with uniform regulations adopted that would provide a method of keeping inventories on a constant unit-value basis. The simplicity of this method recommended it, and cattlemen thought that many futile arguments could be forestalled if the Commissioner of Internal Revenue would rule in its favor. Otherwise, an act of Congress would be needed to put it into effect.

All in all, when 1943 came to a close, the Montana Stockgrowers Association could not complain very much about the lot of the embattled cowmen. Moreover, its spokesman, *The Montana Stockgrower,* had initiated a feature in its columns that added a leavening of humor to even the grimmest situations that confronted the readers. Neckyoke Jones' first letter to "Secertary Phillups" appeared in the May 15 issue of that year, and afterwards became part and parcel of the magazine make-up. Neckyoke invariably reports the wisdom and philosophy of his partner, "ol' Greasewood, who is awful smart." The two old-timers, who "run a few head cows on Long Pine," are responsible for thousands of chuckles derived from Neckyoke's recording of their "augering" with each other and with their neighbor, Sody Crick Smith.

The subjects on which Greasewood orates, "retorks," warbles, and ruminates run the gamut from local to international affairs, with no punches pulled. Highly original in substance and vernacular, they stack up to the humor of Will Rogers and the pungent observations of Finley Peter Dunne's Mr. Dooley. In the June 15, 1945, issue, Greasewood's picture made its appearance and is now a standard accessory to Neckyoke's accompanying letter.

The originator and ghost writer of the inimitable partners is H. F. Sinclair, of Sheridan, Wyoming, combination cowman and literary genius. More than fifteen years of writing letters to the "Secertary" has sharpened, rather than dulled, the wit and profundity of Greasewood's tangy comments on the passing show.

Summarizing the effects of 1943 on the stock industry, the editor of *The Montana Stockgrower* carried a front-page editorial in the January, 1944, issue. It reads, in part:

> The largest demand for meat ever known in America has been in evidence due to the high employment and wage situations . . . most conditions surrounding the production of livestock in Montana have been excellent. . . .

But the affairs of the stockmen have been so constantly interfered with, that as satisfactory returns as have been shown for other years have been prevented by government agencies whose programs lack vision and knowledge of the stockmen's problems and business.

On January 1, 1944, there were an estimated 1,727,000 cattle in Montana, but the feed lots back East were almost empty. The feeders, knowing that they would get the same price for cattle in September as they would in March, due to price controls, could see no percentage in carrying them through the winter. The natural result was a shortage to supply the spring market and the usual repercussions, reaching back to the ranches. Nevertheless, the year turned out to be highly profitable for Montana growers, with its combination of good weather and good prices, and ranch indebtedness was reduced almost to the vanishing point.

The annual 1945 meeting of the Association was not held because of wartime travel restrictions, but the executive committee convened and went on record as opposing the Senate's so-called Murray Bill, introduced by Senator James A. Murray, of Montana, and designed to create a Missouri River Valley Authority of the TVA (Tennessee Valley Authority) type. In deference to the paper shortage, the July issue of *The Montana Stockgrower* was skipped, as it had been in '44. There were 49,000 brands on record in the office of the Montana Livestock Commission.

That summer (1945), at a special election caused by the demise of incumbent James F. O'Connor, Wesley A. D'Ewart, stockman of Wilsall, Park County, was elected Representative from Montana's Second Congressional District, on the Republican ticket. That fall, he began contributing monthly "Congressional News Items" to the Association paper, thereby keeping members informed of Congressional activities, in general, and measures affecting the livestock industry, in particular. This became an important and popular feature for *The Montana Stockgrower* readers, who appreciated having a sympathetic correspondent in Washington.

V-J Day put a finish to the Second World War and, to the satisfaction of everyone except the black market operators, the rationing of meat was terminated.

Efficient operation of the grazing districts was further enhanced in July, 1946, by a consolidation of the General Land Office and the Taylor Grazing Act Service as the Bureau of Land Management in the Department of the Interior, under a director in whom certain functions of the merging agencies were vested. His responsibilities are many and varied. In the Bureau's *Manual,* a succinct paragraph outlines its functions as related to range and grazing. It states:

Through the granting of grazing permits in grazing districts and grazing leases on public lands outside of grazing districts, the Bureau administers grazing and range activities to protect productivity of lands, permit the highest use of forage, and at the same time retard soil erosion and provide watershed areas of interspersed Federal, State, and privately owned lands, for the development and improvement of facilities which permit more effective use of the range.

Montana now has six grazing districts. The state supervisor headquarters is at Billings. The general coordinating supervision for Montana, Wyoming, Colorado, and New Mexico is in the area offices at Denver. The Federal Range Management Program in operation is best described by the Bureau's publication, *Managing the Public Range,* published July, 1954. After citing the critical condition of deteriorated grazing land, the text reads:

A vicious circle of increasing use of a decreasing forage supply, resulting in further depletion, was established and continued unbroken until the passage of the Taylor Act in 1934 made possible the control and management of range use on the public domain. Two generations were considered the minimum of time needed to restore the public land to its original productivity. Such improvement could be attained only through proper control of grazing use, permitting the natural range restorative forces to operate, and applying artificial revegetation and other conservation practices to that part of the range where such practices were feasible. . . .

Through the provisions of the Taylor Grazing Act, the grazing administration of the public lands is accomplished within two distinct categories, those within and those outside of grazing districts. The more concentrated portions of the public lands, generally spoken of as the Federal Range, have been included within fifty-nine grazing districts. . . .

Authorization for the grazing uses within the fifty-nine districts is provided for through the issuance of grazing permits to approximately 19,000 qualified applicants. Annual grazing is authorized for 8.8 million head of livestock for about 35% of their annual forage requirement on the public lands within grazing districts. In addition, more than 800,000 big game animals secure a part or all of their forage from the Federal Range.

Unreserved public domain lands lying *outside* of grazing districts occur as scattered tracts and are usually referred to as Section 15 lands, after that section of the Taylor Grazing Act which provides for the leasing of grazing privileges on these lands. The total area of the Section 15 lands is approximately 27 million acres, of which 17.9 million acres are leased to 11,500 livestock operators. These leases furnish seasonal grazing each year for approximately 900,000 cattle and horses and two million sheep and goats; consequently, the scattered remnants of the public domain form an important part in western livestock operations. The size of existing grazing leases varies from just a few acres to as much as 400,000 acres; however, the average size is about 1,000 acres.

In Montana (1958), there are 5,224,692 acres of public domain in grazing districts and 1,411,153 isolated acres (Section 15 land) subject to lease. In commenting on the local administration of the Grazing Act, E. D. Nielson, Montana State Supervisor of the Bureau of Land Management, recently said:

Of particular significance is the cooperation that we have received from stockmen in providing assistance in the improvement and development of these remaining public lands. Many thousands of dollars each year, particularly in the form of labor and materials, have been furnished by stockmen in the construction of fences, reservoirs, springs, and other water developments, as well as conservation practices, under our Soil and Moisture Conservation program. Our District Advisory Board also has proved most helpful in accomplishing our objectives in proper range management and development, protection of Federal range, and in the stabilization of the livestock industry.

At last there is intelligent conservation and productive use being made of Western range. The Montana Stockgrowers Association and its affiliates can be justly proud of the major role they have played in bringing this about.

# 20. A NEW DECK

Almost from the creation of the Forest Service, many sportsmen and their associations objected to domestic stock grazing on forest forage. To them, a forest was synonymous with wildlife and it should be preserved in a primitive state for the exclusive benefit of Nature's feathered, furred, and cloven-footed creatures.

Enough such organizations were sufficiently vociferous in their protests to arouse attention and enlist a certain amount of sympathy from overzealous nature lovers. Of course, as citizens and voters they had a right to be heard, and heard they were. Some sports writers belabored the cattlemen with caustic phrase and false premise. They forgot, or never knew, that when snow got deep in the timber, hungry deer and elk in overwhelming numbers left their high forest haunts to invade lower fields, where they feasted on the haystacks of neighboring stockmen. The ranchers had grown and harvested the fodder, at a cost of cash and travail, for the wintering of their cattle. No one offered to pay *them* a grazing fee or damages. The stacks were a free lunch counter for visiting wildlife. This condition came to a head in 1939 and reached some degree of solution early in 1940.

With the encroachment of settlements in the lowlands, several species of game animals, notably elk, moved to the mountains where they ranged in national parks, forests, and preserves. Deep snow and a shortage of winter forage drove them down to the foothills and lower meadows, where they had no compunction about appropriating ranchers' hay reserves put up for their own livestock. If a stockman used means to frighten the elk away, the trespassers would sometimes depart without bothering to seek out a gate, and away would go many panels of fence. The State Fish and Game Commission was more inclined to sympathize with the elk than with the rancher. The latter was a firm believer in herd depletion where natural range was insufficient to support his stock.

C. R. Rathbone, a cattleman of northern Lewis and Clark County, and his neighbors, had been beset for several winters by bands of elk descending on their fields from the Sun River Elk Preserve. Rathbone had suffered severe damage and had applied to the Fish and Game Commission for relief and compensation, but without success. His patience became exhausted in the spring of 1939 after elk herds of from ten to two hundred and fifty head had visited his ranch almost daily during February. The attorney general's office had told him on one occasion that he had a right to kill elk out of season "when reasonably necessary to protect his property." Rancher Rathbone acted on the advice and was soon made defendant in an action, with the State of Montana as plaintiff. The case reached the Supreme Court of Montana. Attorney W. D. Rankin filed a brief on behalf of the Montana Stockgrowers Association and the Montana Woolgrowers Association, since both memberships were keenly interested in establishing the principle that game animals could be killed out of season if "necessary to protect property."

On March 5, 1940, the Supreme Court rendered a decision, holding that under the Constitution a person did have such right to protect his property from injury or destruction, but that the mere use of the constitutional guaranty was no defense unless substantial damage had been done. The decision held that every case must be decided on its merits, and that the jury must determine whether or not a reasonably prudent person would have shot in defense of his property under the same or similar circumstances. In short, the mere fact that an elk crosses a rancher's land does not give him license to shoot the animal, but where elk habitually feed on a rancher's haystacks, destroy his fences, and become a continual nuisance, and the rancher is honestly helpless to protect himself from them, the Supreme Court of Montana is of the opinion that he has a right to kill the offending elk, in or out of season. However, the rancher must first advise the Fish and Game Commission of the situation; if no relief is offered, he can then act on his own behalf.

Over the years, there were cases where forest officials refused to permit cattle owners to make certain stock-grazing improvements within forest boundaries even though the cattlemen offered to pay for them and to install them under forest personnel supervision. In other instances, the number of livestock per permit was reduced and the grazing period shortened. No doubt the officials had reasons that they considered good, but stockmen didn't always agree. There were inevitable clashes of personalities. These irritations built up to unfriendliness and recriminations. Many forest supervisors and rangers in the field were practical men, expert in their business, and rated as close friends by many ranchers, but those were not the men who formulated Forest Service policies in Washington, D.C.

*Collier's* (now defunct) published two articles that were considered slanderous by the American National Livestock Association. It was claimed that the staff writer showed decided partiality for the Forest Service, which had provided him with most of his data. With the naïveté of some eastern writers on the subject, he claimed that the stockmen were responsible for soil erosion and for the destruction of range. If the writer had taken the trouble to investigate, he would have found that stockmen *favored* protection of the range because it is the life substance of their industry. A craftsman doesn't deliberately damage the tools that bring him a living.

Other writers cited the muddy Missouri, the Little Missouri, and the Powder River as silt-laden streams that carried Montana's soil to extend the Louisiana delta because wicked "cattle barons" insisted on overgrazing the range. The Missouri, which was muddy for ages before Lewis and Clark fought its currents! The Powder, which had been "too thick to drink, too thin to plow" far beyond the memory of man! It is true that at one time "tramp" cow outfits and nomadic bands of sheep roamed the eastern range at large, the stock being the owner's sole investment. These owners had no compunction about grazing an area down to the last thin blade and then moving on. People of that sort were not condoned by responsible cattlemen and, fortunately, their numbers were relatively few.

Considerable hard feeling was engendered by misunderstandings between stockmen and Forest officials, some of it stirred up by overzealous outsiders. Growing dissatisfaction with management of public domain, including grazing districts in and out of national forests, also stirred up public sentiment, pro and con, until a Congressional Public Lands Subcommittee held hearings in the western states between sessions of Congress. One, dealing with the Taylor Grazing and public domain problems, was scheduled at Glasgow, Montana, on August 27, 1947; another, at Billings a few days later, was devoted primarily to forest lands.

Jack Milburn, subsequently president of the Montana Stockgrowers Association as well as president of the American National Cattlemen's Association, represented the Montana Joint Public Lands Committee, which in turn represented both the Montana Stockgrowers and the Montana Woolgrowers Associations at the Glasgow meeting. His statement to the visiting subcommittee was enlightening. It follows:

Historically, until recent years, it has been the policy of our national government, in the administration of its public land holdings, to so legislate that the land holdings would pass into private ownership. It can likewise be stated that historically, until recent years, it has been the recognized national policy that profits accruing from the public lands should pass to the respective states.

Through the various grants, allocation, and homestead acts, the most desirable areas of the public lands have passed into private ownership or trusteeship, until only the most worthless land is left. So far as public lands in Montana are concerned, there are tracts of isolated public domain land, as well as certain areas of sub-marginal purchase lands, that could still pass into private acreage or public domain land, particularly badland areas, that could not support a tax base under our present tax structure, and, regardless of the type of administration, would always have to be used in common to render the greatest return to the public and the livestock industry from a conservation standpoint.

Pending final disposition of the remaining public domain, and in view of the general demand for economy and efficiency in government, we recommend now, as we have many times in the past, the consolidation of some federal agencies administering the public grazing-use lands. The Forest Service, the Indian Service, and National Park Service have distinct duties in administration of our timber lands, the welfare of the Indians, and the entertainment of the public, hence should not be eliminated or consolidated.

In view of the fact that over 35 per cent of the land in the State of Montana is owned or controlled by the Federal Government, we are unalterably opposed to the acquisition by any federal agency of any additional land. We further recommend that land transfers or acquisition resulting from war needs be restored to former status. It is further recommended that public-owned grazing land, outside of national parks, national forests, and Indian reservations, be re-examined to determine its best final disposition.

In considering the question of final disposition of the surface rights of the remaining public domain in Montana, it is the considered judgment of [the committee I represent] that in preference to outright sale, this land should eventually be passed to the State of Montana to be administered by the state for the benefit of the public schools, and in such case the enabling act should require that the grazing and preference rights of the present users be maintained, as well as game preserves and other public use lands.

The Montana Joint Public Lands Committee proposed a transfer to private ownership of the thousands of abandoned homestead tracts and other lands too arid for other economic use than grazing, at a price to be arrived at by government officials working with stockmen, and based on carrying capacity. As most of the land was of low capacity, a fair price would have run from 70 cents to $2.50 per acre. This was merely a recommendation, but it touched off an uproar from many idealists, who cried that livestock interests wanted to put over a bill to permit the sale of all public land, including national forests, parks, monuments, and primitive areas.

At the Billings meeting, George M. Mungas, of Philipsburg, Montana, also a member of the Montana Joint Public Lands Committee, represented the two state livestock associations. He enumerated the causes of permittee dissatisfaction with Forest Service procedure: the lack of authority of advisory boards and district stock associations, the cutting down of numbers of livestock permitted, the short periods of use, the lack of water development and other range improvements that had been promised permittees, the small amount of grazing fees received by counties in lieu of taxes, and the heavy expenditures for new roads while existing roads and trails were badly in need of repair. He said, "Forest users feel they are in a better position to determine carrying capacity, length of grazing seasons, the range improvement practices through their advisory boards, and a practical and conservative grazing program in their districts than any group of salaried men in the employ of the Federal Government."

Mr. Mungas further expressed an opinion that the advisory boards were being ignored, that Forest Service officials had become arbitrary. "In many cases," he said, "permittees of forest grazing lands who were contacted are fearful of speaking their own minds as to their dissatisfaction with Forest Service administration because of threats made to them regarding the tenure of their grazing permits."

In referring to the wildlife controversy, Mr. Mungas told the committee:

Montana stockmen are definitely interested in the administration of public lands. They are also interested in wildlife. I have yet to contact a stockman who objects to game within reason on his premises. The only complaint concerning game that I have heard comes from excessive numbers where actual damage results. Stockmen in some localities do object to the continued game increase. . . . It must be remembered that stockmen are compelled to furnish a large part of the winter feed consumed by wild life as, for the most part, game is sustained during the winter season on private property.

Stockmen generally recognize that National Forests are for the use and

Natures Cattle.

Montana Stock Growers Convention. April. 16 to 18 - 1918.

The Long Horn.          The Come Lately.

For many years, Charles Marion Russell, cowboy and Western artist, was a familiar figure at the annual meetings of the Montana Stockgrowers Association. To ornament the 1918 program, he designed the page of line drawings shown above. In replying to an invitation to attend the 1919 MSGA meeting at Miles City, he wrote: "Most of my old friends either rode for or owned irons. Many of them have crossed the big range, but they left tracks in history that the farmer can't plow under . . . they were regular men and America's last frontiersmen."

*Right, top:* N-Bar Ranch Angus.
*Below, in order:* Senator "Bill" Mackay registers for the 75th Anniversary meeting of the Montana Stockgrowers Association; putting in hay; the Jubilee insignia of the MSGA.

THE WHITE HOUSE
WASHINGTON

May 15, 1959

Dear Mr. Etchart:

From your letter I learn that the Montana Stockgrowers will celebrate the seventy-fifth anniversary of their Association in Miles City this month.

As a boy growing up in Abilene, Kansas, one of the frontier towns on the old Chisholm trail, I was always fascinated by the legends and stories of life on the plains during the decades immediately following The War Between the States. My personal heroes and heroines were the men and women who had lived through that period and in that region, and who would tell to me their tales of cattle drives, law enforcement and, of course, Indians.

Some of them knew Montana from personal experience; I used to hear much about its vast grazing lands and, even more, I must confess, about the blizzards and snows that seemed, to my youthful mind, to be the principal hazard in cattle raising in that State.

Out of those days the clearest and most lasting impression I developed was that the cattlemen of the unfenced prairie were men of initiative, courage and independent spirit. I cannot help but believe that modern America has been the gainer by the examples of daring, stamina and skill given to us by the sturdy, and fiercely independent, western drover of the latter half of the nineteenth century.

It is a real pleasure to send, through this note, to all the members of the Montana Stockgrowers, my best wishes for a fine anniversary meeting.

Sincerely,

Dwight Eisenhower

Mr. Gene Etchart
President
Montana Stockgrowers Association
Glasgow, Montana

18 84
MONTANA
STOCKGROWERS ASSN.

DIAMOND
JUBILEE
MILES CITY
MAY 20-23

19 59

*Above:* President Eisenhower recalls his boyhood impressions of the West in a letter to the Montana Stockgrowers Association. *Below:* a quarter-century span of MSGA Presidents: (*beginning left*) Jack Milburn, Tom Ross, Carl Malone, Jack Brenner, F. H. Sinclair (famed as "Neckyoke Jones"—the only non-President pictured), George Mungas, Milton Simpson, Jack Arnold, Julian Terrett, and Dan Fulton, all present at the Diamond Jubilee meeting.

The 1960 officers and executive committee of the Montana Stockgrowers Association: (*front row, l. to r.*) Bob Murphy, Assistant Secretary; Gene Etchart, President; Don McRae, Second Vice President; Ralph Miracle, Secretary; Alex Christie; Wes Stearns; Bob Barthelmess; Bill Garrison; Elmer Hanson; (*back row, l. to r.*) Howell Harris; Wayne Bratten, First Vice President; Ford Garfield; Wilford Johnson; Reg Dawes; Alvin Ellis. (Photographed at Miles City Jubilee, May, 1959.)

In 1959, recognizing the terrible plight of the New York City baseball team, Joe Blazek, Bob Ellerd, Gene Etchart, and Robin MacNab, representing the Montana Livestock Markets Association, the Montana Stockgrowers Association, and the Montana Beef Council, sent fifty choice breakfast steaks to "beef-up" the sagging Yankees. They speedily moved from cellar to the top division!

MSGA members are proud of their auxiliary organization, the Montana Cow Belles. These are the 1960 officers, in Jubilee garb and from left to right: Mrs. Bob Barthelmess, Secretary-Treasurer; Mrs. George Voldseth, Second Vice President; Mrs. Pete Hill, President; Mrs. Phil Burke (1959 Jubilee Hostess); and Mrs. Henry Miller, First Vice President.

*Above and left:* a montage of the Stockgrowers' festive Diamond Jubilee at Miles City (May 20–23, 1959), attended by almost 2,000 Montana cattlemen and their friends. Parts of the rodeo, parade, and elaborate preparations which made the occasion so successful are depicted.

Throughout the years, the MSGA has worked for scientific advancement in the livestock industry. Another goal was realized when a venerated MSGA member, the late Wallis Huidekoper (*second from the left*), presented Montana State College with a library for the Livestock Veterinary Research Laboratory.

This is the 1960 scene in the Montana cattle industry. Below is award-winning American Cow Belles photograph, "Branding Time," taken by Mrs. Frank Castleberry, of Ekalaka, Montana.

In the mountains, on the prairies, and in the lush, irrigated Montana valleys—summer and winter—the cattle industry goes on; a tremendous factor in Montana's economy, her prime beef is vitally important to America's health and well-being.

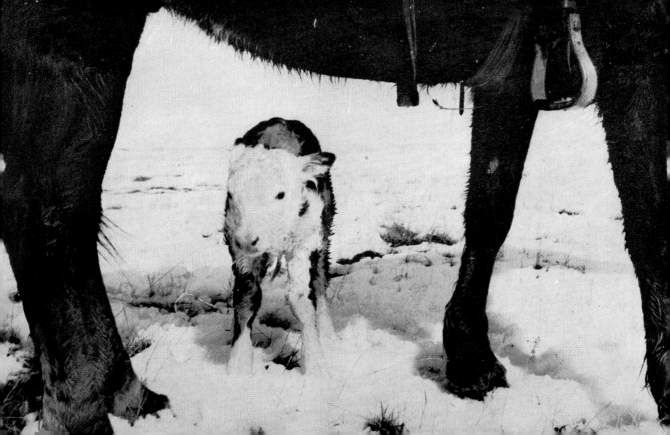

benefit and enjoyment of all of America, and they recognize that the public demands are entitled to consideration and tolerance. We often hear of controversies between stockman and sportsman. We are confident that most of these disagreements are due to misunderstanding and to the unfounded publicity that comes from uninformed writers. We are doing everything possible to create a better understanding of the problems among both groups and we are proud to say that a very wholesome feeling exists between sportsmen and stockmen in Montana, except in a few cases where no effort is made to understand the problems that exist.

The "few cases" mentioned by Mr. Mungas no doubt referred to the kind of "sportsmen" who cut fences, leave gates open, remove fence posts, dump garbage, leave campfires burning, deface property, and kill or injure stock. Such pariahs are fortunately very much in the minority and are as unpopular with sportsmen's associations as they are with stockgrowers.

The upshot of the subcommittee hearings was that its parent body, the Congressional Public Land Committee, with unanimous approval, made preliminary recommendations to Secretary of Agriculture Clinton Anderson just as the subcommittee had submitted them. One of these read: "Effective immediately and extending for a three-year test period, there shall be no reductions made in [grazing] permits." This was explained to the Secretary in a letter of transmittal, which read in part:

> We are convinced that much of the criticism of the Forest Service grazing policies is well founded. . . . We are unanimous in believing it advisable to provide a three-year period during which there shall be a minimum of disturbance in existing range livestock operations in the National Forests. In this period joint studies should be made by the Forest office and livestock men to determine the carrying capacity of each individual range and whether vegetation is improving under present usage.

It seemed to be a logical and practical effort to settle the debatable question of range carrying capacity, but the Secretary rejected it. Certainly, one of the sources of the bickering between users of the forest land and the administrators was the fact that when National Forests were established in 1897, the stated purpose was to protect and conserve timber and watersheds. There was no thought of their use for grazing, preservation of wildlife, or for recreation, and no provision was made for such uses in the Act. Congress, as representing the public at large, had had no hand in prescribing how the forest land should be administered for these supplementary purposes. The rules and regulations in existence had come direct from Forest Service officials.

L. H. Douglas, former assistant regional forester in charge of range management, was quoted by the Committee as saying, "If . . . earnest attempts are put forth by both stockmen and government officers to seek substitutes for reduced permits, much of the dissension . . . will disappear." But the Forest officials wanted no advice from cattlemen, whose interests kept them in constant touch with range conditions. The Public Lands Committee finally deferred to Secretary Anderson, blue-penciled the test-period recommendation, and came up with the following:

1. That the Forest Act be amended to provide that grazing, recreation, and wildlife be made basic uses of national forest lands.
2. That advisory boards on the national forest be given legal status.
3. That present policy of transfer cuts be discontinued, and that any cuts that may be necessary be made for protection purposes only.
4. That the Forest Service undertake a vigorous program of range development, including (a) water development, (b) re-seeding, (c) fencing, (d) rodent and poisonous weed control.
5. That the Forest Service undertake a policy that will enable permittees to participate in and contribute to a greatly extended range-improvement program.

The Committee closed its report by stating, "We are convinced that the national interest demands that the Forest Service adopt these recommendations in the conviction that such a program will bring stability and security to the western livestock industry dependent upon the use of our national forests." So the matter stood at the end of 1948.

There are two sides to every controversy over forest range. During World War I, one of the many slogans was "Food Will Win the War," and the high command passed the word for the federal forests to increase grazing permits to the limit of forage capability. After the war emergency, when reductions were made to get the range back to normal, it was sometimes difficult to convince holders of grazing permits that such curtailment was necessary.

Changing conditions not noticeable to the casual forest visitor, or even to habitual users, are evident to rangers and supervisors who are making forestry a life work. Young timber growth has insidiously encroached on grass and sagebrush areas, thereby decreasing available forage; many ranges, grazed thirty-five or forty years ago, cannot be used now. In 1930 a mountain pine beetle infestation killed hundreds of trees, high winds blew them down, and now, in certain areas, it is impossible to get a saddle horse through the down timber, to say nothing of cattle. At one time, hundreds of horses from adjacent public domain invaded the national forests. It required legal and roundup action in many instances to rid the forest range of these trespassers that diminished the forage supply for legitimate users.

Between Forest Service personnel and livestock owners, there has been better understanding of one another's problems during the past ten years. This has brought about mutual respect and cooperation. In 1958 Montana had eleven national forests, all included in Northern Region No. 1. There were over 4,500,000 acres of range in these forests open to livestock; 117,581 head of cattle and horses were permitted for a five-month season, and 1,706 grazing permits were issued for them.

In the conservation of timber, its economic harvesting, the protection of watersheds, the prevention and curtailment of forest fires, the building of roads, trails, and public camp grounds, research, reforestation, protection of wildlife, fighting blight and insect infestation, and the many other facets of forest administration, the U.S. Forest Service has carried on projects of untold benefit to the American public and, on the whole, has accomplished them efficiently and unobtrusively.

# 21. MADISON AVENUE
# RIDES WEST

Financially, the Montana stockgrowers could not complain about 1948. There were top prices, sometimes followed by busts, it is true, but government spending was still in effect on a grandiose scale. Ranchers now had the advantage of twelve (later thirteen) strategically located, local, livestock auction markets, Billings being the oldest (1934) and Shelby the newest (1947). These markets operate under license from the Montana Livestock Commission and are obligated to meet construction, sanitary, and bond requirements stipulated by the Commission and the Livestock Sanitary Board. Billings, Bozeman, and Great Falls also qualified for interstate trade, under the jurisdiction of the Federal Packers and Stockyards Act of 1921.

The winter of 1948–49 was stormy. So much hay had been sold out of

state that there was a threatened shortage at home. Deep snow made feeding difficult. State Highway Engineer Scott Hart cooperated to the greatest
degree by instructing his maintenance department to keep highways and
ranch roads open. Ranchers even resorted to air lifts to get feed to isolated
cattle.

Aftosa, the vicious foot-and-mouth disease, had been brought into
Mexico in 1946 by two Brahma bulls imported from Brazil in violation
of treaty agreement. A joint United States and Mexican commission was
organized to undertake the tremendous job of inspection, vaccination, quarantine, disinfection, killing, and burying. It covered all cloven-hooved animals, including deer. Mexico is also well provided with goats. The isolation
of so many of Mexico's rural areas, their inaccessibility, the ignorance of
native owners who were loath to part with their herds and flocks, and their
inertia and failure to cooperate, made it a maddening, heartbreaking task.
By 1949, the campaign was reaching a crisis. The cattle industry had been
deeply concerned when the Argentine was a threat; now here it was right
at our door. It was licked, after a struggle that went on until 1955.

That big business could no longer indulge itself in a the-public-be-
damned attitude had been apparent to a number of important industries
for some years. Research had disclosed that many of their troubles, stem-
ming from public criticism, were due to misconceptions on the part of the
great majority, whose opinions were being formed for them by columnists,
press headlines, the movies, magazines, and other mass communication
media. People were becoming mentally lazy. They accepted false doctrines
if these were given sufficient repetition and had an authoritative ring. There
is much talk about the world being smaller because of modern communication and transportation, but many people still have a very restricted horizon
due to limited personal experience and observation. The business of truth-
fully informing the public so that there may be some appreciation of the
other fellow's side of a story, and willingness to see him get fair play, is called
public relations. The cattle industry had been needing something like that
for a long, long time.

The American National Livestock Association took the initiative by
appointing a public relations committee, which met in Denver in the summer of 1948 to formulate a program. Its stated purpose was to bring the
livestock industry of the nation in closer rapport with the public, by presenting to it the facts and a true picture of the industry. It had been discovered that even citizens living in cow country had little knowledge of the
cattle-growing business and that the misinformation existing in the industrial eastern sections of the country was appalling.

Every western cattle state was represented on the committee by men who were willing to further its purpose at the cost of much personal sacrifice—men who had vision and originality. W. A. Johnson, secretary of the committee, in a report to livestock producers, said:

> Misunderstanding between the administrators of some parts of the public lands and stockmen who use public lands for grazing provided a windfall for sensational writers, who wrote highly critical articles which were followed by editorial treatment in the nation's press. During the last days of the O.P.A. stockmen were charged with withholding cattle from the market in order to keep consumers' prices high. The unfavorable publicity, which unquestionably hurt the stockmen, made it clearly apparent that the industry must immediately take some progressive move to keep itself in the good graces of the consuming public. Not only were range cattlemen concerned at the bad press notices which had been so widely and frequently appearing, but feeders, purebred raisers, commission houses, and the agricultural press, all realized that the need of a public relations agency was imperative.

Once awakened to the serious need for public understanding, the industry, through this committee, began a campaign of news releases on the local level, provided stockmen speakers for local civic clubs and other opinion-forming organizations, promoted tours of business and professional men to stockgrowing areas. A file of facts and figures was compiled for use in the refutation of untruthful statements made on the platform, in writing, or on the air. Association members were warned not to expect miracles overnight. It would be a long, uphill pull to convince urbanites that the high cost of their steaks and pot roasts was not due to the nefarious plots of avaricious cowmen who had no conscience about destroying extremely valuable public acres in the process.

The spring of 1949 was late, cold, and stormy. The summer was dry to the point of drouth on much of the range and the "hoppers" were out in force again. The cattlemen weathered it through and declared their rugged independence in a special resolution passed at the 1950 convention of the American National Livestock Association held in Miami, Florida, on January 5:

> We . . . reaffirm our solemn conviction that the future health, strength, and prosperity of our country depend on the re-establishment and maintenance of free and competitive enterprise, and hereby pledge ourselves as individuals and as an association to diligently and actively work toward this objective and toward the defeat of the fallacious philosophies that are beguiling our country into socialism.

This characteristic and uncompromising statement probably never reached the eyes or ears of the Secretary of Agriculture, but he did announce the creation of a National Forest Advisory Board of Appeals, to settle controversial Forest Service problems and to hear appeals on administrative matters in which the Forest Service and stockmen disagreed. The leverage that produced the Board of Appeals was, without doubt, the report of the Congressional Committee on Public Lands. However, there was a catch to it. The board was to consist of five members employed in any agency of the Department of Agriculture except the Forest Service. Again the stockmen were left out.

On March 11, 1950, the Montana Livestock Production Credit Association dedicated a new building in Helena, at the corner of Edwards Street and Last Chance Gulch. It houses the offices of the Montana Stockgrowers Association and the Montana Woolgrowers Association, as well as those of the Credit Association. In the basement there is an auditorium with a seating capacity of one hundred. Located in the business and financial center of Montana's capital city, close to hotels and not too far from the capitol and the Livestock Commission offices, it provides convenient and strategic office space for Association secretaries and their staffs. Membership reached 4,300 that year and was still growing.

The beginning of the 1950's was satisfactory insofar as industry revenue was concerned. International difficulties in the Far East and our bickering with Russia kept the nation in a foreign relations turmoil. Not even our reps in the beetlebacked coats and striped trousers seem to be clear on the subject, let alone that portion of the citizenry who wear Pendleton jackets and California pants. The Korean "police action" was accompanied by most of the by-products of full-fledged war. In fact, the shooting and the casualty lists made it hard for the ramrods in Washington to convince the proletariat that it *wasn't* a war.

There was no O.P.A. This time it was O.P.S. (Office of Price Stabilization) that put a ceiling price on live cattle and administered other federal price controls. President Truman's message of 1952 airily indicated billions more deficit to come. Congressman D'Ewart predicted: "It is going to be difficult for farmers [and stockmen] to meet the high production goals set by the Department of Agriculture when taxes destroy incentive, controls limit profits, allocations deny them equipment and parts, and the Army and industry outbid them for man power."

The over-all picture brightened in 1953. That year saw the greatest production of beef in the history of the United States, to supply the greatest demand. At the close of his Congressional term, Representative D'Ewart introduced a Uniform Federal Grazing Lands Act in Congress that was the result of years of thought and study by many people intent on bringing uniformity and stability to the management of such lands in the West. Approximately 50 per cent of the land in fourteen Western states was still controlled by federal agencies, each with different procedure, fees, rules, and regulations. The bill met with violent opposition and got nowhere.

The year 1953 also brought a change in federal administration. Ezra T. Benson, a westerner, was appointed Secretary of Agriculture. Montana cattlemen were going to miss Congressman D'Ewart as a champion of their causes in the House, but his appointment as a special assistant to Secretary Benson meant that his talents and broad knowledge of Western needs would still be at their service.

In October, an Association membership poll was taken to determine how much sentiment existed in favor of price supports for cattle. The result was conclusive proof that the independent spirit of the old-timers persisted. The ballots returned showed 194 to 51 against price supports for cattle; 169 to 47 favoring heavier government purchase of beef; 46 favoring no help of any kind to stabilize the market.

In 1939 a few Arizona ranch women had met occasionally at the home of Mr. and Mrs. Ira Glenn, north of Douglas, for fun, food, and dancing. The get-togethers were so popular that an enlarged group met that fall at the home of Mrs. Ralph Cowan, where sixteen of them organized a club, calling themselves the Cow Belles. No organization of ranch girls could devote all of their energy to social pursuits, and it wasn't long before the Cow Belles were engaged in community projects of their own devising. When the American National Stockgrowers Association met in Phoenix in January, 1947, the club members acted as hostesses, and took the occasion to organize the Arizona Cow Belles, the first state group, with Mrs. Cowan as president. At the convention banquet, the women from other states were told about the Cow Belle clubs in Arizona. Many of the visitors went home and formed local and state organizations of their own. In 1952, when the national Association met in Fort Worth, there were so many active groups throughout the country that the American National Cow Belles was organized with 300 charter members. Mrs. O. W. Lyman, of Kansas, was elected the first president.

The ladies of the Montana Stockgrowers Association members held their initial meeting at the Butte convention, May 21–24, 1952. Mrs. Jack Hirschy, of Jackson in the Big Hole Basin, was elected president, Mrs. Tom Herrin, of Helena, vice president, and Mrs. I. W. Vinsel, of Dillon, secretary-treasurer. The Montana organization was perfected at the Missoula convention the following year with the adoption of a constitution and by-laws, and re-election of the original officers. Members were urged to form small local groups to keep activities and interest alive throughout the year. The Madison-Gallatin area got away to a fast start by enlisting the Cow Belles of that district under the banner of "The Mad Gals." Today there are over twenty Montana groups, spread from southeastern Montana to the Tobacco Valley at Eureka in the northwestern part of the state. The original idea may have been confined largely to social activities, but such a program was far too passive for Montana ranch girls. They were soon absorbed in projects designed to promote Beef.

Many groups now have regular columns in the weekly newspapers; some maintain booths at county and regional fairs; others distribute litter bags, place mats, and paper napkins printed with cut and caption urging everyone to watch his waistline and "Eat More Beef." The Cow Belles have carried on school programs and entertained (and painlessly instructed) town and city people, including tourists. They meet when the men meet and plan stunts of great variety and ingenuity. They tie in with the national polio drive by raffling steers, the proceeds going to the polio fund. In Montana, the traditional piggy bank is on its way out; "Beefy Banks" are now in vogue with the small fry. The alert ladies not only help collect contributions for the Beef Council treasury, but contribute money earned by their endless and original schemes. Montana is no exception; wherever cattle are raised, groups of Cow Belles are helping their men to promote better public understanding, and are doing a job that is the envy of many a high-powered public relations specialist. The Cow Belles are energetic, shining examples of that time-honored adage, "Never underestimate the power of a woman."

At the 1954 Montana Stockgrowers Association meeting in Miles City, Mr. Jay Taylor, of Amarillo, Texas, then president of the American National Cattlemen's Association, outlined his ideas for helping the beef industry which, at the time, was in a state of low price stagnation. Moreover, beef was not moving across the retail counters at a very encouraging rate. Lay it to war, industrialization, the movies, automobiles, the columnists, TV, or what you will, there had been both abrupt and insidious changes in American ways of living, including dietary changes. A generation of young people who blithely followed the trend towards more children per family awakened to the realization that more mouths to feed meant the need for serious menu planning. In the restricted budget, even pot roasts, hamburger, beef stew, and round steak were no longer the economical, substantial staples of yore. Prime rib roasts, tenderloin and T-bone steaks were no longer casual food purchases. They were reserved for "occasions," special outdoor grilling, and for "dining out."

Competitive foods, aided by aggressive promotional and advertising campaigns, were making startling inroads on national beef consumption. The gorgeous planked steak, royally garnished, was a thing of the past, but you could buy frozen shrimp, lobster tails, and fish filets in the most remote hamlet in the country; you could purchase packaged frozen drumsticks, thighs, breasts, and giblets, or a precooked chicken—stewed, baked or broiled, whole or cut up, in glass or in cans. Mexican food, largely cornmeal, beans, and peppers, attained popularity, as did the American-concocted "Chinese" dishes and Italian cookery that featured macaroni and noodles with incidental meat balls.

Jay Taylor's ambition was to reverse the trend away from good American beef, and to double its consumption, through a ten-year campaign that would require thorough organization and cooperative effort on the part of every branch of the beef industry, from stockgrower to ultimate consumer. Such a project was not a proper function of the American National Cattlemen's Association. It demanded the support of the unaffiliated feeder and dairy people. As the purpose was to feature and increase the sale of beef only, the work must be apart from existing, all-inclusive "meat" boards and institutions, but it could supplement and aid their work, too.

Although between 20 per cent and 30 per cent of the nation's beef is marketed by the dairy industry, most of the total originates in the farm and range country west of the Mississippi and is consumed in the densely populated East. Thus, financing must come largely from the West and the promotional effort be concentrated in the East. The National Beef Council was formed as a separate entity at the 1955 ANCA meeting, held in Reno, Nevada. Forest Noel, of Lewistown, Montana, was the first Council president and C. T. Sanders, then secretary of the Montana Livestock Markets Association, its first secretary. An office was opened in Chicago, the services of an advertising agency were engaged, and the campaign opened with TV plugs on national programs.

So convincing was Mr. Taylor's plan, in embryo, for a National Beef Council, that his Miles City audience of 1954 took the lead with a state council even before the national council became a reality. Its directors represent the Montana Stockgrowers Association, the Montana Livestock Auction Markets Association, the Montana Farm Bureau, the Grange, and the Montana Meat Packers Association. The secretaries of the MLAMA and the MSGA have served as secretary and treasurer, respectively, without compensation. Joe Blazek, of Glasgow, Montana, is president (1959). There have been no office rent and salaries to date. All segments of the Montana beef industry lend the Council their support, with range, dairy, feeder, purebred, and marketing groups, the latter including order and contract buyers.

These people realize that anything done to increase beef demand in Montana is a drop in the bucket compared to the potentialities that lie in the East. They know that in order to win they must excel, or at least equal, the promotional programs extolling competing foods, and that means really important financing. At present, financing is done through voluntary deductions of five cents per head on cattle sold at Montana auction markets, to which is added five cents per head voluntarily mailed in from direct sales at farm, ranch, or feed lot. The projects of the Cow Belles provide another source of revenue. The annual revenue to date has not been overwhelming —about $23,000 for the year ending April 30, 1959. Of this amount, 39 per cent was contributed to the National Livestock and Meat Board, 20 per cent to the National Beef Council, and 41 per cent retained for promotion and advertising on the local level.

The slogan "Montana Makes Beef and Beef Makes Montana" has been adopted and widely publicized through the distribution of windshield stickers, paper napkins, and beef recipe booklets. The Cow Belles have been unstinting in their furtherance of the beef promotion program. In the summer of 1954, the extension service of Montana State College submitted a program to the executive committee of the Montana Stockgrowers Association, which mated perfectly with the public relations and "Eat More Beef" campaigns. Consumer classes were to be held in key Montana towns, to bring complete information regarding production, marketing, processing, and cooking beef to selected groups of housewives. The nutritive value of meat was to be emphasized. The executive committee agreed to sponsor the project to the extent of encouraging producer participation, and providing the meat given as door prizes and used in demonstrations.

Edwin A. Phillips retired in 1954 after thirty-three years as secretary of the Montana Stockgrowers Association, having served the Livestock Commission in a secretarial capacity before that. He was made assistant to the president so that the Association would not be entirely deprived of his valuable services. He held that position until his final resignation went into effect on May 31, 1955. His successor is Ralph B. Miracle, who has had lifelong experience in the livestock industry both as a rancher and as secretary of the Livestock Commission after the death of Paul Raftery in 1946. (Raftery had become Commission secretary in 1929 when Ed Phillips became full-time secretary of the Association.) Bill Cheney, another Montana stockman's son, followed Mr. Miracle as secretary of the Commission.

The West has always fascinated Americans, including those who live in it, and the cattle phase of its history seems to dominate their interest. The small-fry, never-ending craze for cowboy regalia is only exceeded by adult addiction to "westerns," be they "paperbacks," movies, or on TV. To those born too late to have seen Buffalo Bill's Wild West Show and Congress of Rough Riders, the westerns typify the West. To a slightly earlier generation so did certain individuals whose origins were as western as the sage and cactus, but who also excelled in show business. Will Rogers, master of homespun quip and philosophy, was one of them. Tom Mix, screen idol of the juveniles, was another. Incidentally, both had native American blood in their veins—Cherokee, to be specific.

C. A. Reynolds, of Kansas City, and one-time Colorado settler, while on a trip in 1947, saw the statue of Will Rogers in the beautiful memorial at Claremore, Oklahoma. Mr. Reynolds, later retired, was then in the prosaic business of garment-making and knew very little lore of western cow country; yet, as he mused at the Will Rogers shrine, he evolved a scheme to help preserve western tradition. Much of the drama of the West's development centered in the cattle industry, with virile roles played by men whose names and deeds deserved lasting recognition. Why not inscribe the names of the best of them in a shrine dedicated to that purpose?

Reynolds did not let his vision dim. He enlisted help and secured the pledge of seventeen states to participate in the construction of a National Cowboy Hall of Fame. Bids were entered for the location by well-qualified cities, from Fort Benton, Montana, to Fort Worth, Texas. A board of trustees selected a thirty-seven-acre site, just east of Oklahoma City. A design was chosen out of 229 submitted, the complete plans calling for an expenditure of $5,000,000. Prior to the completion of the first unit, each state was privileged to nominate two candidates for the Hall of Fame, subject to approval of a 75 per cent majority of the board of trustees. Montana's representation on the board was filled by Governor Hugo Aronson, Frank L. Spencer, of Great Falls, and G. R. ("Jack") Milburn, of Grass Range.

Quite appropriately, the choice of Montana's candidates was left to a special committee appointed by the Montana Stockgrowers Association's executive committee. The special committee chose Robert S. Ford and Conrad Kohrs as Montana's initial representation in the Hall of Fame. Charlie Russell and Tom Mix were "at large" nominees, selected as two of eleven for the entire West. Charlie Russell is Montana's own, of course, and the state can also stake a claim to Tom Mix, who rode the range between the Milk River and the Missouri as a cowhand for the Circle Diamond when John Survant was ramrodding that well-known outfit.

Every old-timer who knew Charlie Russell liked him, just as all Montanans now revere his memory—not only for his marvelous record of frontier life done with pigment, bronze, and ink, but for himself, his humor, his tolerance, his understanding of the old West. He was part of it. He caught scenes from the passing pageant and immortalized them on his canvasses. Indians, cowhands, freighters, and other earthy characters; humor, pathos, drama; action, color, and a story; cattle, horses, and buffalo—each type is exactly drawn, every detail perfection, yet not photographic. You can smell sagebrush, frying bacon, and sweat-soaked leather; you can hear the pop of bullwhip, the jangle of trace chains, the pounding of hooves. Maybe it's the dust of a trail herd getting in old-timers' eyes that makes them water when they look at Charlie's pictures.

There are drawbacks to having total annual income arriving in a lump sum, a circumstance that makes diversification desirable for almost any industry so afflicted. Woolgrowers escape it because they have two cash crops—wool in the spring, lambs in the fall. Cattlemen usually market in the fall. The year's take comes in a chunk. The once-a-year pay-day system has a disadvantage. Even thrifty, conservative budgeteers can get slightly reckless with their cash when the fall bank deposit runs to large figures. But as the balance approaches bottom during the next summer, any means of relieving the strain and adding a few dollars to the dwindling exchequer is welcome. Some ranchers have tried a side line.

In the frontier days of the cattle range, eastern visitors were dubbed "tenderfeet" by jocular westerners and were sometimes induced to fork a languid-looking bronc that promptly broke in two. Nowadays, dudes are too valuable to waste in that way. Dude ranching started a good many years ago when the astute owner of a western cattle spread discovered that its business and environs fascinated many adult easterners. Those innocents had the firm conviction that wrangling range stock was a glamorous and virile vocation. They were fifty per cent right. Investigation by this pioneer proved that substantial and seemingly sane citizens from urban areas were not only willing to acquire saddle galls, but were even eager to pay liberally for the privilege. Old-timer Howard Eaton is credited with having been the dean of dude ranchers, although many years before his time—in fact, in 1855—Sir George Gore of Sligo, Ireland, was Montana's first dude.

Forty-five-year-old Sir George traveled leisurely and luxuriously from old Fort Laramie on the North Platte via the Powder River route to the Yellowstone, and thence upstream to the Tongue, with an entourage of forty-one men, including the valiant and entertaining Jim Bridger. His rolling stock consisted of six large wagons and twenty-one bright-red French carts. His livestock tallied twenty-four mules, twelve oxen, forty-two cart horses, three milch cows, plenty of saddle horses, and fourteen dogs.

This sportsman de luxe had one cart loaded solely with his personal firearms, which totted up to seventy-five rifles, over a dozen shotguns, and a small arsenal of pistols and revolvers. Two other carts carried nothing but fishing tackle, and one retainer was employed solely to tie Sir George's trout flies. He camped in comfort each night in a spacious linen tent equipped with a folding brass bed, collapsible iron table, and washstand.

Attempts were made to impose upon Sir George but that gentleman was not as gullible as he may have appeared. Indians were prompted to complain about his slaughter of their game until the government took measures to curtail his buffalo hunting. Sir George's party didn't make a dent in the buffalo hordes and the government's concern over his kill was amusing in view of the policy of extermination officially adopted twenty-five years later. Sir George's legacy to Montana is the name Glendive.

Today, Montana's dudes are not as elaborately outfitted as was Sir George. After all, city people intent on a western vacation are content to find a place where informality is perfectly natural; where they can soak up western lore and lingo by fraternizing with the booted and spurred characters lounging around the horse corrals. Many—in truth most—dude ranches of today are not "working ranches," or even ranches. Summer resorts, camps, and lodges have usurped the name. Nevertheless, there are Montana stockgrowers who will accept a few select dudes on a by-product basis. The cattlemen consider it good business, and the dudes love it. After they have been "ranching" for a few days you can't tell the girls from the boys unless they are going away from you.

Dudes can get on a Westerner's nerves and they can also be amusing. Pretty Nora Leighter, daughter of Jos Leighter of the U Cross spread in Wyoming and sister of Lady Curzon (wife of the Viceroy of India), elected to ride on roundup. She had a pronounced British accent. She and Sage Collings of the U Cross were coming in from circle and crossed a badly damaged ranch bridge. She said to Sage, "Mr. Collings, your breeges are very much in need of repair." Sage meekly replied, "Yessum, I'm going to get a new pair if I ever get to town."

Another by-product of the range, in whose profits the stockgrower does not participate, is the rodeo, which is becoming more and more conventionalized and bound about with rules, regulations, precedent, and prize money. In a degree, the rodeos perpetuate the work and skills of the cowhand craft while mixing honest competition with no small measure of showmanship. They are the spectacular outgrowth of the bronc-peeling, calf-roping, steer-busting routine of bygone cowhands, who worked at these crafts for $40 a month.

# 22. LAST OF THE MAVERICKS

Economic cycles, variables, and other complexities of the cattle industry were very much in the minds of Montana stockgrowers when the 1957 annual convention of MSGA was held in Butte. President Jack Brenner rode point on the program and, like all good presidents before him, set the tone for the meeting. He said:

> I recently read what a big job associations such as ours had to do in their pioneer days. Our forefathers moved into a new and different land and founded a new and different business. They not only had to learn how to survive and prosper but they also had to make their own laws and enforce them. They had to protect themselves and their communities from all conceivable hazards, natural, governmental, and self-made. They had to band together as the Montana Stockgrowers Association to do the job. Unfortunately, not all of their wisdom and experienced advice was heeded in the formation of our government, the use of our lands and water, and the laws we must live by. That is our heritage and we are still at it.

It often seems to me that our basic problem is still the same. We are more in the minority than ever. Our laws are written, our land use prescribed, our credit furnished, and our product used in main by people who do not understand us, our business, or our country. It all calls for more thought, more cooperation, and a stronger organization with your active support.

With this starter, President Brenner launched into pressing matters of the moment. There was the customary discussion about taxes and various phases of the industry; then, as usual, the subject of cycles came up. Ferrington ("Ferry") Carpenter, of Hayden, Colorado, former U.S. Director of Grazing under the Taylor Act, was a guest speaker. He asserted that labor and some industries had found that they could exercise certain well-defined controls over cycles. He pointed out that preplanning had assured them some degree of stabilization for definite intervals, which permitted the reasonable expectancy of fair profits. He cited the accomplishments of the organized dairy industry and intimated that no teat-squeezing milkmen should outdo the cowboys. He proposed that self-regulated selling quotas should be put into practice that would run the cyclical wrinkles through the ironer and flatten them out. Mr. Carpenter, who enjoys a bit of mild rabble-rousing now and then, may not have been too sincere in his pronouncements, knowing the intricacies of beef cattle marketing as he does.

Still, the Carpenter suggestions did not fall on totally deaf ears. Western cattlemen have long been aware that closely related demand and price for feeders are dependent to a considerable extent on the current status of crops in feeder areas, over which the stock producer has no control. They have learned that industrial output or curtailment affects employment and the purchasing power of the public, which, in turn, affects the price of cattle. They know that strikes, war, and threats of war affect their market. They also realize that the beef cattle industry is different from dairying or manufacturing. So, naturally, the Carpenter address was received with some skepticism.

The volume of a mechanically manufactured product can be regulated almost instantly by throwing a switch or throttle. A farmer can rotate his crops or let the land lie fallow from year to year. A stockman cannot make such quick changes. The steer that leaves the ranch has been a long time in the making, be he feeder or grasser; he cannot be held over for an indefinite period. He is a perishable product. Montana stockmen had been indoctrinated with the theory of "orderly marketing" for a long time. This share-the-market idea was just a variation of this, and the plan to give suppliers of beef cattle a base quota, with each group of producers voting on the number of their cattle that would be sent to slaughter, and when, met with apathy. No one got very excited over Mr. Carpenter's talk dealing with amendments to the law of supply and demand, but a Market Stabilization

Study Committee of seven was appointed to think it over. Only a year later, a special National Association committee was formed to delve into the same subject.

What cattlemen do know full well is that their own marketing practice was slipshod in the old days, loosely and sporadically organized since then, and that there is still much room for improvement. Tired of being berated and harangued by the uninformed, and of taking it on the chin financially, cattlemen associations in recent years have been analyzing field investigations of modern marketing methods, both in their own firsthand transactions and in the final disposition of their product by others. The results have been illuminating.

It has been determined that, while Chicago and the river markets have long been in high favor with many large western operators, there is a decided movement towards decentralization of packer activities and a corresponding shift from Corn Belt to intermountain feeders located in Utah, Idaho, Washington, and California. Even Montana has a fast-growing trend towards feeding at home near sugar beet refineries, grain, and silage-feed sources. No longer is a stockgrower restricted to driving his herd to the nearest railroad loading point in the fall and consigning them to an agency 1,500 to 2,000 miles away, to be disposed of on a glutted market. Now he can choose terminal sale, in or out of state auctions at any of Montana's thirteen licensed yards, or direct sale to order buyers. He is free to sell one head, a truckload, or a trainload, when and how he thinks he will get the best price at the least expense. If he sours on one method of disposal, he can switch to another or utilize two.

Each outlet has advantages and disadvantages. Where one man may profit to his complete satisfaction, another may have cause for complaint. Nowadays, a commission man or packer's representative in Chicago or Omaha can pick up a telephone and talk to a Montana producer at his ranch in a matter of minutes. He can catch a plane and be in Montana to close a deal in a matter of hours. Market quotations reach the ranch by radio in a matter of seconds. A rancher can telephone a local stockyard in the morning, a truck will roll over improved roads to pick up his cattle, and the money can be deposited in town to his credit that afternoon. They haven't sold them over TV yet, but keep your fingers crossed.

A producer of beef cattle, like Neckyoke's friend Sody Crick Smith over on the Fryin' Pan, may not realize that his marketing responsibility should continue after he collects payment from a direct buyer for a truckload of long yearlings. He has just turned over the raw product to a string of intermediary services that will probably end with a ninety-pound customer who knows what she wants for her family and who is extremely price-conscious. Before a steer reaches the display stage as hamburger, roast, or steak, it runs the gantlet of charges imposed by transport companies, stockyards, commission houses, feed lots, packing plants, refrigerating units, distribution centers before it is finally packaged and placed on sale in a super-self-service store. Then, the frugal housewife may take a look at the cumulative price-tag and decide to have spaghetti without meat balls for dinner. Who is blamed for the "exorbitant" price? The stockgrower!

In truth, none of the intermediary services has made an excessive charge when the increasing cost of their separate operations is analyzed. They are pretty much in the same category as those on the production line of a loaf of bread in its progress from wheatgrower to consumer, but the rise in price of that loaf from the five cents of the nineties to the near thirty cents of today is seldom blamed on the wheat farmer, coddled though he is by price controls. However, that accumulation of costs from ranch to kitchen can influence the consumer's buying habits.

This has been a matter of concern to the feeders, the packers, and the retailers who make up the chain reaction and, as the last two are in highly competitive businesses, it behooves them to be ever on the alert for cost-cutting innovations that will redound to their profit. If the saving is of sufficient magnitude, some of it may be slipped on to the consumer, but rarely does it go to the producer at the other end of the line unless beef supply is short. The producer is beginning to find this out. He would like to get away from booms and busts—especially the latter. It was something of this sort that Ferry Carpenter had in mind.

It all revives and involves the perplexing questions of price adjustments by the producer. Are they feasible and are they permissible? Can and shall ranchers manipulate supply to keep prices at reasonable profit levels? If they can and do, will the housewife turn to competitive products—pork and poultry—or can that impulse be offset by a well-conceived and persistent advertising campaign to keep beef out in the lead of American diet preference as it always has been?

To find the answers, the American National Cattlemen's Association appointed a fact-finding committee at its 1957 convention in Phoenix, Arizona. The committee's research director, Dr. Herrell DeGraff, of Cornell University, submitted its first progress report in 1958. The report did not draw premature conclusions. It outlined sources that might be available for aid in its future investigations of changes and conditions affecting the economics of the beef cattle industry. It called attention to a number of trails that might prove worthy of thorough scouting—the thought processes and emotional reactions of that ninety-pound mistress of the cuisine, for example.

The fact-finding committee's report, released in January, 1959, concentrates on two major problems of the beef industry: (1) the cause and possible alleviation of the violent cyclical changes that have characterized the business for the past forty years, and (2) the influence of consumer acceptance on beef production and marketing. The report reverted to the beef market "bust" of 1952–53, which brought consternation to cattlemen because it occurred in a period of high employment, flush consumer spending, and national prosperity. Individual stockmen could not account for it although the blame could be laid at their own door. In the two years 1951 to 1953, the number of cattle marketed for slaughter increased 41 per cent and the price dropped 43 per cent in consequence of the often-deplored glutting of a rising market.

Price fluctuations are desirable when they act as a barometer to give warning and as a gyroscope to keep supply and demand within a reasonable balance that will give the producer a fair profit and yet not discourage retail sales. But when abnormal marketing volume grossly overruns demand, an abrupt and exaggerated boom-and-bust cycle that does no one any good occurs. Even the boom returns must be shared with Uncle Sam, although he fails to participate in losses occasioned by the bust.

Excessive marketing volume can be the result of drouth-caused feed shortage that forces liquidation, but it has more frequently been due to over-production on the ranch, stimulated by attractive prices. Price-fixing would never be a panacea. If the disastrous boom-and-bust wave is to be flattened to a benign ripple, it will require a method of forecasting marketing volume and cattle prices that will take much of the speculation out of production planning by the individual rancher. Even then, the successful working of such a system would be dependent on the ability and alertness of individual stockmen in making constant adjustments, keeping a close scrutiny on marketing statistics, and taking immediate action when a shift in ranch operations is indicated.

The committee believes that cattle growers have an advantage in their never-ending competition with pork and poultry producers because Americans have always had a natural preference for beef, possibly a heritage from our English beginnings, and acquired by settlers from other countries. This choice was given momentum by World War II. The armed forces became accustomed to liberal rations of good red meat and the high wartime earnings of industrial workers sharpened their taste for juicy steaks. If the supply of beef of the kind that consumers want remains stable, they will pay a price for it that brings a fair profit to the producer even though it be somewhat higher per unit than competitive meats.

The investigators cite well-defined trends in national beef production and analyze their impact on the cattle growers. They find that expansion of the cattle industry has continued over the past ninety years in a ratio consistent with increasing population. The consumption of beef per capita has not decreased, at least to an appreciable extent. The cattle census of 1867 was about 29,000,000 head; at the beginning of 1959, about 97,000,000. The big increase has been in beef cattle and not in dairy stock. The type of slaughter animal has changed from heavy to light or moderate, and from four-year-old steers to steers and heifers ranging from eighteen to thirty months old. There has been a vast expansion in feeding, thereby giving better control of grade, early maturity, rate of gain, and smoothness of finish. Feeding undoubtedly adds quality as well as weight, and permits an even, all-seasonal flow of meat from rancher to consumer.

Too often, prophets in the past have tried to predict coming demand with a crystal ball, but the use of occult arts and hunches in divining the future beef supply and demand cannot compete with intelligent deduction based on sound statistics. One solution to the boom-and bust, or exaggerated cycle difficulty might be the maintenance of a competent national advisory staff of research specialists who will closely follow general trends and specific market variations and issue general recommendations. Then, if the individuals of the beef cattle industry can be induced to act in unison and follow such recommendations promptly, the roller coaster sequence of price inflation and sickening slump can be smoothed out.

Another important finding of the committee deals with the cause and effect of changes in the distribution and retailing of foods. The impersonal but efficient supermarkets are only 10 per cent of all retail food stores in the U.S.A., yet they handle 66⅔ per cent of all retail food sales. The mass distribution of food has become an intricate combination of diversified crafts, assembly-line methods, mechanism, and standardization of raw products, their processing and packaging. There is no sales force in such stores suggesting to customers that they buy this and that, extolling the virtues of any particular brand, or catering to neighborhood buying habits. Each product on display is sold on its own merits or reputation, built by national advertising and satisfied users. Once accepted, a product must maintain uniformity of quality and appearance, be easily identified by brand or label, and be packaged in convenient sizes if it is to hold public favor.

Knowing this, and knowing that the success of each individual unit in a corporate chain of food stores, or in an "affiliate-independent" group, lies in consumer approval of its meat display, the mass distributors require suppliers to furnish them with beef carcasses tailored to specification. The meat department is the heart of their establishments. It can be the traffic-builder that makes auxiliary sales of other foodstuffs. A shopper can pick up well-known brands of staples at any corner grocery. The quality of a shop's meat is what brings customers from miles around, so astute managers try to make available the kind of beef the housewife wants, and to have it packaged the way she likes it. Their mass buying power gives them leverage to deal direct with a packer and dictate what he must furnish if he is to hold the account. Compliance with such rigid and arbitrary requirements must go right back to feed lot and ranch.

The housewife stocks her larder with nationally advertised brands because she is familiar with them and has confidence in their standard quality and uniformity. Can she buy a cut of beef in the same manner? She cannot! It may be graded as "Choice." Just what "choice" means is problematical and vague. It gives no clue to the age, sex, breed, or source of the animal nor to the length of time that the piece of meat has been aged. Two T-bones lying side by side on the counter and looking like identical twins, can differ materially in texture and flavor, yet their price tag is the same.

Research has determined what the housewife wants in beef. She does not want to gamble. She wants that ideal, and seemingly unattainable, combination of lean meat—no waste trim—with superb quality, taste, and texture, in cuts packaged and designed to fit her refrigerator, the size of her family, and her pocketbook. Impossible? Not at all, but it will take teamwork, and the man who is responsible for the raw material is part of the team. Whether they like it or not, that is the situation confronting cowmen. It is making the cattle grower study and plan to produce the slaughter cattle to suit the feeder, who must suit the packer, who must suit the distributor, who must suit the mistress of the household.

There are other details that the producer should know. Bedeviled packers, once dictators of price and quality to producer and corner butcher shop alike, are now in the throes of radical changes. They, too, must bow to the wishes of the housewife as conveyed through the medium of the mass distributor. Increasing wage demands, attempts to arrive at year-round, uniform, processing volume, desirability of being closer to production sources, shifting of population balance—these have all worked to bring decentralization of the packing industry. In their effort to maintain a level operation, some packers are doing their own feeding and some are contracting for specified delivery dates. Swift and Company ended cattle killing and processing at their Chicago plant on June 13, 1959, considering it no longer economically sound. The Chicago stockyards which handled 17 per cent of the nation's commercial livestock slaughtering in 1919 handled only 3 per cent in 1958.

It is a shortsighted stockgrower who cannot see that he and the "services" have a mutual interest in the ultimate consumer, the lady who does the shopping. In the study now in progress, there are so many pieces to the jigsaw puzzle of fact-finding that it is bewildering to the layman, but eventually the pieces should fit into place and present a clear picture.

An invaluable and convenient source of immediate assistance to Montana stockmen in their quest for stock improvement to keep pace with changing marketing demands is the State College at Bozeman. Montanans at large may lament the financial burden of higher education as provided by our widely dispersed University system, but for the stockgrowers the "cow college" portion of it has been invaluable. Established in 1893 as a land-grant college, the classroom instruction in agriculture and animal husbandry has been augmented by experimental stations for research, and an extension service, represented in the field by county agents, to bring research results to those who can directly benefit by them.

For the study of livestock problems, the seven branches of the Experimental Station provide the best of research facilities. The personnel have delved into matters that never occurred to old-time cowmen, to whom grass was grass and most any kind of prairie plant, barring loco weed, was good cattle forage. The modern investigators have probed the metabolism of a cow's digestive processes and have arrived at ways to correct mineral and organic deficiencies in feed. Range management has been a major subject for their attention, and their efforts to improve natural forage and to advance its season with supplemental seeded grass—notably crested wheat—have been successful.

Experiments in irrigated pasture, the control of range pests, veterinary research, have all added fruitful, scientific knowledge to the once haphazard occupation of growing beef cattle. The Beef Cattle Research Advisory Committee of the Montana Stockgrowers Association meets once or twice a year with the research and extension staffs of the college to discuss methods and programs for the betterment of the industry, thereby keeping the academic and the practical in liaison.

The American taste that once preferred steaks cut from mature carcasses now demands beef not far past the veal stage. This has started the trend to lighter-weight cattle and small, quality cuts. No longer is hamburger that is impregnated with lots of suet the family standby that it once was. National infatuation with reducing diets, encouraged by "health" articles in magazines and the sage advice of the family physician, calls for high protein content in menus, and lean meat fills the bill. Rejection of fat by the consumer left packers wondering how to get rid of the consequent excess. Since detergents were cutting into the soap market for fats, the situation grew more acute. Packers began asking for steers weighing not over 1,100 pounds and requested feeders and breeders to eliminate as much by-product material as possible—bone, fat, and offal, the very things that once gave them their profit. They wanted steers of the type that Dr. A. D. Weber, of Kansas City College, called "those boneless, gutless wonders."

Here again, the production of such critters was passed on to the ranchers who were desperately trying to oblige everyone by growing adolescent steers of required size and weight in a period of time that would give them a profit. The U.S. Experimental Station at Miles City, suspecting that the king of the show ring might not always be the best-performing bull when it comes to records of gain by his progeny in the feed lots, began a series of performance tests in 1936 that resulted in a unique accomplishment termed "bull indexing." Ten years later, the Experimental Station at Bozeman inaugurated a program that laid a foundation for bull indexing, with fourteen bull calves furnished by seven Montana breeders. If heredity had anything to do with a calf's rate of gain on a prescribed ration, a bull calf's record in the feed lot would give an index of what might be expected of *his* progeny under the same conditions.

This was a brand-new experiment in the line of beef cattle improvement—the first of its kind in the United States. The calves were fed a standard fattening ration and were weighed at four-week intervals. Average daily gains were tabulated and a record kept of the amount of feed and time required by each calf to gain one hundred pounds. By a comparison of weight-gain and amount and cost of feed, the experiments proved that the best bulls could be determined independent of the value set on them by visual appraisal. It was also shown that while heredity was a major factor in the feed lot performance of a bull calf, there was no conflict between that trait and the established hereditary quality of beef type. The commercial breeder can now select bulls that not only sire calves that make more rapid gains on less feed than the average, but that are top carcass quality, producing more beef per cow bred. The records are open to the skeptical and they show a variation in average gain of a pound a day between the best and the poorest performing bulls. It is fair to assume that a fast gainer in the feed lot will parallel his performance on grass.

Bull indexing has demonstrated the benefit of well-conducted college experiments to the bank accounts of stockgrowers, for operators in feeding areas are finding that feeders from indexed bulls net them more out of the feed lots. Some have paid a premium—three to six cents per pound—to the breeder for such animals. To Montana and her State College goes the credit for pioneering the program which is being accepted throughout the United States. Buyers still come to Montana for the pick of the crop. This has resulted in the formation of the Montana Beef Cattle Performance Registry Association, whose members breed and raise so-called I.P.R. (Individual Performance Record) bulls. A checking system has been established whereby an unbiased examiner can verify the claims of a breeder as to the invisible qualities of birth-weight, inherent growth ability, and fertility that have been passed on to his yearlings by their sire.

On the basis of a trained fieldman's impartial inspection of methods and indexing records employed by the breeder, an Association I.P.R. certificate is issued for each qualified calf or range bull. The certificate is expected to give a prospective buyer convincing evidence of the invisible characteristics that the bull's progeny may be expected to inherit. The buyer may then make his own estimate of the animal's visible qualities.

To quote *Circular 264* (June, 1957), Extension Service, Montana State College:

The whole purpose of this performance testing program—and the Montana Beef Cattle Performance Registry Association—is to "maintain and improve the type, quality, and conformation of Montana beef cattle and to increase their efficiency and productivity through the application of proved economic factors." The Individual Performance records are the written evidence and they must be accurate and dependable.

The State College, in addition to its Department of Animal Industry and Range Management, maintains a Veterinary Research Laboratory, an Extension Service, and State Experimental Stations, all of which are associated with, or cooperate with, the Montana Stockgrowers Association, independent stockgrowers, the Livestock Sanitary Board and its State Laboratory. At one time, the Department of Animal Industry was prone to make the development of show cattle its major project. Today the emphasis is on research applied to breeding, feeding, heredity, disease, and range management. Findings are brought to the attention of stockmen through such media as circulars, bulletins, Association publications, field days at branch stations, and through the agency of the College's extension service. Upon request, any Montana stockgrower's name will be put on the mailing list for printed information.

There has been nothing static about the Montana beef cattle industry since its inception, including changes in breeds and breeding. In the span of years covering the existence of the Montana Stockgrowers Association, the industry has altered from a highly speculative venture that made the Wild West wilder, to a more systematized, more scientific business with calculated risks slightly reduced but still existing.

A glance at the current ads in *The Montana Stockgrower* gives clue to modernity on the ranch—mechanical chutes and tipping calf tables, cattle guards and steel corrals, portable scales and sacked feed. The feature articles deal with such subjects of the moment as income taxes, publicity, and public relations, while still devoting much space to ever-recurring legislative problems in new guise.

Today, Montana ranch houses are built where stacked or baled hay in quantity are available to beat drouth and blizzards. Summer range on leased land, grazing district, forest reserve, or privately-owned pasture under fence—all are within easy distance. Attractive, furnace-heated, electrically equipped ranch homes have replaced the mud-daubed log cabins that squatted in cottonwood groves. Nondescript Texans and Durham crosses have relinquished the grass to bald-faced Herefords and sturdy Angus, whose conformation attests their selective breeding and scientific feeding.

The decided change in ranch life has been expressed by Jack Brenner, past president of the Montana Stockgrowers Association and lifelong cattle-man of southwestern Montana:

When I was young we would do our buying in town about twice a year. Canned goods, sugar, flour, coffee, that we had shipped out on a branch rail-road that has long since folded up. From a farming country we would ship in a carload of potatoes, root vegetables, and a little grain to feed a few hens and a pig or two. Bacon and eggs when the hens laid, hotcakes when they didn't. We would get a car of coal and be set for the winter. For haying— the big job in our kind of ranching—we would go to the hills and run in some fifty head of supposedly broke horses, plus a few unbroken colts. We had hundred-dollar mowers and seventy-five-dollar rakes that lasted for years—if those ridge-running horses didn't wreck them. Buckrakes and stackers were just old patterns that we rebuilt with hewed-out native timber. All we needed was a side of leather, some rope, a can of oil, rivets, monkey wrench, pliers, and a hammer. If we got seven cents for two-year-old steers and five cents for cows, we were in the chips.

*Now* look at us! The root cellar is caved in and the icehouse torn down. We have electric coolers and freezers and we are in town every week or so. We stock up on all kinds of frozen foods that we had never heard of then, and we buy our eggs, bacon, bread, and fresh fruits and vegetables that we never knew grew outside of a can. The half-broke horses are replaced by several tractors at $3,000 to $6,000 apiece, and those tractors pull mowers that cost $400 and last about two seasons. The pliers have grown into a full-sized shop stocked with welders and power tools and all kinds of gadgets to keep the tractors going. Our fifty-gallon gasoline drum that we filled once a month has grown into a five-hundred-gallon tank that won't last a week. With all of that we need twenty-cent yearling steers to keep our heads above the banker's desk.

In the early days of the range-cattle industry, no stockman suspected that both longhorns and Shorthorns would be superseded by the prolific progeny of white-faced immigrants from Herefordshire, England. The first importer of the English oddities was gentleman farmer Henry Clay, of Lex-ington, Kentucky. He made a modest investment in a cow, a heifer, and a young bull. He found that they had the desirable ability to fatten on the bluegrass without being grain-fed, and that the bulls possessed prepotency that marked their get in appearance and traits as being unmistakably Here-ford, regardless of maternal heritage. However, his base stock was too limited to preserve a pure line without disastrous interbreeding, and the Hereford strain, despite its tenacity, became diluted to the point of extinction.

It was not until 1840 that a Hereford herd of any importance was to be found in America. In the 1880's, several thousand head were imported and cattle owners soon showed a marked preference for these conversion units that turned grass into beef so efficiently. Breeders in Ohio, Illinois, Michigan, Iowa, and Missouri lost no time in establishing notable family lines. They initiated advertising campaigns that lauded the qualities of the breed—qualities made to order for western range. This was coincidental with the boom in range cattle that was exciting the owners and management of western herds. Some of them experimented by grazing Herefords side by side with their other cattle and found that the newcomers lived up to their advance billing.

That giant among other cattlemen of great stature, Colonel Charles Goodnight, of the Texas Panhandle, was an early and fervid Hereford man. He found that the whitefaces had the stamina needed to survive and thrive in western range environment. They fattened on grass when other stock grew gaunt. They stood the heat of southwestern summers and the vicious winter cold of the northern plains. They rustled and traveled far to water under conditions that made their less aggressive herd mates suffer and languish.

The first arrivals on the plains probably came to Colorado soon after the Civil War. During the 1870's, they spread to the southwest as stockmen, eager to improve their herds, recognized their superiority. In the late 1870's, the Swan Brothers and Frank and the Swan Land and Cattle Company, of Wyoming, went in for Herefords on a grand scale. It was their ambition to build and maintain a breeding herd of 20,000 cows or more. They bought tons of barbed wire to protect the harem from contamination by bovine Lotharios of lesser pedigree than their distinguished white-faced bulls. Con Kohrs bought some of the Swan herd for the Pioneer Cattle Company to try out on the Sun River range, and found them to his liking. His were among the first, if not the first, in Montana.

One of Montana's greatest herds was built by A. B. Cook, of Helena, at his Missouri River ranch below Townsend, a ranch now flooded by a government reservoir. "A.B.," whose career as a successful construction contractor made it possible for him to indulge his liking for animal husbandry, bought a seven-year-old Hereford cow named Cuba 4th, in 1911, at a dispersion sale in Savannah, Missouri, not far from St. Joseph. He paid the top price of $300. The lady was the daughter of an imported sire and had been serviced by a bull of illustrious ancestry, a double-grandson of the famous Beau Brummel. A month after A. B. Cook acquired Cuba 4th, she dropped a bull calf, Cuba's Panama 372431, who was to become the patriarch of one of the important Hereford families of his time.

A. B. Cook began acquiring blue ribbons at the National Western in Denver in 1909. In 1917 the Panama blood came into its own when he took Senior Grand Champion bull on Panama 431986 by Cuba's Panama 372431; Senior Grand Champion female on Lady Panama 7th, 451991; and Get of Sire on Cuba's Panama 372431, at the National Western, Panama topping the sale at $5,100. From then on for the next ten years, the Panama family were the aristocrats of the show ring, and in 1922 climaxed their record with Panama 110th, 816250, greatest of them all, who won the Senior Grand Championship at the International and who sired Joy 4th, 1119875, Senior Grand Champion female at the American Royal in 1925.

Lamentable and forced liquidation of the famous Cook herd occurred in the fall of 1928 when 2,537 head were sold for $453,475 at the largest registered Hereford sale of record. There are today many Montana breeders of Herefords whose enviable performance at the big shows have made their cattle nationally known and sought. Although whitefaces dominate Montana landscapes, other breeds are not without their admirers. Shorthorns, the foundation stock of early Montana herds, persist in important numbers. Their early history also goes back to Kentucky, where Henry Clay had his famous herd of Durhams, some of whom went to Oregon in 1847.

The first serious fancier of Aberdeen-Angus cattle in Montana was T. C. Power, of Fort Benton and Helena, who started in 1883 with superior foundation stock drawn largely from a Canadian herd in the Province of Quebec. Many of the first animals had been imported from the herds of noted Scotch breeders. This foundation stock produced many winners at the International. The exceptional herd was sold about 1892 to Charles Escher and Son, of Iowa, thereby depriving Montana of that marvelous blood strain.

Favoritism for Angus cattle is not confined to any particular part of Montana. The registered descendants of aristocratic ancestry continue to bring honors to Montana breeders, and commercial herds have increased through the years. Three of the largest are at the Cremer Ranch near Melville, the N Bar Ranch near Grass Range, and the Montgomery Ranch at Lima. These black, hornless cattle have proven hardy and prolific. They mature early and stand the rigors of winters at high altitudes. One quality claimed for them is that the cows' udders do not sunburn and become sore from snow-reflected sun rays. This is because of the dark pigmentation in their skin. When crossbred, their progeny, like that of the Herefords, retain the characteristics that make high-grade beef stock. The Montana Aberdeen-Angus Association was formed August 5, 1942, at Great Falls.

The introduction of novel breeds continues. There is now a Montana Galloway Breeders Association, and very enthusiastic it is about the shaggy descendants of the wild, black cattle of the Scottish Highlands, who thrive on poor forage to make high-quality beef. Out west of Great Falls, near the old cow town of Augusta, A. B. Cobb, Jr., has a Charollaise breeding herd, something new in Montana. Crossed with Hereford cows, their calves are also alleged to give more weight for less feed, and to yield finer, tenderer, smoother meat cuts with a minimum of waste-fat cover.

But even the most sentimental old-timer didn't shed tears when 20-year-old "Roscoe," Texan fugitive from the law of averages, succumbed at last at the Billings stockyards, leaving Montana without a longhorn or a place to throw it.

Cattle research, unheard of in the days of the open range, now concentrates on a dozen phases of animal husbandry and land management. Jeeps, trucks, and other mechanical equipment make ranch life easier, but there is still plenty of hard labor left for the successful rancher and his horses. With calves worth what they are today, wise stockmen just don't sit and let nature take its course. They are in the saddle during calving time for long, long hours, keeping track of where this or that secretive cow dropped her calf, reading their minds, and seeing that the calf has a shot of milk. If the mother fails to provide it, the rancher will. The percentage of calves saved shows that such treatment pays well. Then there are branding, haying, shipping, with other chores wedged in. Come sunshine or stormy weather, the cowman who doesn't want to go broke makes a hand right with the boys on his payroll. If the ranch is a family operation, and many of them are, everyone turns to and does his or her stint. There is still a place in the cow business for work horses, both equine and human.

# 23. BOLD NEW BLOOD LINES

The year 1958 was not a bad one for Montana cattlemen. Numerically they are a small segment of the state's population. Not so small is their contribution of taxes, investment, and production to the state's economy. About 35,000 farms and ranches of all sizes in the state are paying about one-third of the property taxes. Stockgrowers are still gallantly fighting for principles that seem inherent to self-reliant people who live in the open and cherish the sense of freedom inspired by their environment.

On December 11, 1958, a hearing was held in Kalispell by the U.S. Senate Public Works subcommittee, headed by the late Richard L. Neuberger of Oregon, an advocate of public ownership. The hearing was in connection with the proposed creation of a Columbia River Development Corporation, another tax-exempt federal corporation offering competition to private industry. Wesley Stearns, of Plains, Montana, MSGA executive committee member, appeared to represent the Association in its opposition to the legislation. He said that, if enacted, it would impose a threat to Montana water laws and to owners of water rights under them.

With the advent of 1959, western stockmen were maintaining an independence of thought that seemed to have been lost by those who let columnists, commentators, and cinema producers formulate their opinions for them. No collectivism for the cowmen. As defenders of individual dignity and rights, they ask no favors, seek no subsidies. When the American National Cattlemen's Association met in mid-January at Omaha, President G. R. Milburn, of Grass Range, Montana, said to the press, "We cattlemen are the last segment of agriculture resisting government interference." Resolutions passed at the annual convention a few days later were an index to the sentiment of the members. One of them called for a national referendum on whether to continue or repeal the federal income tax amendment. In another, Congress was urged to keep spending within the budget. The resolution cited the fact that "each succeeding year brings greater spending of taxpayers' money, much of it for non-essential services based on political expediency." It called upon Congress to realize "the fact that we have already gone a long way towards ruinous inflation that can only be corrected by turning away from profligate spending and recognizing the government's role is to govern and not to spend us into bankruptcy and chaos."

The January 15, 1959, edition of *The Montana Stockgrower* carried F. H. Sinclair's "New Year Message from Neckyoke to Secretary Miracle." Abandoning the vernacular, Neckyoke wrote what he termed an "off trail" letter, taking inventory of developments since his epistles to the "secertary" were inaugurated as a monthly feature sixteen years before. He called attention to the fact that three Presidents had occupied the White House in that time; that two wars had ended with American troops scattered all over the globe; that our foreign policy had involved us in fantastic financial contributions to nations in far-away places with strange-sounding names. He referred to the astounding advances of science: nuclear energy, man-made satellites, communication, transportation, and television. He opined:

> The economic philosophy of Americans has changed and the welfare state has become a reality and socialistic ideas which would have been abhorrent but a few years ago have been accepted by the public, who have been educated to believe that the government has the answer to all problems. Those who were teen-agers sixteen years ago are now grown and have families. They have lived under a growing collectivism all their lives and know nothing else. Thrift at one time was considered a virtue, but not today. The public is constantly pounded to buy and buy and the business fraternity, which has in the past advocated sound economic policies, has abandoned old, tried ideas until today everything from homes, cars, and utilities can be

bought on the cuff with the buyer having very little equity in his purchase. There is no stigma attached to heavy debt as there was in former years.

We may as well face the fact that we are entering an era of labor government. Labor unions have grown in power until they are in position to completely stall the economic train of the nation. By the use of union funds they have made national legislators subservient to their will. Increased demands for higher wages together with benefits have been major causes of the present inflation that threatens the country. Members of unions often have no voice in the expenditure of their funds. Congress fears to make any laws governing labor because of political retaliation at the polls. Some union leaders openly propose socialistic programs.

Today statesmanship on the part of national officers and legislators has given way to political expediency. Taxes have risen to the point where nearly half of the national income is going to governmental agencies. Municipal, state, and national debt has reached a point which responsible economists say means that the nation is virtually bankrupt. . . . More and more government interference with living and competition from government has been increasing.

The alarming aspect of all this is that the public in general shows apathy and even unwillingness to give much thought to economic affairs and the trend in government. No attention is paid to the economic history of the world or the experience of other countries. If people can be made to think, America is in no danger. . . . The cattle producers can take pride in the fact that, as a group, they have steadfastly fought for free enterprise without the controlling hand of government regimenting their activities, and they have been one group that has respected American tradition and the ideals which were set up by the wise forefathers who founded a nation that has been envied by all other countries.

Many wonderful things have come out of the age in which we are living —and then, too, we have "swept wing" automobiles, parking meters, the hula hoop, and bubble gum! The next sixteen years may see pioneers opening up a new country on Mars or the moon. To those of us who are fast approaching the evening of life, it probably won't make much difference, but . . . as Greasewood might say, "I'd like to stick around a spell just to see what the hell is going to happen next!"

Regardless of what happens next, past performance of the Montana Stockgrowers Association has amply demonstrated that continued, aggressive organization is essential to meet change. Through organization, a member of MSGA is the recipient of information and services impossible for him to obtain as an individual. A trained secretarial staff in the central offices provides each member with a personal representative and consultant in the capital city and keeps him posted on current affairs of interest to cowland through the pages of *The Montana Stockgrower*. Other work is done by six representative standing committees and eighteen cooperative committees, the latter frequently working with outside groups whose objectives parallel or contact those of stockmen.

Today there are many local stock associations in Montana which concern themselves with conditions peculiar to their particular range. Some of their meetings have an attendance comparable to that of the State Association meetings of a few years ago. Attendance is large, programs are excellent. Since state membership has reached present proportions, a program of grass-root meetings has been inaugurated, with agenda sponsored by combined groups of local associations. The State Association staff and officers lend a helping hand. By scheduling the meetings at strategic points, every member of MSGA has an opportunity to attend and to take part in the action and discussion pertinent to his area and to the industry at large without traveling excessive distances to do so.

The local associations are indispensable. They provide the strength and push that help the state organization to function in their behalf. There is no fixed pattern for their *modus operandi* or their individual goals. Some lean heavily on the leadership of an individual or a board of directors and meet but once a year. Others put every member to work on continuing programs and require frequent conferences. Some originated as a combined defense against rustlers and some are offshoots of forest grazing associations. Some are well-heeled, with a substantial stack of blues in the kitty, while others are content to collect token dues, relying on special assessments for emergencies. All in all, they are the fiber from which the fabric of State Association accomplishment is woven. By the same token, the State Association is independent of all outside influences, and it is democratic.

From May 20 to 23, 1959, Miles City bulged at the seams. Every old cow-waddie who could rope himself transportation was there. It was the Diamond Jubilee of the Montana Stockgrowers Association, and it made cow town history, thanks to the hardworking committee, headed by Milt Simpson, that had been meeting, "augering," plotting, and planning for months. There are kill-joy mathematical sharps who cite the fact that only seventy-four years had elapsed since the organization meeting in 1885. Others get technical and allege that it was not even the seventy-fifth yearly meeting, inasmuch as the 1945 convention was vacated. But why quibble? It *was* the Diamond Jubilee. Sons and grandsons of founding members had stellar parts in the proceedings. Nothing was spared to make it a memorable occasion of accomplishment, fellowship, and entertainment from the moment of registration at the Elks Club to the last dance at the Stockgrowers Ball in the Exhibition Hall at the Fair Grounds. Parades, pageants, Follies, an old-fashioned roundup, barbecues, White and Black Horse Patrol drills, a square dance jamboree, tailgate breakfasts, a steak fry, and Indian powwows were sandwiched in between the serious affairs of the convention. A highlight was the panel composed of ten Association past presidents, monitored by F. H. Sinclair, each panel member reviewing the conditions, problems, and accomplishments of his administration—really a symposium covering a span of twenty-five years.

Miles City is no green hand at dispensing exceptional hospitality to the Montana Stockgrowers Association. The second MSGA meeting, held April 20, 1886, set the precedent. The *Weekly Yellowstone Journal and Livestock Reporter* was evidently impressed. Its story of that convention reads in part:

> The convention was inaugurated with that truly American institution, a street parade with a brass band at the head. Preparations for this event were commenced early in the morning. The street presented a scene of more than usual bustle and activity, the center of which was the Macqueen Hotel. Cowboys, a squad of whom was to form a part of the procession, were gathered in great numbers and their gyrations were witnessed with great interest by the visitors, many of whom were from the East and strangers to such scenes. The band from the post [Fort Keogh] discussed [*sic*] stirring music on the steps of the hotel.
>
> Finally the preparations were completed and the procession was organized by the Grand Marshal, W. M. Carter. The band led, followed by the carriages in which rode the ladies, guests, and officers of the Association, the body of mounted cowboys, 100 or more in number, and lastly the members of the Association on foot, the head of the pedestrian column being the visitors from St. Paul. . . .
>
> The concluding exercises of the stockmen's convention were of a terpsichorean character, being a grand ball tendered to the visitors by the merchants and stockmen of Miles City. The ball took place in the spacious dining room of the Macqueen House which had been cleared of tables for the occasion, and a temporary platform raised in one corner for the orchestra of six pieces from the post. The elite of Miles City and Ft. Keogh were there, the ladies wearing their prettiest toilettes and the army officers appearing gorgeous in their full dress uniforms. . . .
>
> The dancing was continued until nearly midnight when the intermission for supper took place, the banquet being served in the basement of the hotel. It was of the same elegant description which characterized all the arrangements of the event. The committee in charge deserve great credit for the successful manner in which the affair was conducted.

A similar compliment can appropriately be paid the Miles City Diamond Jubilee Executive Committee and the Montana Stockgrowers Convention Committee for 1959.

Due to numerous causes, there is not strict uniformity in Montana ranch operations today, so in closing, let us take a quick survey of the cattle situation in various corners of the state. Although there were over 2,000,000 head of beef cattle in Montana as of January 1, 1959, they are so widely scattered on range and in pastures that they are not in great evidence and it would be hard to convince tourists driving our highways that they exist in such numbers.

It's been only ninety-three years since Nelson Story drove that first herd of longhorns over the Bozeman Trail into the Gallatin Valley. Today the prosperous basin, with rich fields of grain, peas, and alfalfa, basks in contentment, well assured that its future is secure. Its irrigated expanse doesn't worry about drouth. Its people go to town on Saturday in family-laden cars to mill around the commercial section of Bozeman, the county seat. Farm boys in skin-tight Levi's and the ubiquitous high-heeled boots, attract as little attention as do the State College students in the current mode of dishabille as they collapse in booths at their favorite fountain and dawdle over cokes or coffee.

The upper and lower Madison Valleys are still dedicated to stockgrowing, although big spreads are owned by comparative newcomers or absentee proprietors as hobby or investment. The Ruby, Jefferson, and Beaverhead Valleys west of the Tobaccoroot Range have never ceased to be cow country since Captain Grant and his friends brought in the first cattle from the Oregon Trail.

When Con Kohrs walked into the Deer Lodge Valley, he and his companions were broke. They camped near the village of Cottonwood (now Deer Lodge) and caught trout which they had to boil or roast on the embers of a campfire because they had no money to buy frying grease. Today the valley is bisected by an arterial highway and traversed by two transcontinental railways, one electrified, and is sprinkled with state institutions. It has never deviated from its production of fine beef cattle since the days of Johnny Grant, Bob Dempsey, Fred Burr, and, of course, Con Kohrs and his half-brother, Nick Bielenberg.

The mountain basins of western Montana that sheltered her first herds were never bothered by interlopers. Their ranges were well defined by natural barriers and, barring sporadic Indian trouble with the Shoshones, there were no clashes between neighbors. In the summer of 1886, the Dillon *Tribune* noted that "some 300 Indian warriors camped near Mr. Brenner's last week. They indulged in their pale-faced brothers' luxuries—fire water and gambling."

Many of the difficulties that beset open-range operators of the plains were nonexistent, or at least minimized, for the mountaineers. In the sprawling Big Hole Basin no railroad whistles disturb the tranquility, and the drone of an occasional plane merely signifies that a rancher is flying to town. The meadows once provided natural pastures for deer, elk, and antelope; out of the surrounding mountains come chuckling trout streams that unite to form the Big Hole River. Fur trappers, Indian hunting parties, Captain Billy Clark's contingent of the Lewis and Clark Expedition, Chief Joseph and his fugitive band of Nez Perce, troops, and gold-seekers have passed through it in colorful parade.

In 1882 the first permanent settler and his bride "took up" land and soon they had neighbors. Those pioneers trailed cattle in from Idaho and Oregon. The stock thrived on the natural forage that includes a nut grass peculiar to the area and full of fattening oil. The high altitude, climate, feed, shelter, and abundant pure water combined to produce prime, finished grassers. Today, in the eighteen-mile stretch between the towns of Wisdom and Jackson, there is probably the greatest concentration of fine beef cattle anywhere in the United States. Broad-backed, sturdy whitefaces graze under fence the year around. No open range, no roundups. If an owner wants to inspect or move a herd, riders saddle the horses at the home ranch, move them in trailers to the field, sometimes fifteen or twenty miles away, and the stock is leisurely gathered and moved without unduly exciting them. To inspect the herds in winter, ranchers glide across country in a ski-mounted fuselage pushed by an airplane prop—sometimes taking time out to run down a coyote.

In early summer the fields are soggy with irrigation water and mosquitoes rule the range. Haying starts in August and it takes a lot of hay to winter the 30,000 head of cattle in the Basin—about 1,500 tons per 1,000 head. The Clemows, Hirschys, Huntleys, and McDowells go into action and, with the help of itinerant hayhands, some of them college boys, dot the bottom land with blowsy blimps, the eighteen-ton piles of forage that give the Big Hole its nickname, The Valley of the Ten Thousand Stacks. Production-line methods are used. At top speed, a well-coordinated crew can run up an eighteen-ton stack in thirty minutes and skid the stacker to a new setup, ready to start another. Eight stacks in an eight-hour day is a good average. By Labor Day, the Big Hole is a well-stocked, or stacked, larder and the hands go fishing.

Drop over the Continental Divide via Trail Creek and make a breathtaking descent to Ross's Hole at the head of the Bitterroot Valley. This is the country where Major Owen, Louis Maillet, and other early settlers, traded in cattle. Now the eighty-five miles of river bottom is packed with prosperous small ranches and apple orchards. Travel from the State University city of Missoula, located astride those two streams of sinister name, the Hellgate and the Rattlesnake, to the Mission Valley where the Jesuits and their Indian parishioners had a thousand head of cattle in the 1860's. The beautiful basin is fenced, plowed, and closely settled. Dairy herds are more in evidence from the highway than is beef stock.

Cut back across the Continental Divide, traveling to the east, via U.S. Highway 2, along the south boundary of Glacier National Park. The scenic road will take you down through the Blackfeet Indian Reservation and bring you into another world very abruptly. You won't see many cattle in the vicinity of the reservation town of Browning. In the summer season the erstwhile braves, who at one time were intent on raiding white men's herds, are now selling souvenirs to tourists while their own herds graze peacefully to the Canadian line.

Around the old cow towns of Cut Bank and Shelby the rolling plains now sprout oil derricks, and the conversation runs to kindred subjects. To the south, along the Teton, Marias, and down past the Sun and Dearborn Rivers, much of the vast grass country west of the Missouri is still in range but fenced and spattered here and there with wheat fields. Around Great Falls wheat farmers reign, but east of the Shonkin Sag and beyond to Judith Basin, the Flatwillow, and the Musselshell, cattlemen are still entrenched. To the north, in the shallow valley of the Milk River, former pastures and sod-roofed ranch houses have been replaced by irrigated farm units and modern, if less picturesque, homes. On the rippling benchland to north and south, where the Circle Diamond, Circle C, and Matador steers used to range, alternate green and dun stripes of strip-farming stretch to the horizon, but you will find stockgrowers, too, fortified with commensurate deeded land and utilizing nearby Taylor Grazing District, or LU, land.

Over by the Little Rockies and the breaks of the Missouri, rough, rugged, and remote, are the ghost towns of Zortman and Landusky, far off the beaten trail. There is where mining camp bordered cow country—wild, broken land where man or bronc could dodge a loop and hide out indefinitely with kindred spirits, a land once ruled by Colt and carbine. Cross the Missouri where the buffalo hordes used to ford and enter the range where the DHS, PN, 79, and a dozen other famous irons used to run their wagons; then drift east to the Big Dry and on to Circle, still cow country, although the CK, XIT, and W Bar steers are no longer there.

Head south again over billowing benchland and reach that jaunty, ever-vibrant hub of Montana's southeastern cowland, Miles City on the Tongue and Yellowstone. Here the tradition of trailherds and roundups is preserved and revered by the descendants of the original old-he-ones—the first Terrett, Simpson, Holt, Barthelmess, Brown, Brewster, Spear, and other stalwarts who helped found and hold together the Montana Stockgrowers Association. It isn't only along the Tongue and Powder Rivers that you find the sons and grandsons of the pioneers in their trade. They are scattered all over the state and mingled with cattlemen of many origins. Changes have been inevitable. Six of our early stockmen of western Montana, Con Kohrs, Bob Ford, Dan Flowerree, Nelson Story, Phil Poindexter, and Billy Orr, through native acumen and shrewd timing, used the cattle business as a steppingstone to fortune across the morass of hazards that bogged down so many pioneers. They knew nothing about consumer preference, production planning, controlled marketing, or public relations. For each success story, there are hundreds that tell of loss and downright disaster. Though the "early days" were just yesterday, itinerant cowboys are hard to find. In many instances, ranching has become a family operation out of necessity, with neighbors and women helping each other when extra hands are needed.

Treasure State cattlemen have inherited itching feet from restless ancestors. They are as familiar with the canyons of Manhattan as they are with their own cutback coulees. They are at home in the Vieux Carré of New Orleans and on San Francisco's Embarcadero. They frequently cut each other's trails in foreign lands, but they are always glad to get back to the smell of pines and sage and to the hush of the hills, where anyone within a hundred-mile radius is a reasonably close neighbor.

Chuck wagons no longer appear except as a name for cafés. Jeeps and trucks do many chores and a haystacker is a major piece of equipment on a ranch. Nevertheless, the bona fide cattleman of today is unmistakable when you see him in town. There is no particular manner of speech that marks him. He isn't shooting up barrooms or bucking a faro layout. He is minding his own business, with some of his women folks not far away. His frontier pants, his Stetson felt, his Pendleton shirt, and his Justin boots aren't needed to identify him. Other Westerners know the comfort and utility of such sartorial items. It is his air of detached serenity and self-confidence that peg him as an outdoor man with the same clear-eyed outlook that has belonged to herdsmen ever since their half-savage predecessors followed the grass and protected their stock from predators, both men and beasts, on the steppes of ancient Asia.

# Montana Stockgrowers Association
## Conventions and Officers—1885–1960

| No. | Place | Date | President-Elect | 1st V. P.-Elect | 2nd V. P.-Elect | Secretary |
|---|---|---|---|---|---|---|
| 1. | Miles City | 4/ 4/85 | Col. T. J. Bryan | Gov. B. F. Potts | Capt. Wm. Harmon | R. B. Harrison |
| 2. | " | 4/20/86 | " | " | " | " |
| 3. | " | 4/19/87 | " | " | " | " |
| 4. | " | 4/17/88 | " | Henry Klein | " | " |
| 5. | " | 4/16/89 | Jos. Scott | W. B. Hundley | Henry Tresler | " |
| 6. | " | 4/15/90 | " | Conrad Kohrs | J. M. Holt | " |
| 7. | " | 4/21/91 | " | John T. Murphy | " | W. G. Preuitt |
| 8. | " | 4/19/92 | " | " | " | " |
| 9. | " | 4/18/93 | " | " | " | " |
| 10. | " | 4/17/94 | " | " | " | " |
| 11. | " | 4/16/95 | " | Conrad Kohrs | J. W. Strevell | " |
| 12. | " | 4/21/96 | " | " | " | " |
| 13. | " | 4/20/97 | S. F. B. Biddle | John Harris | H. R. Phillips | " |
| 14. | " | 4/19/98 | J. M. Holt | " | " | " |
| 15. | " | 4/18/99 | " | " | " | " |
| 16. | " | 4/17/00 | Jos. T. Brown | C. J. McNamara | L. W. Stacy | " |
| 17. | " | 4/16/01 | " | David Fratt | J. I. Phelps | " |
| 18. | " | 4/15/02 | " | " | " | " |
| 19. | " | 4/21/03 | " | " | " | " |
| 20. | " | 4/19/04 | J. M. Holt | Conrad Kohrs | Thomas Cruse | " |
| 21. | " | 4/18/05 | " | " | " | " |
| 22. | " | 4/17/06 | " | David Fratt | Conrad Kohrs | " |
| 23. | " | 4/16/07 | G. F. Ingersoll | " | " | H. R. Wells |
| 24. | " | 4/21/08 | " | " | " | " |
| 25. | " | 4/20/09 | " | " | G. B. Kesley | { W. G. Preuitt / E. K. Preuitt * |
| 26. | " | 4/19/10 | Judge C. H. Loud | " | Geo. W. Brewster | D. W. Raymond |
| 27. | " | 4/18/11 | Geo. W. Brewster | " | Kenneth McLean | " |
| 28. | " | 4/16/12 | Kenneth McLean | Chas. O'Donnell | N. J. Humphrey | " |
| 29. | " | 4/15/13 | Col. F. M. Malone | Jno. Bielenberg | R. P. Heren | " |
| 30. | " | 4/21/14 | Rolla Heren | Wallis Huidekoper | W. W. Terrett | " |
| 31. | " | 4/20/15 | " | " | Randolph Dribel | " |
| 32. | " | 4/18/16 | " | " | " | " |
| 33. | " | 4/17/17 | " | " | " | " |
| 34. | Great Falls | 4/16/18 | " | E. O. Selway | W. K. Flowerree | " |
| 35. | Miles City | 4/15/19 | Wallis Huidekoper | G. B. Pope | " | " |
| 36. | Billings | 4/20/20 | " | " | " | " |

* After the death of W. G. Preuitt, his son, E. K. Preuitt, filled out his term as secretary.

| No. | Place | Date | President-Elect | 1st V. P.-Elect | 2nd V. P.-Elect | Secretary |
|-----|-------|------|-----------------|-----------------|-----------------|-----------|
| 37. | Helena | 4/19/21 | J. H. Burke | W. K. Flowerree | Chas. M. Simpson | E. A. Phillips |
| 38. | Butte | 4/18/22 | " | " | " | " |
| 39. | Miles City | 4/ 7/23 | " | C. M. Simpson | Roy F. Clary | " |
| 40. | Dillon | 4/24/24 | C. M. Simpson † | R. F. Clary | E. O. Selway | " |
| 41. | Great Falls | 4/ 7/25 | Roy F. Clary | Chas. M. Dowlin | Geo. M. Clemow | " |
| 42. | Billings | 3/30/26 | C. M. Dowlin | Geo. M. Clemow | Julian Terrett | " |
| 43. | Miles City | 4/ 7/27 | " | " | " | " |
| 44. | Havre | 4/12/28 | " | " | " | " |
| 45. | Butte | 5/27/29 | Geo. M. Clemow | Julian Terrett | W. H. Donald | " |
| 46. | Lewistown | 5/27/30 | " | " | " | " |
| 47. | Bozeman | 5/ 7/31 | " | " | " | " |
| 48. | Great Falls | 5/25/32 | C. L. Ancenny | W. H. Donald | John Arnold | " |
| 49. | Bozeman | 5/25/33 | Wallis Huidekoper | Julian Terrett | B. J. Metlin | " |
| 50. | Miles City | 5/24/34 | Julian Terrett | B. J. Metlin | T. A. Ross | " |
| 51. | Great Falls | 5/23/35 | " | " | " | " |
| 52. | Billings | 5/21/36 | B. J. Metlin | Thos. A. Ross | John Arnold | " |
| 53. | Bozeman | 5/19/37 | Thos. A. Ross | John Arnold | Carl K. Malone | " |
| 54. | Helena | 5/18/38 | " | " | " | " |
| 55. | Livingston | 5/18/39 | John Arnold | C. K. Malone | G. M. Mungas | " |
| 56. | Butte | 5/23/40 | " | " | " | " |
| 57. | Great Falls | 5/22/41 | C. K. Malone | G. M. Mungas | R. J. Miller | " |
| 58. | Missoula | 5/27/42 | G. M. Mungas | R. J. Miller | W. P. Sullivan | " |
| 59. | Billings | 5/27/43 | " | " | " | " |
| 60. | Miles City | 5/25/44 | R. J. Miller | W. P. Sullivan | C. K. Warren | " |
| 61. | (vacated) | 1945 | " | " | " | " |
| 62. | Great Falls | 5/16/46 | W. P. Sullivan | C. K. Warren | M. C. Simpson | " |
| 63. | Butte | 5/22/47 | " | " | " | " |
| 64. | Bozeman | 5/13/48 | M. C. Simpson | " | G. R. Milburn | " |
| 65. | Missoula | 5/26/49 | " | " | " | " |
| 66. | Billings | 5/25/50 | C. K. Warren | G. R. Milburn | Dan Fulton | " |
| 67. | Great Falls | 5/24/51 | " | " | " | " |
| 68. | Butte | 5/22/52 | G. R. Milburn | Dan Fulton | Jack Brenner | " |
| 69. | Missoula | 5/14/53 | " | " | " | " |
| 70. | Miles City | 5/22/54 | Dan Fulton | Jack Brenner | Gene Etchart | Ralph Miracle |
| 71. | Helena | 5/21/55 | " | " | " | " |
| 72. | Billings | 5/20/56 | J. S. Brenner | Gene Etchart | Wayne Bratten | " |
| 73. | Butte | 5/23/57 | " | " | " | " |
| 74. | Great Falls | 5/22/58 | Gene Etchart | Wayne Bratten | Don McRae | " |
| 75. | Miles City | 5/20/59 | " | " | " | " |
| 76. | Missoula | 6/16/60 | Wayne Bratten | { Don McRae ‡ <br> Wesley Stearns | { Wesley Stearns <br> (office vacant) | " |

† Jack Burke had died.

‡ When Don McRae died, on July 23, 1960, Wesley Stearns succeeded him, leaving the office of second vice president vacant.